Law, Politics and Society
in the Ancient Mediterranean World

Edited by
Baruch Halpern
and
Deborah W. Hobson

Sheffield Academic Press

Law, Politics and Society in the Ancient Mediterranean World

Edited by
Baruch Halpern
and
Deborah W. Hobson

Sheffield Academic Press

Published by
Sheffield Academic Press Ltd
343 Fulwood Road
Sheffield S10 3BP
England

Typeset by Sheffield Academic Press
and
Printed on acid-free paper in Great Britain
by Biddles Ltd
Guildford

British Library Cataloguing in Publication Data

Law, Politics and Society in the Ancient
Mediterranean World
    I. Halpern, Baruch II. Hobson, Deborah W.
    909.091822

ISBN 1-85075-350-4

CONTENTS

ABBREVIATIONS

Papyri are cited according to J.F. Oates *et al.*, *Checklist of Editions of Greek Papyri and Ostraca* (*BASP*Sup, 4; Atlanta, 1985).

Aeg	*Aegyptus*
AE	*L'Année épigraphique* (Paris: Leroux, 1888–1940; Presses Universitaires de France, 1941– [1919–1964 published in *Revue Archéologique*])
AHw	W. von Soden, *Akkadisches Handwörterbuch*
Archiv	*Archiv für Papyrusforschung*
BA	*Biblical Archaeologist*
BASOR	*Bulletin of the American Schools of Oriental Research*
BASP	*Bulletin of the American Society of Papyrologists*
*BASP*Sup	*Bulletin of the American Society of Papyrologists*, Supplements
CAD	*The Assyrian Dictionary of the Oriental Institute of the University of Chicago*
C d'E	*Chronique d'Egypte*
CIE	*Corpus inscriptionum etruscarum* (Leipzig, 1893–1902)
CIL	*Corpus inscriptionum latinarum*
CQ	*Classical Quarterly*
FIRA	*Fontes iuris romani antejustiniani* (ed. S. Riccobono; Florence: Barbera, 1940–43)
GRBS	*Greek, Roman and Byzantine Studies*
IFAO	L'Instituit français d'archeologie orientale du Caire
IG	*Inscriptiones graecae* (Berlin: de Gruyter [1873–])
IGRR	*Inscriptiones graecae ad res romanas pertinentes* (ed. R. Cagnat, J. Toutain and P. Jouguet; Paris: Leroux, 1901–1927)
ILLRP	*Inscriptiones latinae liberae rei publicae* (ed. A. Degrassi; 2 vols.; Florence: La Nuova Italia, 1957 [rev. edn, 1965], 1963)
ILS	*Inscriptiones latinae selectae* (ed. H. Dessau; Berlin: Weidmann, 1892–1916)
JAOS	*Journal of the American Oriental Society*
JCS	*Journal of Cuneiform Studies*
JHS	*Journal of Hellenic Studies*
JJP	*Journal of Juristic Papyrology*
JQR	*Jewish Quarterly Review*
JRS	*Journal of Roman Studies*
JSOT	*Journal for the Study of the Old Testament*

LR	*Roman Civilization, Sourcebook I: The Republic* (ed. N. Lewis and M. Reinhold; New York; Columbia University, 1966)
OGIS	*Orientis graeci inscriptiones selectae* (ed. W. Dittenberger; Leipzig: Hirzel, 1903–1905)
PG	J. Migne (ed.), *Patrologia graeca*
RB	*Revue biblique*
RDGE	*Roman Documents from the Greek East: Senatus Consulta and Epistulae to the Age of Augustus* (ed. R.K. Sherk; Baltimore: Johns Hopkins University, 1969)
RGE	*Rome and the Greek East to the Death of Augustus* (ed. R.K. Sherk; Translated Documents of Greece and Rome, 4; Cambridge: Cambridge University Press, 1984)
ROL	*Remains of Old Latin*. IV. *Archaic Inscriptions* (ed. E.H. Warmington; Loeb Classical Library; Cambridge, MA: Harvard University Press, 1940)
SBLDS	SBL Dissertation Series
SBLSP	SBL Seminar Papers
SEG	*Supplementum epigraphicum graecum* (eds. H.W. Pleket and R.S. Stroud; Amsterdam: Gieben, 1976–)
*SIG*³	*Sylloge inscriptionum graecarum* (ed. W. Dittenberger; 4 vols.; Leipzig: Hirzel, 1915–17)
TAPA	*Transactions of the American Philological Association*
ZPE	*Zeitschrift für Papyrologie und Epigraphik*
ZSS	*Zeitschrift für Savigny Stiftung*

INTRODUCTION

The essays in this volume were delivered and submitted in writing in 1987–1988 in Ontario as part of the inaugural York University Seminar for Advanced Research. They constitute part of the Gerstein Lectures at York University 1988. The seminar in which they were delivered, 'Law in its Social Setting in the Ancient Mediterranean World', represented an attempt to promote dialogue among social historians and historically minded philologians dealing with all aspects of antiquity in the Mediterranean basin. Three other papers presented in the seminar appear in a volume entitled *Law and Ideology in Monarchic Israel*, where the focus is on cultural changes in Judah in the eighth and seventh centuries BCE.

The range of the contributions in this volume fully reflects that of the seminar. It focuses on the social context of the law in such areas as old Babylonian Mesopotamia, biblical Israel, classical Athens, Rome and Roman Greece, Italy and Egypt, the Byzantine Levant, and the Middle Ages. The strongest common interests are in the functions of kinship groups and kinship status in the administration of disputes and conveyances. Also represented, however, are widespread interests in ancient public policy and its social goals and impact, in the theory and reality of legal institutions and in the status of legal documents in society. The thematic unity of the collection, on the rope model (no single common thread, but a running fabric of overlapping themes), mirrors the sense of the seminar that reflection on one pre-modern culture often produces opportunities to put similar questions to others.

Funding for the Seminar in Advanced Research was provided by the Gerstein Lectures at York University, by the Social Sciences and Humanities Research Council of Canada President's Fund and Conference Programme, and by the York University Faculty of Arts and Senate Committee on Research. The seminar's organizers would like to express their gratitude that a joint effort by scholars in a variety of fields met with support from such a diverse range of programmes.

The specific contributions included in this volume are as follows: Reuven Yaron's address, 'Social Problems in the Ancient Near East', opened the seminar, and adumbrated many of the issues that occupied subsequent sessions. Yaron confronts the issue of theory and result in ancient public policy, principally in connection with the distribution or redistribution of land, but with particular attention to the role of social inequality in land transfer and other transactions. In Mesopotamia, from the mid-third millennium forward, legislators attempted to regulate the conditions of conveyance. Even the earliest texts exhibit a consciousness of the economic distortions to which disparities in status and wealth can lead. They reflect, in fact, a concern that the state, too, may be seen to usurp the property rights of its citizens unfairly. The status of even the weak citizen before the law is equal to that of the strong. In the Mesopotamian tradition, however, enforcement of this norm fell to the king, and where royal interests were involved, no social agency had the power to reverse the king's act. In biblical Israel, however, protection of inferiors against social superiors was part not just of the king's portfolio, but of the prophet's, as the cases of David and Bathsheba and Ahab and Naboth's vineyard illustrate. The publication of the misdeed was in this instance conceived as the sanction against it. Moreover, Mesopotamian and biblical law codes introduce limitations on the sale of land aimed at precluding its alienation from functioning kinship groups (patrilineages)—the right of close kin (and thus potential heirs) either to first refusal or to subsequent redemption of land, and, in the Bible, reversion of property at the jubilee. Thus, not surprisingly, it is the social network of the kin groups that ancient legal theory recognized as the chief protection of the individual landholder, and the latter as the chief benefactor of the network.

Maynard Maidman's essay, 'Some Late Bronze Age Legal Tablets from the British Museum: Problems of Context and Meaning', richly illuminates not just the society of ancient Nuzi (now northeastern Iraq) in the 15th and 14th centuries BCE, but, more importantly, the dialectic between philological recovery of a text's significations and the historical recovery of the text's institutional and social context. The texts published here derive from private archives, typically repositories of business and adoption contracts, deeds, wills and conveyances. These, however, are 'trial' texts, concerning breach of contract or of the law, and permit a fairly detailed reconstruction of a trial process involving no codified law, other than royal edicts, a bench of examining magistrates, and several appellate procedures. Despite the existence of a professional judiciary at Nuzi, no 'trial' texts have been found in any public archive; rather, these texts, sealed by the judges, were deposited in the winner's archives not as descriptions of proceedings, but as a record of the essential facts to be held against future litigation; they thus belong precisely in the private archives that produced them, with the other contracts and conveyances. In particular, many of the texts presented here document the economic life of one successful entrepreneur and financier, and his legal relations with debtors and vendors.

Robert Wilson's reflections on 'The Role of Law in Early Israelite Society' touch on social organization, legal procedure and the relationship between the two. Wilson, too, denies that certain texts, namely, metaphorical legal pleas in prophetic literature, can be understood, as they have been understood, as mirror images of court proceedings. However, with limited appeal to comparative evidence, and on the proviso that new evidence or new insights will require perspectival revision, an agenda for the study of Israelite law in its sociological dimensions can be set. In the premonarchic era, kinship studies models are most powerful. Lineages are hierarchical in nature—each component of a segment is related to its counterparts only through filiation to a superior (hereditary) element in the social taxonomy. Dispute adjudication, thus, is smoothest when living lineage heads are able to enforce customary law on those under their jurisdiction; it involves difficult negotiation when disputes cross the lines of authority enjoyed by such lineage heads. In the monarchical period, increasingly centralized leadership took in the judicial system, engendering conflict with lineage custom. Foreign powers, too, will have introduced novel legal elements. Domestically, priesthoods gradually developed a body of religious law, not necessarily identical with civil law. And prophets, commissioned by God rather than by the laws, will have had the potential to create conflict with existing law. The Persian era, however, saw the decline of prophecy, and the separation of priestly law from civil, the latter under the control of foreign overlords. The judicial history of ancient Israel remains imperfectly, yet generally, open to investigation.

'Agnatic Kinship in Athenian Law and Athenian Family Practice: Its Implications for Women', by Virginia Hunter, places Athenian women, after marriage, in the context of their natal kin-groups. Agnatic kinship, which was stronger in the network of Athenian bilateral kinship than recent studies allow, also cemented ties between a woman and her own agnates, the natal family. The individual's secondary kinship group extended to children of first cousins on both the mother's and the father's side. In homicide prosecutions and cases of intestate succession, agnates had precedence, including, however, female agnates (sisters before uncle, cousins and uterine half-brothers, for example). The right of agnatic female inheritance in particular was yoked with attenuated property rights inside the husband's household. Sisters' children, who were heirs in law, comprise the largest group of adopted agnates in the extant legal corpus, though brothers' children were perhaps preferable as adoptees. Indeed, the practice developed of having an inheriting daughter's son adopted posthumously by her father, thus furnishing him with a male heir; inheriting sisters also were expected to provide a son to his estate. In marriage, too, the natal family remained responsible for a woman, who only slowly assimilated to her husband's household, particularly before she had borne a son. Where a woman was an heir, complex pressures could develop from various branches of her family; it was her eventual male issue who guaranteed succession, such that she was potentially the equivalent of a daughter to any agnate. Generally, the kinship structure of classical Athens reflects bilateral orientation, which prohibited the complete absorption of women into their conjugal families.

Marguerite Deslauriers's essay, entitled 'Some Implications of Aristotle's Conception of A   uthority', excavates the philosopher's undeveloped view of the justification of the state's right to govern without constant coercion, which lies at the basis of his concept of the legitimate (city-)state (polis). Authority in this sense is to be distinguished from threat and persuasion, as dependent in the individual on expertise or special knowledge, and, in the state, on constitution (it then manifests itself in laws). Modelling his concept of state authority on one part of an individual's soul ruling the rest—a natural state— Aristotle distinguished the state's councillors from its warriors (and took these only, as distinct from labourers, to be the part of the state). This structural comparison of state with individual contrasts with the functional comparison of state to household—each serves the purpose of supplying the individual's wants. If the societies constituting the state are natural, and if households and villages had it as a goal to live in the state, then the state is natural. Within the household, however, the male head has authority by dint of a deliberative faculty absent in slaves, by nature, undeveloped in children, and, by convention, not attributed to women (the last judgment derived from a structural parallel of the husband–wife relationship with that between ruler and ruled). Within the individual, the deliberative faculty has authority when it governs the appetitive. And within the state, the constitution enjoys authority when it ensures governance geared to the common good, not the interests of the rulers alone. Overall, Aristotle assumes that people concur on authority by convention only. Conversely, Aristotle models his concept of state authority on questions involving the individual, and contrary to received wisdom and the seeming implication of *Politics* Book 1, makes this the basis for his modelling of authority in the household.

Working from Cicero's published speeches, and thus, like Maidman, not from actual trial records, Paul Swarney analyzes 'Social Status and Social Behaviour as Criteria in Judicial Proceedings in the Late Republic'. He argues that a defendant's place in society, and the prose-cutor's inferiority or social deviance, were central to Roman jurisprudential rhetoric. The defenses of Sex. Roscius, A. Cluentius Habitus and M. Caelius Rufus, spoken before the kin and dependents of defendant and prosecutors alike, all reflect the fact that the state played the role, at best, of an impartial referee in a contest between two social blocs. Portraying his defendants and particularly their friends as upstanding models of the ancient virtues was Cicero's strategy to compel the prosecution to make its accusations psychologi-cally plausible. The prosecutors, conversely, are characterized as violent libertines, driven by cupidity, or as opponents in feud, driven by family pressure and by hate. Such legal duels offered opportunities for young advocates to enhance their standing in society, and for the principals to vindicate the dignity of their own parties. Completely absent, however, is any appeal to concrete evidence of innocence or guilt. The trials in question, thus, were less examining tribunals than social occasions.

Jonathan Edmondson's '*Instrumenta Imperii*: Law and Imperialism in Republican Rome' contributes to the ongoing discussion, not of the Roman elite per se, but of the impact of Roman domination on peripheral zones. The concern here is with Roman administrative instruments in the empire, both in their concrete and in their symbolic valences. Focusing on edicts and decrees displayed as stelae or as plaques, mounted ritually on temple walls, Edmondson discerns a mix of evidence that includes both the unexpected and the predictable. Rome sometimes required public display, such as at the initiative of a general, anxious to claim a place as the founder of a new order after subjecting a region or population. The same requirement was made of subjects and clients alike, and was attached to certain weighty *senatus* consulta and Latin law codes—an extension of the antique tradition of erecting monumental victory dedications—especially in the late second century BCE, leading perhaps to the Social War. Yet gradually, Roman legal style and presentation infiltrated the writings of affected communities. In this way, Roman constitutional and legal culture informed the peripheries of the empire. Conversely, dependents of Rome in the provinces sometimes took the initiative to display decrees from the centre, in order to solidify their own local standing, whether among competing communities, or, for example as envoys to Rome, among the elite within a particular state. The very act of public discourse between Rome and the empire thus comes into focus as one of mutual reinforcement between the Roman and the peripheral elites. The effect was a tendency toward the effacement of local differences, particularly in legal procedures and elite culture—one of the hallmarks of a trading empire. The results of this study correlate quite closely, thus, with Gray's remarks on the politics of Byzantine administration.

Deborah Hobson examines 'The Impact of Law on Village Life in Roman Egypt' from the perspective of the rural inhabitants of Egypt. In the early Roman era, fiscal, administrative, military and legal authority were not distinct categories, particularly to the ignorant villager—it is questionable whether such a person could have had a clear understanding of what constituted the law. Though imperial edicts were widely disseminated throughout the country (as demonstrated by Edmondson), comparison of texts from different sites discloses that access to the legal machinery was differential. Hobson draws much of her information from petitions from three communities, two of them relatively insignificant villages (Tebtunis, Soknopaiou Nesos), and one of them a district capital or metropolis (Oxyrhynchus). In these documents, individuals appeal to officials for assistance in settling disputes; thus they provide first-hand evidence of how the inhabitants interfaced with the legal system. Yet petitions are only the end of the disputing process; most disputes are settled informally, the law being invoked when less formal processes fail. Comparing petitions from the metropolis with those of the villages, Hobson finds that only those from the metropolis reflect a knowledge of specific laws which might be applicable in a particular case. Furthermore, those from the metropolis are more often directed to the prefect, who was the supreme authority in the country and the personal representative of the Roman emperor, whereas those from the villages tend to be addressed to a more regional or local authority. Petitions reflect a judicial system which is heavily dependent on self-help, and thus works inevitably to reinforce the rights of the most powerful—the winners, as in Maidman's archival setting, to which the present evidence is most similar, or the advocates, as in the cases of Hunter and Swarney. Many of the petitions from the metropolis refer to previous levels of adjudication of cases—evidently, villagers were far less likely to persist with their cases until they reached a level at which an authoritative adjudication was made. Hobson concludes that to the rural inhabitants of Egypt the imperial legal system would have been more perceptible as a source of authority or obligation than as a means of protecting their personal rights.

In 'Slavery and Society in Late Roman Egypt', Roger Bagnall directs attention to a phenomenon accorded little scrutiny in the rest of the collection, namely slavery and the socioeconomic status of slaves. The basis for the regnant consensus that slavery declined precipitously in Egypt starting in the third century CE is a decline in the percentage of slaves and manumissions recorded in surviving papyri. Yet similar evidence could be adduced to indicate that slavery suddenly boomed during the early Roman period over against the Ptolemaic. In fact, however, the picture is distorted by the nature and distribution of the surviving documentation. Deducting from the comparison those genres of documents not found after c. 300 CE produces comparable percentages of references to slaves. Furthermore, critical examination of the evidence for rural slavery reveals a consistent pattern of limited slave ownership among holders of modest properties, who not only benefited from augmented labour at harvest, but also undertook civic duties. Slaveholding would have been at a special premium on farms whose owners did not enjoy integration into a large kinship network. Slaves also constituted a significant complement of the staff—though not plainly in agriculture—of 'great houses'. In the towns, slaves tended to be their masters' business aides or domestics. Conditions were such that slaves attempted escape, or pursued the possibility of manumission. Masters seem not to have reposed great trust in them, despite their having to shoulder weighty responsibilities. Slaves also figure prominently not just in reports of theft, but also of urban violence. Indeed, with the wealthy urban elite continuing to rely on slaves and tenant farmers, slaveholding in late antiquity appears to have all the economic and social characteristics of the earlier period.

Patrick Gray's 'Palestine and Justinian's Legislation on Non-Christian Religions' surveys conditions in sixth-century Palestine to advance the thesis that Byzantine legislation reflected pressure exerted upon the centre by officialdom and the elite in the peripheries. Though immigrant Christian monastics, in the main of an elite, literate, pro-Chalcedonian bent, had established themselves in the region of Jerusalem and in the desert, Jews, Samaritans and pagans comprised the bulk of the population. In some cases, these enjoyed considerable rank in the local officialdom of the empire when, probably in reaction to Christian nervousness about them, Justinian banned heretics, Jews, Samaritans and pagans from any public or military office. Yet this measure reflects pressure exerted by Christians upon the centre as much as a personal zealotry. At the local level it manifested itself in brutalization in the cause of speeding pagan conversions. However, paganism, though in existence, was by this time marginal and unorganized in the region. Christians also had a long history of attempting to stamp out Samaritanism. In the sixth century, one influential Jerusalemite archimandrite is known to have encouraged the immolation of a prominent Samaritan; Samaritan baiting was common. The legislation from the centre reflects these circumstances, including Jews and Samaritans, for example, among those forbidden to disinherit orthodox Christian children—a provision geared to fracturing agricultural communities. And even after the resultant uprising of 529, the emperor made a point of ordering the destruction of all Samaritan synagogues and banning all non-orthodox heirs. Indeed, when Jewish and heretical testimony against Christians was banned, Samaritan testimony was outlawed in all proceedings. And, as Samaritan fields lay increasingly fallow and a heavy tax burden began to accrue to Christian landowners, at the intercession of the Archbishop of Caesarea, Justinian retracted the harshest elements of the legislation. How Justinian's legislation affected Jews is less clear; a novella of 545 applied the sanction of confiscation against the construction of buildings for non-orthodox religious use; construction continued, perhaps because the institutions of the church did not extend into the inside of rural Jewish villages. Yet, as in the matter of legislation against excommunication of those who read the Bible in Greek, rather than Hebrew, and against appeal to the Mishnah, the pressure for these innovations seems to have stemmed from divines interested in eradicating ethno-religious heterogeneity in the province. The urge to homogenize the empire, thus, was not just a product of central initiative, but also of central response to agencies of the centre located in the peripheries.

'Truth or *peśāt*? Issues in Law and Exegesis', by Martin Lockshin, examines the awakening of interest in the plain sense of the biblical text among Jewish exegetes in the eleventh and twelfth centuries CE. Midrash, the standard form of exegesis, especially of legal texts, showed little regard for the complex signification of a whole text, focusing its attention instead on minutiae in a single word or passage and imposing the resulting interpretation on the context. Primarily a means of applying law, midrashic method enabled rabbinic authorities to adapt ancient legislation to changed communal circumstances. The medievals interested in the plain sense of legal texts therefore lacked a precedent for their inquiries; Ibn Ezra thus argued that it was midrash which was authoritative for the life of the community, but that midrash was not identical with exegesis. Rashbam admitted midrash as the most important method of exegesis, but sought the plain sense in addition to the midrashic. Nevertheless, this concession led to impasses, such that the plain sense of the biblical text, according to an exegete, might contradict the law (the midrash on the text). The implication of such contradictions would be that the plain sense of the biblical text is irrelevant to its authoritative, traditional, midrashic construction, which is perhaps one reason why Rashbam's commentary on the Pentateuch did not capture the attention of later traditional Jews.

Overall, then, this volume locates law in pre-modern Mediterranean societies in its context in constitution and other elite theory, in the state, in urban and village life, in the interaction among the kinship networks and between kinship organization and the state. The degree of comparability of issues across societies is probably less remarkable than it may seem at first. The same questions may profitably be levelled at most complex societies with a history of legislation and especially of constitutional thought. Fortunately for the historian, the ancient societies under scrutiny here have left adequate documentation to wrestle with. Even so, as perusal of the collection will reveal, scholars are driven, explicitly or implicitly, to anthropological models to furnish conceptual frameworks for their analyses. It is our experience and expectation that exposure to a broad range of corpora and ancient cultures will cast light on the types of overtures that may in any single case prove fruitful. In the hope of fostering such a cross-cultural dialogue, then, we offer this volume.

Baruch Halpern
Deborah Hobson
November 1992

Social Problems and Policies in the Ancient Near East

Reuven Yaron

From the very early times ancient Near Eastern sources display considerable awareness concerning social problems. Beyond mere awareness, there is the desire to deal with such problems in a practical way; if not to resolve them, at least make them easier to live with. Yet these were not, nor were they meant to be, egalitarian societies. Even the Bible, which so often takes note of the poor and wishes to care for them, only rarely speaks in abolitionist terms, expressing a desire for the elimination of poverty, or envisaging a distant future, when poverty will have disappeared. Usually it combines a recognition of poverty as a constant phenomenon, with the exhortation to do something about it: 'For there will never cease to be needy ones in your land, which is why I command you: open your hand to the poor and needy kinsmen in your land' (Deut. 15.11). Even where—in later times—equality was proclaimed to be a major aim and purpose of society, there was a considerable gap between ideals and achievement, between programme and performance.

It should be obvious that in the sphere of welfare the actual state of affairs in the ancient Near East does not bear comparison with modern practices. In stressing the practical aspects over the programmatic ones, I wish to bridge the gap between the apparently conflicting attitudes which one encounters in modern societies. One may cast a glance at two materially rather comfortable countries, like the United States and Sweden, and find much more discrepancy in dogma than in practice. What is praised in one place, may well be regarded in the other as no more than a necessary evil. But when one turns from rhetoric and examines what is actually being done—the attempt, for example, to measure the investment in education or health-care—the differences may shrink very considerably.

It is this generalized picture of modern, developed welfare practice which I would juxtapose with what one finds in the ancient world. And when one does so, one comes up with stark contrasts. One difference is slavery—that pillar of ancient economic life. Today human beings no longer constitute a mere economic asset, to be disposed of just like other live or inanimate property. People are no longer, due to their inferior status, deprived of *Freizügigkeit*, the right, that is, to move from one residence to another, nor are they prevented from contracting a legally recognized marriage.

Let me start with some general remarks concerning the need for assistance or protection felt by some when they find themselves in collision with someone stronger. In a given situation even a strong person (in terms of wealth and influence) may be facing someone who is yet stronger, and they might then wish to fall back on some supportive institution. Such a person or institution might be the head of the society, the state—whether they are called 'king', or bear some lesser title.

The earliest material that is relevant to our topic, in Sumerian, goes back to the middle of the twenty-fourth century BCE. While this is early, it does not take us back to Sumerian beginnings. At that time their past extended over many centuries, about half a millennium. During this prolonged period, their ideas had developed and matured over a wide range of topics and so we encounter sometimes formulations and sentiments which are quite advanced, and may appear to be anachronistically modern. It is not that the sources are out of step with the realities of social life, rather that our assumptions are mistaken. Sumer of the third millennium was far from primitive.

The earliest source is also one of the most detailed. These are reforms proclaimed by Uruinimgina, king of Lagash, who ruled about 2350 BCE, a scion of a dynasty which had established itself in the city about 2500 BCE. The text deals at length with various malpractices and abuses, which the king wishes to suppress. Excessive taxes are to be abolished or reduced. High-handed behaviour of functionaries and bureaucrats is to be restrained. Here I shall concentrate on two passages which refer to land.[1]

---

1.   For the full text of the reform documents, see S.N. Kramer, *The Sumerians: Their History, Culture and Character* (Chicago: University of Chicago Press, 1963), pp. 317-22. Especially important, not only for the Uruinimgina text but also for the topic in general, is D.O. Edzard, '"Soziale Reformen" im Zweistromland', in

Humanity's acquisitiveness, its desire to accumulate and to hoard, is not confined to a particular type of property. In that respect humankind is truly omnivorous. It will derive its income from a great variety of activities, and will employ the means at its disposal in many fashions. But there is a significant difference between the acquisition of most movables and that of land. As long as one disregards unique pieces (a famous painting, an ancient manuscript might be stock examples), the acquisition of movables does not ordinarily imply the deprivation of others, the prior owners.

With land, however, the urge to acquire may frequently find expression in the effort to displace the neighbour, to add a piece of land to the estate of the acquirer, the one who is socially or financially stronger. The rich man 'needs' the land of his neighbour, and resents his refusal to move aside. Only in very exceptional circumstances will the desire for more land find satisfaction in transferring to a place where there is as yet no competition, or only little of it, to conquer virgin lands. Usually, the one who is able to do so will be tempted to flex his muscle, physical as well as financial, to make his neighbour an 'irresistible' offer, irresistible because of the stick wielded by the big neighbour, or because of the carrot he offers.

This phenomenon is by no means confined to a specific country, say to Mesopotamia. One finds it practically everywhere, and at all times. The negative impact of big estates upon the social structure of a country was recognized (and deplored) already in antiquity; 'the great estates have destroyed Italy', writes Pliny.[1] It was only to be expected that man's lust for more and more land should lead to various attempts to remedy the situation, to curb acquisition. But it should be obvious that, running into opposition of powerful interests, attempts at containment will often have failed in achieving their aim. The problems of land reform have retained their topical relevance to this day.

In one passage, Uruinimgina describes the excessive concentration of land in to a very few hands:

> The houses of the *ensi* (the ruler) and the fields of the *ensi*, the houses of the (palace) harem and the fields of the (palace) harem, the houses of the (palace) nursery (and) the fields of the (palace) nursery crowded each other side by side.

J. Harmath and G. Komoróczy (eds.), *Wirtschaft und Gesellschaft im alten Voderasien* (Budapest: Akadimiai Kiads, 1976), pp. 145-56.

1. *Historiae Naturales* 18.7.35.

These formulations find a distant, yet unmistakeable echo in the words of Isaiah, some 1600 years later: 'Ah, those who add house to house, and join field to field, till there is room for none but you to dwell in the land' (Isa. 5.8).

In a subsequent passage, the king addresses himself to the need of restraining undue pressure in the acquisition of land:

> When the house of a king's retainer was next to the house of a 'big man' (and) that 'big man' says to him, 'I want to buy it from you', and if when he (the 'big man') is about to buy it from him, he (the king's retainer) says, 'Pay as much as I think fair', or 'Pay me in barley equivalent to my house', then when he refuses to sell it, that 'big man' must not coerce him to do so.

While one would not say that all is clear in this text, its general background seems fairly certain. It appears to reflect at least some earlier instances of coercion, in order to make people abandon their land which is coveted by their 'big' neighbour. The provision itself seems to be dealing with two objectives; first, to make sure that the holder, in case he is willing to sell, will receive a fair price; and secondly, and more importantly, to enable the holder to refuse to sell, to withstand pressures brought to bear upon him. What impact would such a provision have had in practice? In the last resort, the answer would depend upon the readiness of the authorities to intervene, to give redress to the person who was being coerced. Documents from somewhat later old-Babylonian times show the king dealing with complaints concerning the involuntary transfer of possession from one holder to another; occasionally orders are given to restore the *status quo ante*. However, these cases concern lands held from the king (or the palace), not sale brought about by undue pressure. In Rome, if transactions resulted from coercion or threats, redress could be obtained by a special procedure, the *actio quod metus causa*. Here the complainant could obtain the annulment of his undertaking; if he had already performed, he could claim restoration. The action would lie not only against the person who had actually exerted the pressure, but also against the person who had ultimately benefited from it, the purchaser. Penalties might also be imposed.

The beginnings of the dynasty of Ur III, some 300 years after Uruinimgina, bring the laws of Ur-Nammu (now more exactly attributed to his son Shulgi). Fragments of these laws have been discovered and published in the course of the last three decades, the last (so far) in 1981. This is the earliest collection of laws known up to the present. In a structure typical for such collections, the laws proper are preceded by a prologue, setting out the military feats and domestic achievements of the promulgator. (The body of the laws is usually followed by an epilogue, containing exhortations to observe these laws, and imprecations against those who do not. For the laws of Ur-Nammu—or Shulgi—we do not yet have an epilogue; this is probably due only to the fragmentary state of the material.)

Ur-Nammu's prologue contains, amongst others, a series of negative declarations of the king, concerning acts which he proclaims not to have done. One is at once reminded of the well-known 'negative confessions', found in chapter 125 of the Egyptian *Book of the Dead* where the soul of the deceased declares not to have committed 42 specific offences. Each declaration is addressed to a specific deity. (Professor Daube's gloss: 'No. 43 got lost: "I have written no papers"'.)

This, then, is what Ur-Nammu declares:

> The orphan I did not deliver to the rich, the widow I did not deliver to the
> mighty. The man of one shekel, I did not deliver to the man of one *mina*
> (= 60 shekel), the man of one lamb I did not deliver to the man of one ox.

Note the cautious phrasing of the passage. The king does not assert that he has taken active steps for the protection of the orphan, the widow, the relatively weak person. It would not have been difficult to formulate a positive sentence, like 'the orphan called out to me, and I protected him against the rich; the widow approached me, and I assisted her against the mighty'. The very restrained tone of the declaration sounds almost apologetic. Note, on the other hand, the repetitive style, which adds emphasis; orphan and widow form a pair, vis-à-vis their potential oppressors, the rich and the mighty. The man of 1 shekel and the man of 1 lamb are parallel in their weakness, vis-à-vis the man of 1 *mina* and the man of 1 ox. I shall return to the last pair in this quartet, '1 lamb–1 ox', when I discuss its biblical echo, in the famous parable of the 'poor man's lamb'.

The Ur-Nammu prologue continues at once with the following statement: 'I se[ttled] my generals, my mother, my [sister]s (and) my brothers, their acqu[aintances] (and) their [loved ones]. I did not [put] myself [at the disposal?] of [the]ir. . . I did not impose labour(?)'.

The verb in the first part of the passage, rendered by 'se[ttled]', is largely restored, but it makes good sense, and I can but proceed on the assumption that the proposed restoration is correct. Towards the end, the tablet is again impaired and altogether open to doubt. Accepting, then, the basic validity of the suggested restoration, namely that the passage concerns favours rendered by the king to his entourage and to his family, one must ask oneself, what the purpose of such a declaration may have been. Since human nature is what it is, favouritism and nepotism are to be expected, but the king is unlikely to have boasted about favours he has shown to those close to him.

For a speculative solution, I take my cue from Ezek. 46.16-18: 'But the prince shall not take property away from any of the people and rob them of their holdings. Only out of his own holdings shall he endow his sons, in order that My people may not be dispossessed of their holdings'.

My suggestion is that the passage quoted from Ur-Nammu's prologue in fact continues his negative confession. The king mentions that he gave land to his associates, and to members of his family, but stresses that he did so without depriving anyone of what was his (note that there are, twice over, negations at the end of the passage, but unfortunately the context is altogether unclear). If this speculation were confirmed, it would still have to be understood *cum grano salis*; times of political upheaval (such as the establishment of a new dynasty, here that of Ur III, by Ur-Nammu) bring about not only a shift in power, but also often involve the transfer of property. The 'ins' of yesteryear have become 'outs', they may have had to flee the city, and in doing so would have forfeited all that they could not take with them; in the first place any land of theirs, owned or held otherwise (when one has to move, land is the least useful of possessions). The same would apply to others who at any time found the ground under their feet too hot for comfort. Confiscation of property of anyone entangled in political crime (or suspected of it, rightly or wrongly) will since early times have been a widespread phenomenon. Very interesting in this context is a fourteenth-century document from Alalakh.[1] A groom had brought a *nidnu* (bride-payment) to his prospective father-in-law. The latter had turned into an evil-doer (*bel masiktim*), and consequently 'he was killed according to his offence'; and his property 'entered to the king', was forfeited. The groom, an inhabitant

---

1. Text 17, in the edition by D.J. Wiseman, *The Alakah Tablets* (London: The British Institute of Archaeology at Ankara, 1953), p. 40. I follow the interpretation of the text given in the *Chicago Assyrian Dictionary* M, part i (1977), p. 324.

of another city, now comes and claims the return of what he had given as *nidnu* (which had become part of the property of the girl's father, and had shared its fate). His request is granted. It is a necessary corollary that he had renounced the idea of marrying the daughter of an executed offender. Were he still willing to have her, there would be no ground for claiming the return of the *nidnu*. It is the groom's refusal to consummate the union, a refusal deemed justified in the situation which had arisen, which is the starting point for the demand of *restitutio in integrum*, if one may use a Roman technical term in an early Oriental context. But what concerns us here is the way in which forfeiture of the offender's property is regarded as a matter of course.

The most important law text which Mesopotamia has bequeathed to posterity is the Code of Hammurabi (king of Babylon, c. 1729–1686). The text is written in Akkadian and engraved on a stone stele. It was found in 1901, during excavations at Susa, and is currently at the Louvre. The king sets out the essential purpose of his compilation of laws, as follows: 'That the strong man may not oppress the weak (*dannum enšam ana la ḫabalim*), to give justice to the orphan (and) the widow, I have inscribed my precious words on my monument' (epilogue xxivb. 59-62; the words quoted here in Akkadian are given identically in the prologue i. 37-39). The progress in formulation is noteworthy. No need now for detailed negative confessions, as offered by Ur-Nammu, which at the side of Hammurabi's elegantly brief slogan looks rather clumsy.

Scholars have recognised the central significance of the statement *dannum enšam ana la ḫabalim*[1] and I concur. I suggest that one may, without exaggerating, put this maxim on a par with some famous later formulations, such as *we'ahavta l^ere'akha kamokha*—'love your fellow as yourself' (Lev. 19.18). In the early Talmudic period, Hillel restated this, quoting a popular proverb: 'What is hateful to thee, do not do to your fellow'—*ma d^elakh śani l^ehaverakh la ta'aved* (b. Šab. 31a). Hillel goes so far as to proclaim this proverb a central tenet of Judaism, treating all the rest as secondary. Incidentally, one may note that the principle, as expressed by Hillel, is much more concrete and meaningful a criterion of behaviour than the rather vague positive formulation in the Bible. Everyone feels instinctively what is

1. See in particular F.N.H. Al-Rawi, 'Assault and Battery', *Sumer* 38 (1982), p. 117.

distasteful to him, and hence ought to be able to estimate full-well what he ought not to do to others. What, by contrast, are suitable limits of *amour propre*, of 'loving oneself'?

To these two maxims, of Hammurabi and of Hillel, one may add a third one, identical in spirit and import. This is Ulpian's triple precept *honeste vivere, alterum non laedere, suum cuique tribuere* (Dig. 1.1.10.1). For our context I would emphasize the middle one *alterum non laedere*—'not to hurt another'. So, over a period of some 2000 years, the same central idea appears, expressed in a rather similar fashion, in three different societies, in old Babylonia, in early Talmudic Jewry and in Severan Rome. But, focusing again on Hammurabi, the interesting fact is that such an advanced, abstract and concise formulation could be achieved at so early a time, in the seventeenth century BCE. It reflects the distillation of a basic postulate for the proper functioning of a society; everyone is duty-bound to respect the rights of others, not to hurt one who is weaker.

Hammurabi was not the last Mesopotamian ruler to speak of the need to protect the weak, to prevent his oppression by the stronger. Without going into detail, similar sentiments can be noted in much later times—so in a neo-Assyrian inscription of Esarhaddon (early seventh century), and in a neo-Babylonian one of Nebuchadnezar II (early sixth century). It has been said that the 'motif of protection and just judgment for widows and orphans is a traditional literary topos in ancient oriental royal texts since early times'.[1] This is indeed so, but it should not be taken to indicate that these statements were devoid of purpose and impact. Rather, the very repetition may testify to a considerable degree of genuine concern.

In fact, the protection of the weak will have depended upon the readiness of those occupying the top of the pyramid to intervene on their behalf. It was the king who was traditionally cast in the role of the defender of the weak. Yet, whatever the scope of his protection, the system would hardly offer a remedy in case the king himself happened to covet what was not his; say, a beautiful woman (married to another) or a piece of land (belonging to someone else). Not only coveted, but used (or abused) the power inherent in his position to obtain what he longed for. There is no reason to doubt that such situations will have arisen again and again.

1.   H.M. Kümmel, in W. Schuller (ed.), *Korruption im Altertum* (Munich: R. Oldenbourg, 1982), p. 59.

There is a more concrete picture for ancient Israel, owing to the emergence of a new and highly influential element. Prophecy is not an exclusively Hebrew phenomenon, but it seems to have developed and flourished in Israel more than elsewhere. 'The term prophet refers to an inspired person who believes that he has been sent by his god with a message to tell. He is, in this sense, the mouthpiece of his god.'[1] The prophet represents a non-institutionalized facet of religion (in contrast with the priest). He will pronounce his views—as inspired by his principal, whom he serves—over a wide range of topics—religion, foreign affairs, problems of social justice. Even this last aspect, which is our immediate concern, is the topic for books, not for the fragment of a lecture. Here I shall confine myself to quoting, from Isaiah, the prophet whom I have mentioned in discussing a passage from Uruinimgina. Following this, I shall relate, in some greater detail, two instances which have a king as the villain of the tale.

The prophet is a radical. Often his words will arouse the enmity of those against whom they are directed. He might face persecution, even death. His only shield is his divine mission, which is a source of inner strength, and might often, though not always, restrain his adversaries.

In Isaiah, we find in 1.23: 'Your rulers are rogues and cronies of thieves, every one avid for presents, and greedy for gifts; they do not judge the case of the orphan, and the widow's cause never reaches them'. Again in 3.13-14: 'The Lord stands up to plead a cause, he rises to champion peoples. The Lord will bring this charge against the elders and officers of His people: "It is you who have ravaged the vineyard: that which was robbed from the poor is in your houses"'. And in 10.1-2: 'Ah! Those who write out evil writs and compose iniquitous documents, to subvert the cause of the poor, to rob of their rights the needy of My people; That widows may be their spoil, and orphans their booty!'

I turn now to the two cases of royal abuse of power, recorded in the Bible. These stories have been much discussed, and opinions differ on their *Entstehungsgeschichte*, how they were given the shape in which they are presented in the biblical texts. This is a discussion in which we need not participate. Whatever their history, the stories, as they are before us, are of great interest; they reflect the views and attitudes of their authors, and have had their impact on their readers.

The first case concerns the affair of David with Bathsheba, related

1.   *The New Encyclopaedia Britannica, Macropaedia,* vol. XV, s.v. Prophecy.

in 2 Samuel 11 and 12. From the roof of his house the king saw a
very beautiful woman washing herself. He establishes her identity—
she is Bathsheba, the wife of Uriah the Hittite, who is at the time in
the king's army, laying siege to Rabbath Ammon. David has the
woman brought to his house, 'she came to him and he lay with her. . .
and she went back home. The woman conceived, and she sent word to
David, "I am pregnant".' David now attempts to cover his tracks. He
summons Uriah from the field: 'When Uriah came to him, David
asked him how Joab (the commander of the army) and the troops
were faring, and how the war was going'. David then dismisses Uriah
to his house; 'but Uriah slept at the entrance of the royal palace, along
with the other officers of his lord, and did not go down to his house'.
David is told of Uriah's surprising behaviour and he queries him:
'Why did you not go down to your house?' Uriah answered David:
'The Ark and Israel and Judah are located at Succoth, and my master
Joab and Your Majesty's men are camped in the open; how can I go
home and eat and drink and sleep with my wife? As you live, by your
very life, I will not do this.' David keeps Uriah in Jerusalem for one
more day. Uriah eats with the king, who uses the opportunity to make
him drunk. To no avail—the loyal Uriah does not go to his house, and
thereby signs his death-warrant. David sends a letter to Joab, by hand
of Uriah: 'Place Uriah in the front line where the fighting is fiercest:
then fall back so that he may be killed'. The king's orders are carried
out. Uriah dies and Joab has it reported to the king:

> The messenger said to David, 'First the men prevailed against us and
> sallied out against us into the open; then we drove them back up to the
> entrance of the gate. But the archers shot at your men from the wall and
> some of Your Majesty's men fell; your servant Uriah also fell'.
> Whereupon David said to the messenger, 'Give Joab this message: Do not
> be distressed about the matter. The sword always takes its toll. . .' When
> Uriah's wife heard that her husband Uriah was dead, she lamented over
> her husband. After the period of mourning was over, David sent and had
> her brought into his palace; she became his wife and she bore him a son.

End of Act I. Evil has triumphed, but not for long. Already, the
clouds are gathering; the story takes its course, and nothing can
prevent it.

> But the Lord was displeased with what David had done, and the Lord sent
> Nathan to David. He came to him and said, 'There were two men in the
> same city, one rich and one poor. The rich man had very large flocks and

herds, but the poor man had only one little ewe lamb that he had bought.
He tended it and it grew up together with him and his children: it used to
share his morsel of bread, drink from his cup, and nestle in his bosom; it
was like a daughter to him. One day, a traveller came to the rich man, but
he was loath to take anything from his own flocks or herds to prepare a
meal for the guest who had come to him; so he took the poor man's lamb
and prepared it for the man who had come to him.'

The king is not yet aware that the prophet's story refers to him.

David flew into a rage against the man, and said to Nathan, 'As the Lord
lives, the man who did this deserves to die! He shall pay for the lamb four
times over, because he did such a thing and showed no pity.'

Unwittingly, the king has pronounced judgement against himself. The
dénouement follows at once:

And Nathan said to David, 'That man is you! Thus said the Lord, the God
of Israel. . . Why have you flouted the command of the Lord and done
what displeases him? You have put Uriah the Hittite to the sword; you
took his wife and made her your wife and had him killed by the sword of
the Ammonites. Therefore the sword shall never depart from your
House—because you spurned me by taking the wife of Uriah the Hittite
and making her your wife. Thus said the Lord: "I will make a calamity
rise against you from within your own house; I will take your wives and
give them to another man before your eyes, and he shall sleep with your
wives under this very sun. You acted in secret, but I will make this
happen in the sight of all Israel, and in broad daylight".'

David admits his sin, and is granted a qualified pardon. He will not die
because of what he has done, but the son begotten from Bathsheba
will. Curiously enough, one rather obvious sanction is missing, as if
the prophet knew the limits of the attainable. David is not made to
renounce his relationship with the dead man's wife. He has another
son by Bathsheba, his eventual successor to the throne, Solomon.

Let me return briefly to Ur-Nammu's declaration 'the man of one
lamb I did not deliver to the man of one ox'—I have already
suggested that this dictum has its echo, albeit a faint one, in Nathan's
parable. Since more than a millennium separates the two kings, the
Sumerian and the Judaean, I do not claim that Nathan's parable can be
directly traced to Ur-Nammu, but the image invoked may have been
commonly known in the ancient Orient. If one connects, in this way,
Ur-Nammu's 'negative confession' with the parable of Nathan, then
David's offence becomes compounded. Not only has he, in the role of

'the man of one ox' committed a grave transgression, but he also failed in his duty as ruler, to protect those who are relatively weak. And, in addition to its moral and legal implications, the story of David and Uriah is also a literary masterpiece. Nothing could be more striking than the contrast between a soldier's loyalty and his king's treachery.

The second drama, some 150 years later, is also performed by four participants, a king, his subject, a woman (this time the king's wife) and the prophet. The actual circumstances are different as we return from a tragedy engendered by illicit love, to the rather more prosaic story of a king who covets a piece of land bordering on his estate. It is the story of Ahab, king of Israel (c. 874–853), as related in 1 Kings 21 and 22:

> Naboth the Jezreelite owned a vineyard in Jezreel, adjoining the palace of King Ahab of Samariah. Ahab said to Naboth, 'Give me your vineyard, so that I may have it as a vegetable garden, since it is right next to my palace. I will give you a better vineyard in exchange; or, if you prefer, I will pay you the price in silver.'

The royal offer meets with a stubborn refusal. Naboth is attached to his paternal land: 'But Naboth replied, "The Lord forbid that I should give up to you what I have inherited from my fathers!"' He relies on his right, he does not want to convey his land, and he will not. Yet he acts in total and fatal disregard of the realities of the situation (what the Germans call *Machtlage*), and will soon suffer for it. As the Bible tells the story, he even might have got away with his daring. The king returns to his house, angry and truculent, and this might have been it, but for the intervention of his evil genius, his wife Jezebel, the foreign princess.

> His wife Jezebel came to him and asked him, 'Why are you so dispirited that you won't eat?' So he told her, 'I spoke to Naboth the Jezreelite and proposed to him, "Sell me your vineyard for silver, or if you prefer, I'll give you another vineyard in exchange"; but he answered, "I will not give my vineyard to you"'.

Jezebel decides to take the matter into her own hands. She urges her royal husband along, 'Now is the time to show yourself king over Israel'; but she does not rely on him to assert himself: 'I will get the vineyard of Naboth the Jezreelite for you'. Deeds follow at once:

> So she wrote letters in Ahab's name and sealed them with his seal, and sent the letters to the elders and the nobles who lived in the same town with Naboth. In the letters she wrote as follows: 'Proclaim a fast and seat

> Naboth at the front of the assembly. And seat two scoundrels opposite
> him, and let them testify against him: "You have reviled God and king!"
> Then take him out and stone him to death.'

The recipients of the letter did as instructed (just as Joab had done in
his time); Naboth is brought to trial on trumped-up charges of treason, false evidence is given against him and he is executed. Jezebel is
informed.

> As soon as Jezebel heard that Naboth had been stoned to death, she said
> to Ahab, 'Go and take possession of the vineyard which Naboth refused
> to sell you for silver; for Naboth is no longer alive, he is dead'. When
> Ahab heard that Naboth was dead, Ahab set out for the vineyard of
> Naboth the Jezreelite, to take possession of it.

In so taking possession, Ahab presumably acted in accordance with the
rule providing for the confiscation of the property of persons
convicted of political crime.

The stage is now set for the entry of the prophet; only, this time
there is no parable. Everything is to the point.

> Then the word of the Lord came to Elijah the Tishbite: 'Go down and
> confront King Ahab of Israel, who (resides) in Samaria. He is now in
> Naboth's vineyard; he has gone down there, to take possession of it. Say
> to him, Thus said the Lord: "Would you murder and take possession?"
> Thus said the Lord: "In the very place where the dogs lapped up Naboth's
> blood, the dogs will lap up your blood too".'

There are legal overtones to Ahab's plaintive question: 'So you have
found me, my enemy?' In this context, 'to find' means 'find *in
flagranti delicto*, with guilt clear beyond doubt'. Similarly in Elijah's
reply: 'Yes, I have found you; because you have committed yourself
to do what is evil in the sight of the Lord'. The king repents, and
displays his repentance: 'When Ahab heard these words, he rent his
clothes, and put sackcloth on his body. He fasted and lay in sackcloth
and walked about subdued.' He is granted a reprieve: 'Then the word
of the Lord came to Elijah the Tishbite: Have you seen how Ahab has
humbled himself before Me? Because he has humbled himself before
Me, I will not bring the disaster in his lifetime; I will bring the
disaster upon his house in his son's time.'

The cases of Uriah the Hittite and of Naboth gained their
prominence in the Bible from the fact that in each instance a king was
involved. Things of this kind may have happened also in less exalted
quarters. We should note that the topics of both are enshrined also in

the 'do-not-covet' exhortations of the decalogue: 'You shall not covet your fellow's house; you shall not covet your fellow's wife...or anything that is your fellow's' (Exod. 20.14).

The kings who were responsible for the death of Uriah and of Naboth incurred divine intervention, through the agency of prophets. This then is the Bible's reply to the question *quis custodiet custodes*? In circumstances which frustrate earthly justice, divine justice will have to take its place. Moreover, let us note, divine retribution is not something remote, to be feared only due to the belief that there is a God who will not suffer grave injustice to go unpunished. In both instances, a very prominent, even though in the last analysis subordinate, part is played by the human messenger, the prophet. His appearance on the scene turns a hazy foreboding, a vague feeling of discomfort, into a virtual certainty.

It is also noteworthy that in neither case is a cover-up attempted. This is not surprising in the case of Ahab; it was above all his policy in matters of religion, his toleration of Canaanite idolatry (possibly reflecting the influence of his queen, Jezebel), which has earned him the lasting enmity of the circles from which the historical books of the Bible originated. So they may have relished telling about the outrage perpetrated by the royal pair ('What else would you expect of an Ahab, of a Jezebel?'). But the situation regarding David was radically different. In the eyes of the biblical narrator he is the Lord's favourite, the prototype of the good king, the founder of the Davidic dynasty. In David's case, the need 'to go public' must have been regarded as a distasteful necessity. There is—in neither case—anything discreet in the way the prophet goes about his business. On the contrary, it would seem to have been part of their task to ensure a great measure of publicity, not for its own sake, but to deter others from acting in a similarly atrocious fashion, should opportunity present itself. The idea may have been that kings would not relish publicity concerning wrongs committed by them.

Turning from general observations which have occupied us so far, I had to make my choice between various topics which might merit enquiry within the theme of 'protecting the weak'. Probably the most significant is that arising out of the relationship between lender and borrower. However, this intricate subject ought to be examined in a more detailed way than is possible within the given framework. So I propose to continue with the ownership of land.

I shall look at a variety of provisions purporting to curb acquisition and to prevent accumulation of land in one hand, by buying out the owners, in perpetuity. Such provisions are then designed either to protect the *status quo* in land ownership, or else to restore the *status quo ante*, after a change has already taken place. Closely interrelated are two devices, pre-emption and redemption. Pre-emption is a right of priority, granted to the next of kin of an owner of land, in case he contemplates selling it; redemption concerns the right of a seller (or of his next of kin) to repurchase the land which had been sold. Much more sweeping is the jubilee provision, calling for the periodic return of land to its previous owner (the seller) or to his successor(s).

The difference between pre-emption and redemption is in the main one of time; redemption takes place after the land had been conveyed to an outsider, pre-emption prior to such an occurrence. One might regard pre-emption as anticipatory or preventive redemption; it is meant to forestall a situation which could be remedied, if at all, by way of redemption. In pre-emption a close relative of the seller will have—by custom or by law—a power to intervene, that is to acquire for himself a piece of property which has been put up for sale (and which a third person, someone outside the family, might wish to acquire). In certain circumstances, such a power might harden into a concrete 'right of first refusal'. In other words, it would be incumbent on the would-be-seller, as a first step towards sale, to offer his piece of land to his closest relative (and in case of refusal possibly also to others, more remote). Incidentally, these relatives are also potential heirs of the seller. The power of redemption, or repurchase, might be exercised by the seller himself, but also by members of his family. Our information concerning pre-emption and redemption is limited to two main sources, to the Laws of Eshnunna and to the Bible. Some private documents refer to it, but the institution does not seem to have been very widespread.

> If one of the brothers will sell his share, and his brother wishes to buy, the *average (price)* of another he shall pay in full.
> If a man became impoverished and sold his house—the day the buyer will sell, the owner of the house may redeem (LE 38–39).

> If your brother is in straits and has to sell part of his holding, his nearest redeemer shall come and redeem what his brother has sold. If a man has no one to redeem for him, but prospers and acquires enough to redeem with, he shall compute the years since its sale, refund the difference to the

man to whom he sold it, and return to his holding. If he lack sufficient
means to recover it, what he sold shall remain with the purchaser until the
Jubilee; in the Jubilee year it shall be released, and he shall return to his
holding.

If a man sells a dwelling house in a walled city, it may be redeemed
until a year elapsed since its sale; the redemption period shall be a year. If
it is not redeemed before a full year has elapsed, the house in the walled
city shall pass to the purchaser beyond reclaim throughout the generations;
it shall not be released in the Jubilee. But houses in villages that have no
encircling walls shall be classed as country: they may be redeemed, and
they shall be released through the Jubilee (Lev. 25.25-31).

On the face of it, Eshnunna 38 might mean that the seller's 'share'
must be offered to his brother. But it is possible that this interpretation is too rigorous, and nothing more than a subsequent right of
intervention is implied, which would compel the purchaser to resell
the 'share' to the brother of the (original) owner. The actual provision
deals with the price which the intervening brother will have to pay;
this is not the actual price paid or offered by the actual or prospective
purchaser, rather the 'average' offered by others. Opinions differ on
the exact meaning of *qablitum* (here rendered 'average'); I believe this
rendering, first suggested by de Liagre Böhl, to be the best one. Pre-
emption, as considered in this section, is a privilege based not on mere
kinship, rather on actual common ownership. A part-owner can avoid
having an outsider foisted on him.

Eshnunna 39 and the passage quoted from Leviticus seem to be
closely related, in that they share a common feature—in each the sale
is described as being consequent to impoverishment. If the lack of
means is a material element, the implication would be restrictive; the
provision would assist only weaker strata of the population. This
would put the emphasis on the social element. While I incline to take
this view, one cannot be certain. Perhaps impoverishment is mentioned only as part of the ordinary course of events, in a society in
which attachment to land is cherished. Why else should one part with
an ancestral holding (see the story of Naboth)? If poverty is essential,
how would it be established? By declaration of the seller? Adequacy
of the price has been suggested as a possible criterion. According to
this view, redemption is allowed only where an adequate price has not
been paid; by contrast, payment of a full price results in a full conveyance, not to be reversible. Westbrook has forcefully taken this
stand, but I am not altogether convinced. How far below the normal

would the price have to be, to trigger redeemability? Also, in a given case, the 'normalcy' of the price might itself be a matter of contention.

Our two sources differ in the way in which they define the occasion for redemption. Leviticus introduces a distinction between rural and urban property, but beyond that thinks purely in terms of time. Property situated within a walled city can be redeemed within one full year after the sale. Rural land can be redeemed, at the original owner's discretion, any time between the sale and the year of jubilee. However, since the rule concerns primarily agricultural land, one would assume that the suitable time for redemption would in each year be after the harvest and before sowing (otherwise complications might arise). The jubilee entails the gratuitous reversion of the land to its former owner (or to a successor of his). Eshnunna 39 envisages redemption only in case the buyer in turn chooses to sell (a matter which is in his absolute discretion). If he does so, this is the original seller's opportunity; now he can step in and assert his earlier rights. It will remain an open question whether it is a one-time opportunity, or whether the power of redemption could be exercised also on some subsequent occasion, in case of a further conveyance (but if so, how often and how long?).

Who is entitled to redeem? Eshnunna 39 mentions only the original seller (to whom one might add his successor[s], should he have died). By contrast, the Bible envisages in the first place redemption by a next of kin (called for this purpose *go'el*—'redeemer'). Redemption by the seller himself is mentioned only as a secondary possibility, in case a man has no redeemer. It is further open to question whether the system of redemption applied only when the sale was to an outsider, or if it would work also within the clan. For example, would a person be able to redeem what he has sold to his brother? The answer would depend upon fundamentals which are hidden from us; we do not know whether Leviticus wishes to protect the family at large, or specifically the original owner (and his descendants).

Neither Eshnunna nor Leviticus tell us about the price payable at redemption. Some scholars would fix it at the price paid originally by the buyer. However, a price freeze coupled with an indeterminate period allowed for redemption (as in Eshnunna 39) might entail some significant drawbacks. It would fail to take into account possible change in the value of land; more significantly, it would discourage development of the property by the buyer. It would also constitute an

effective barrier to subsequent transfer of the land, if on that occasion
the original seller would be able to reacquire the land for what had
become an altogether unrealistic sum.[1]

Two biblical stories touch upon (or concern) pre-emption or
redemption. One is the story of Ruth (Ruth 3.7–13.1), the young
Moabite widow following her mother-in-law Naomi to Bethlehem.
Ruth gleans in a field belonging to Boaz, who treats her well. Naomi,
when told about it, says to her, 'the man is related to us; he is one of
our redeeming kinsmen'. When the harvest is over, Ruth—instructed
by her mother-in-law—goes to the threshing floor, where Boaz was
spending the night. After he went to sleep,

> she went over stealthily and uncovered his feet and lay down. In the
> middle of the night, the man gave a start and pulled back—there was a
> woman lying at his feet! Who are you? he asked. And she replied: 'I am
> Ruth, your handmaid. Spread your robe over your handmaid, for you are
> a redeeming kinsman.'

Boaz reassures her:

> And now, daughter, have no fear. I will do on your behalf whatever you
> ask. . . But while it is true I am a redeemer, there is another redeemer
> closer than I. . . if he will act as redeemer, good! let him redeem. But if
> he does not want to act as redeemer for you, I will redeem you myself, as
> the Lord lives.

That redeemer is indeed willing to redeem the land which had
belonged to Naomi's dead husband, but withdraws upon being told
that acquisition of the land coincides with acquisition of the dead
man's wife. The Hebrew text (followed by the Septuagint) is equivo-
cal, and the anonymous 'redeemer' may have been led to believe that
the statement referred to Naomi. Boaz knew full well what *he* had in
mind; he acquires land and the young widow—Ruth.

It is a complex story, since it combines two separate customs or
practices which have their origin in different spheres of law. The
'acquisition' or 'redemption' of Ruth should be viewed as a kind of
extended levirate marriage (*yibbum*), which in normative biblical
texts applies only to a childless-deceased's brother, which the unnamed
go'el and Boaz were not. Then there is the pre-emption or redemption
of land (our concern in the present context). It is made clear that

---

1.   For further remarks on redemption, and references, see R. Yaron, *Laws of
Eshnunna* (Leiden: Brill, 2nd edn, 1988), pp. 232ff.

every member of one's paternal family is a potential redeemer, but only the very next is the actual, immediate redeemer (there can of course be several relatives of equal proximity; in this case, it is likely, that everyone could have acted on his own). So Boaz cannot act unless the *go'el* renounces his right, his priority stemming from closer proximity.

The story related in Jeremiah 32 takes us into a very different milieu. The kingdom of Judaea is on the verge of collapse. God bids Jeremiah acquire a field owned by Hanamel, son of his uncle Shallum. The field was at Anathoth, to the north of Jerusalem. The city was under siege, and the region of Anathoth may be assumed to have been under Babylonian occupation. Jeremiah himself is detained at the royal prison, for having prophesied the imminent fall of Jerusalem.

> Jeremiah said: The word of the Lord came to me: Hanamel, the son of your uncle Shallum, will come to you and say, 'Buy my land in Anathoth, for you are next in succession to redeem it by purchase'. And, just as the Lord has said, my cousin Hanamel came to me in the prison compound and said to me, 'Please buy my land in Anathoth, in the territory of Benjamin, for the right of succession is yours, and you have the right of redemption. Buy it.' Then I knew that it was indeed the word of the Lord.

Jeremiah does as bidden, 'So I bought the land in Anathoth from my cousin Hanamel. I weighed out the silver to him, seventeen shekels of silver'. A document is executed, signed and sealed, and put into an earthen vessel, to be preserved for a long time. The purpose of this transaction is spelled out in v. 15: 'For thus said the Lord of Hosts, the God of Israel: Houses, fields and vineyards shall again be purchased in this land'.

This is a prophecy going beyond mere declaration, mere statement. The prophet performs an act, and thereby gives concrete emphasis to his words. There are, it is well known, other instances of symbolic concretization. Jeremiah is told to acquire a potter's earthen bottle, which he is later instructed to break into pieces in public, as a prelude to a divine declaration: 'Thus said the Lord of Hosts: So will I smash this people and this city, as one smashes a potter's vessel, which can never be mended'. In another case (ch. 27) we find Jeremiah putting bonds and a yoke on his neck; he sends these to the kings of the anti-Babylonian coalition, whose representatives are assembling in Jerusalem. The message: 'The nation which puts its neck under the yoke of the king of Babylon, and serves him, will be left by Me on its soil—declares the

Lord—to till it and to dwell on it'. In both cases, the act is purely symbolic, has no intrinsic meaning, no purpose other than the demonstration.

When Jeremiah acquires his cousin's land, this too is a symbolic act. But it takes us one step further; while a symbol, it is not a mere symbol. It is a real act, has meaning and purpose of its own, beyond the desired demonstration.

The purchase was meant to boost morale. The witnesses to the transaction, and others present that day in the courtyard of the prison, would spread the story about Jeremiah's act of faith, which was doubly remarkable because it was performed by a prophet whose untiring message was one of doom and gloom, foretelling the imminent downfall, the collapse of Judaea. Indeed, Jeremiah does not change one iota of his prophecies for the immediate future, but he holds out a modicum of hope for distant days: 'Houses, fields and vineyards shall again be purchased in this land'.

This might have been the end of the story, but interestingly enough, it is not. Jeremiah continues with a lengthy prayer, at the end of which he gives muted—but unmistakeable—expression to his unhappiness about the act which he has just performed in obedience to the divine command. To reach this operative point, Jeremiah embarks upon a kind of magnificat, glorifying God's actions throughout history. He goes back to the very beginnings, to the creation of the world, which shows divine omnipotence, unlimited in scope (v. 17). There follows a discourse on the exodus and the occupation of the land by Israel. History is then brought down to the very present; they sinned, and it is because of this that all this evil is happening to them, and the city is doomed to fall into the hands of the Chaldaeans. Here, at long last, Jeremiah arrives at the real purpose of his historical survey: 'Yet you, Lord God, said to me: Buy the land for silver and call in witnesses—when the city is at the mercy of the Chaldaeans'.

It is a very human passage, showing Jeremiah in his attractive weakness, an anti-hero with whom one will easily sympathize. One may assume that Jeremiah was far from well-to-do, yet here he was told to invest seventeen *shekalim* of the little he had in what he appears to have regarded as a poor deal—to perform an act of faith in which he had insufficient faith.

Next comes the divine reply, the divine 'defence' so to speak. It too goes into considerable detail, justifying the punishment meted out to

Judaea, primarily because of grave religious transgressions. But in the end there is a sudden switch to consolation and restoration, leading back to the original theme, the acquisition of land (vv. 43-44):

> And fields shall again be purchased in this land of which you say, It is a desolation, without man or beast; it is delivered into the hands of the Chaldaeans. Fields shall be purchased, and deeds written and sealed, and witnesses called in the land of Benjamin and in the environs of Jerusalem, and in the towns of Judah; the towns of the hill country, the towns of the Shephelah, and the towns of the Negeb. For I will restore their fortunes— declares the Lord.

Does the story of Jeremiah's purchase of his cousin's land relate to an actual occurrence? I have little hesitation in giving a positive answer to this question. I do so particularly in view of the lengthy sequel from v. 16 to the end of the chapter, v. 44. Jeremiah's restrained expression of dismay is too fine a detail to be explained away as just another literary, fictional stroke of the brush, superimposed upon an imaginary, fictional tale concerning a purchase of land. This does not preclude the possibility that Jeremiah's soliloquy and the divine reply, may both have undergone editing and padding. But the prophet's dismay sounds genuine enough.

As for the price paid, the sum of 17 *shekalim* silver: we do not know how this relates to the real value of the land which was being conveyed. The prevailing external circumstances may indeed have had a negative impact on the price of real estate. But I do not accept the suggestion that Jeremiah may have bought at a bargain price (so Westbrook). True, adequacy of price is not mentioned, but we need not hesitate in postulating it; if Jeremiah had acquired his cousin's field particularly cheaply, the story would have lost much of its point. Could Hanamel, if he so wished, redeem, repurchase the land he had just conveyed to Jeremiah? It seems likely, but the possibility goes unmentioned.

So far, we have seen pre-emption and redemption aimed at safeguarding the interests of the seller's family, to keep the land from passing into the hand of outsiders. One might add that much later, Talmudic law knows also a very different type of redemption, based on a 'law of neighbours'. Under these rules, when land is being sold, neighbours whose holdings border directly on it, have a power of preventing the sale from taking effect. To do so, they have to offer immediate reimbursement; to the buyer, if conveyance has already taken place, or else to the seller, if they were in time to forestall it. The stress is upon the swiftness of the action. For a very short, not otherwise defined time, the law supports the neighbour's wish to enlarge his holding, but takes care to ensure that the owner who is about to sell, should suffer no detriment.

In passing, mention was made of the jubilee. From the main passage, again in Leviticus 25, I quote the parts concerning land. After decreeing (vv. 1-7) that every seventh year the land is to be left fallow (the so-called sabbatic year), it goes on to provide as follows:

> You shall count off seven weeks of years—seven times seven years—so that the period of seven weeks of years gives you a total of forty-nine years. Then you shall sound the horn aloud; in the seventh month, on the tenth day of the month—the day of Atonement—you shall have the horn sounded throughout your land and you shall hallow the fiftieth year. You shall proclaim release throughout the land for all its inhabitants. It shall be a Jubilee for you: each of you shall return to his holding and each of you shall return to his family. . . In this year of Jubilee, each of you shall return to his holding. . . In buying from your neighbour, you shall deduct only for the number of years since the Jubilee; and in selling to you, he shall charge you only for the remaining crop years; the more such years, the higher the price you pay; the fewer such years, the lower the price; for what he is selling you is a number of harvests. . . But the land shall not be sold beyond reclaim, for the land is Mine: you are but strangers resident with Me. Throughout the land that you hold, you must provide for the redemption of the land.

These provisions are very far-reaching. It is quite categorically laid down that conveyance of rural land cannot be in perpetuity; there is a fixed, rigid framework of fifty-year periods, and no transaction can effectively convey land for a period beyond the next jubilee, however far or near that may be. In effect the conveyance of ownership in land is supplanted by a system of leasehold. It would differ from ordinary lease in the potentially longer period, and there might also be a significant difference in the mode of payment; payment might, as in ordinary sale (e.g. of movables) take the form of a one-time lump sum, to be rendered immediately, the moment the transaction is to take effect.

The obvious purpose of such a scheme would be to freeze the *status quo* of land ownership, as it existed at a given moment—this set of rules would prevent not only transfer from tribe to tribe, but also within it, from family to family. Reality chafes at arrangements of such a nature. The question whether jubilee regulations, first and foremost the fifty-years-reversion cycle, were ever put into effect, is in dispute. Scepticism is widespread; some scholars would deny the jubilee altogether, regarding it as essentially no more than a utopian blueprint. Others take a more conservative view. In fact, there is little by way of concrete evidence, and the arguments marshalled in support of one thesis over the other are far from conclusive.

One point is agreed by all. By Talmudic times the jubilee provisions were devoid of import and had become a reference to a distant past, real or imaginary. It is stated that the jubilee was effective, or incumbent, only as long as it could be applied 'to all the land, and to all the people' (*b. 'Arak.* 32b). This means that Talmudic theory relegates the jubilee to the eighth century; it would have disappeared with the Assyrian conquest of the parts of the kingdom of Israel which were east of the Jordan. Practical lawyers that they were, the Talmudists could not be sorry to be free of this particular burden of the law.

I have dealt only with one aspect of the relationship between unequals. We have seen kings, sages and lawyers struggling to give suitable expression to rules which ought to guide peoples' behaviour to each other. And, beyond principle, I have considered actual cases of grave injustice, and the consequences that ensued. It was a vivid procession of kings, covetous and wilful; of their women, complying or vicious; of their subjects-victims, too loyal or too stubborn; and the supporting cast of those who blindly implement royal wishes, right or wrong. The story of David/Bathsheba–Uriah–Nathan, and its counterpart, different yet in many ways so similar, the story of Ahab/Jezebel–Naboth–Elijah. The beautiful story of a young Moabite widow, whose progeny were a long line of kings; the tale of a prophet of doom, engaging in his human weakness.

This paper has been framed widely and thus it clamours for continuation. So I take my leave with a Hebrew phrase: *tam welo nishlam*—'it has ended but it is not complete'.

SOME LATE BRONZE AGE LEGAL TABLETS FROM THE BRITISH MUSEUM: PROBLEMS OF CONTEXT AND MEANING

M.P. Maidman

1. *Introduction*

The material on which my paper is based is a series of cuneiform texts describing court trials. These records derive from Nuzi, a community which flourished some 3500 years ago in northern Mesopotamia. The thrust of my paper is the exposition of the contexts of these documents and how these contexts affect our understanding of their putative legal content.

At first blush, the issue seems amenable to simple and painless resolution. After all, with respect to original context, we know where and when these texts were written. With respect to the history of transmission of these manuscripts, there was none. They are originals. And the circumstances of their discovery aids us further in defining their context. These tablets were found where they were stored in antiquity. They were excavated from archival complexes in the very community where the legal proceedings described in the texts took place.

Compared to the daunting task of the scholar of the Bible or of the Greek and Latin literary sources, the Assyriologist appears blessed indeed. And yet, as I hope to demonstrate, the hazards facing the scholars of late antiquity are also shared by the students of early ancient history. Just because a document is written in clay, describes an event of the immediate past, and gets to us directly by means of the archaeologist's spade, this does not indicate that we can immediately apprehend that document. Even under these circumstances, we must struggle in order to achieve a functional definition of the document. And only with such a definition in hand may we hope to achieve insight into the intricacies of law and legal procedure embedded in the document's content.

I begin with definitions of the various contexts of the Nuzi trial texts. Nuzi itself was a town located near modern Kirkuk in northeastern Iraq, near the foothills of the Zagros Mountains. The community which interests us flourished in the Late Bronze Age, from about 1500 to 1350 BCE. In political terms, Nuzi was part of the expansionist state of Mittanni. But, in its later stages, it was also within the orbit of Assyrian and Babylonian political interests.

The economy of Nuzi was based on cereal farming; there was substantial pastoral activity as well. In addition, there was production of bricks, cloth and other commodities, although this activity seems not nearly as important as agriculture or herding. Finally, Nuzi displayed a good deal of commercial activity. This involved import and export of finished and unfinished goods as well as transshipment of items originating in and targeted to various parts of Mesopotamia (e.g. Babylonia) and beyond (e.g. the Zagros).

The archaeologists who excavated Nuzi in the late 1920s and early 1930s discovered the Nuzi texts in a series of discrete archives. Some of these archives were private; others were institutional. The tablets were eventually distributed, in the main, among two museums. The Semitic Museum of Harvard University became custodian of the urban, mostly institutional archives, comprising about 4500 tablets. The Oriental Institute of the University of Chicago received the suburban, private archives, representing close to 3000 items. However, my interest lies more with a third body of material, one less easy to define. Prior to the organized excavations, there took place illicit digs and pilferage of Nuzi archives. Tablets from this activity surfaced in the antiquities market. As a result, several European museums, most notably the Louvre, the Pushkin in Moscow, the Hermitage in St Petersburg, and especially the British Museum, acquired perhaps about 550 additional tablets and tablet fragments. On grounds of internal evidence, including that of text genre and of the personal names of principal parties, two facts became clear. First, the acquisitions of the several museums indeed come from the same places within Nuzi. Secondly, these collections, although lacking archaeological data regarding their precise provenience, comprise a series of distinct archives, archives as distinct and as distinctive as any of those unearthed in licit excavations.[1]

The British Museum possesses some 352 of these Nuzi texts, 247

---

1. The problem of identifying archival units among texts whose archaeological provenience is imperfectly known is broached in Maidman (forthcoming).

still unpublished.[1] And it is from this group that I have chosen the material to be discussed in this paper. For purposes of illustration, I could just as easily have chosen published material, whether from Harvard, Chicago, or any other museum. To be sure, the unpublished texts contain features unique in the Nuzi corpus and, furthermore, they add substantially to our appreciation of the details of Nuzi society. However, they are also largely typical of the kinds of texts already known. The ideas I shall be presenting, therefore, although illustrated by 'new' documents, are nevertheless based on widely attested facts, deriving from sources all over the area of ancient Nuzi.

The British Museum tablets stem mainly—probably even exclusively—from private archives. Discrete private archives are a phenomenon well attested at Nuzi. Archaeologists have unearthed many such collections, each deriving from a single chamber or from adjoining chambers. The character of many of these archives is similar. They describe private economic activity extending from one to six generations. Business contracts predominate. These would include deeds of sale of real estate, assorted loans and sale of mobilia, and, sometimes, memoranda relating to household production of goods such as bricks and textiles. They might even include so-called 'family law' documents, such as testaments and contracts establishing adoption.

2. Law and Legal Procedure in the Nuzi Trial Records

These archival documents might be supplemented by 'trial' texts of the type upon which I am focusing in this paper. These latter texts almost uniformly deal with issues arising out of the economic life of the household as described by the former class of documents. That is, trial texts describe the abrogation of contractual arrangements or criminal activity predicated on the kind of environment described in those contracts. Non-repayment of loans (exemplified by text no. 5),[2] trespass or theft (3:4), break and enter and illegal distraint are examples of issues raised in these trial records.

---

1.   I examined and published a catalogue of these texts, including descriptions of the 286 items then unpublished (Maidman 1986). Since then, Katarzyna Grosz has published 39 of those texts (1988: 159-82).

2.   In this article, numbers enclosed by parentheses, but without further identification, signify numbers of the texts published here (i.e. texts nos. 1-11). Where these numbers are followed by a colon and other numbers, the latter are line numbers.

The documents themselves record trials conducted in the region of Nuzi. They identify contesting parties and define the issues in dispute. They frequently describe courtroom dynamics and almost always note the outcome of the case. At first glance these texts appear to yield a wealth of information regarding law and legal procedure at Nuzi. And, indeed, we may summarize some of the salient features of the court system, based on the content of these texts.[1]

First, the cases themselves were very likely tried in a chamber or interior area devoted to this function, although, as will be emphasized below, archaeologists have not yet identified any such chamber at Nuzi. Court cases, whether criminal or civil, arose when a private party hauled an accused into court (1:1-3; 3:1-3; 5:1-4). The litigants were most typically free males (5:1-2; 6:1-3). Yet both women and slaves brought suit (2:23-24 [cf. 1:26-29]; 3:1) and, as far as we can tell, were legally indistinguishable from men in the dynamic of the court.

The state seems not to have initiated lawsuits. Disputes were articulated by the parties directly involved or, in the case of plaintiffs, by their non-professional proxies (3:1, probably). No lawyers are attested in these documents.

As far as we can tell, no legal decision was rendered on the basis of an officially promulgated code of laws. At least, no such code is ever cited or even mentioned. On the other hand, royal edicts are both mentioned and cited and are important in determining the legality of some acts. The contents of several such edicts are known, or at least may be surmised. They deal with the maximum price to be paid for the safe return of ransomed hostages (*JEN*[2] 195); the release of palace dependents from their service (*P-S* 51); the general remissions of debts (probably; '*šūdūtu*': *JEN* 27:22; 98:37; and *passim*; cf. '*šūdūtu e ššu*': *JEN* 102:40; *HSS*, XIX, 97:32; etc.); and other, unknown subjects (*IM* 50805:25 [published by Lacheman 1976: 129-31]; Donbaz and

---

1.   This topic has been dealt with most recently and extensively by Hayden (1962). Liebesny's studies (1941; 1943) remain the most detailed published studies on the subject. These works may be consulted for further details of points discussed below.

2.   All abbreviations follow *CAD* (1958–) with the following additions:

G [#] = text published by Gadd (1926)

EN 9/1 [#] = text published by Lacheman *et al.* (1987)

P-S [#] = text published by Pfeiffer and Speiser (1936)

Kalaç 1981: 209 [1:32]; etc.). But apart from the instances in which these edicts are mentioned or cited, practically all cases appear to have been decided on the basis of customary, presumably unwritten, law as this law was interpreted by the bench.

This is not to say that legal procedure was haphazard or organized in a rudimentary fashion. On the contrary. The texts suggest a well-developed and largely uniform court system with elaborate personnel and standardized procedures.

The personnel consist of several court officers. Presiding is a bench of judges, usually three or five in number. In our texts, five and even more appear to have constituted the bench.[1] Judges appear to have been professionals. In any case, the same names of judges recur in a significant number of documents.

Verdicts could be appealed again. Such appeals were heard either by similar benches or by the king or by special officials appointed by the king. Together with the judges and contending parties, there were present in the courtroom bailiffs (that is *manzatuḫlu* [sing.]), who also seem to have been at least part-time professionals. To them fell the task of summoning witnesses (1:22-24?)—done with elaborate and precise ritual—and the task of carrying out other procedural orders of the court. One of these possible orders was officially informing a defendant not present of the charges brought against him. Recognized authorities could also be summoned by the court to give expert testimony in matters such as real estate location or dimensions. Officials described as 'crier' (*nāgiru*) and 'mayor' (*ḫazannu*) occasionally appear carrying out specific duties. Each party could also produce witnesses to events (3:8-16; 4:6)[2] and expert witnesses to establish facts of a case.

Our knowledge of courtroom procedure is limited and, as we shall see presently, with good reason. Interrogation of the litigants by the judges seems to have been the backbone of procedure (5:10-17). Judges could demand evidence and litigants could present evidence voluntarily. Such evidence could consist both of witnesses, expert or otherwise, and of written corroboration of claims or of material evidence of a crime alleged to have taken place; for example, wood from stolen furniture or the hide of a stolen animal.

The testimony of witnesses in criminal cases could be challenged in

1. Among the texts presented here, 4 is sealed by a judge (4:21).
2. In the first case, and perhaps the second, this was at the court's request.

specific ways (1:24-29) but was not subject, as has sometimes been supposed, to challenge by ordeal.[1] As far as written corroboration is concerned, this could take the form of a contract or even a prior trial record dealing with the same issue or property. We are in the happy position, in some cases, of having both a trial record and a piece of documentary evidence actually mentioned in that record.[2]

In cases of theft or dispute regarding title to real estate, where no evidence was available to either party, a river ordeal may have been undertaken. The exact nature of this ordeal is not spelled out but drowning is not part of this procedure since failure at the ordeal could lead to capital punishment while success could lead to victory.

Outcomes in criminal cases include corporal and capital punishment. In property cases, verdicts most usually involve restoration of property to the party illegally denied that property (1:30-33; 2:21-27 [perhaps]; 5:26-32). Punitive damages are infrequently applied (as they are not applied in 6:21-30) except where the issue is stolen livestock. When a losing party appeals against a verdict in a property case and loses again on appeal, damages are awarded to the victor and sometimes to the judges who delivered the original verdict. Fines payable to the state are rarely if ever attested.[3] Perhaps this makes sense in light of the fact that the state does not bring suit and is never, as such, an injured party.

The elements of Nuzi law thus described could easily be detailed further. However, the main elements have been touched upon and the point of this outline is not to present a picture of legal life at Nuzi but to demonstrate that the trial texts *are* capable of yielding up a picture of that legal life. This becomes important because, in essential respects, these texts cannot divulge important aspects of law and legal procedure at Nuzi.

3. *Context, Pattern and Meaning in the Trial Records*

Before committing character assassination of my primary sources, I wish to return to the theme I have already adjudged fundamental to investigation of these sources, the theme of context. What, first of all,

---

1. This point has been demonstrated by Frymer-Kensky (1981: 120-31).

2. For example, the trial record, *JEN* 662, mentions (11.68-72) a prior real estate exchange tablet. That tablet is preserved as *JEN* 144.

3. See Hayden (1962: 62-63) for possible exceptions.

is the archaeological context of these trial texts?

The trial texts, and not only the British Museum trial texts, seem uniformly to be found in private archival contexts. That is, where the findspots of these tablets are known and where other artifacts allow for interpretation as to the nature of their physical environment, the trial texts derive from architecturally small units and, more specifically, from chambers containing other tablets. All these tablets seem to have in common descriptions of economic activity by individuals acting in a private capacity and not on behalf of government, temple, or other institution. These trial tablets are found nowhere else, certainly not in any court archive. In fact, although a standing court system is clearly implied by our texts, we have, as already noted, no idea where the court sat, let alone where the court kept its records, that is if the court kept records at all. Given the functioning of courts at Nuzi which I have posited, it is unclear to me why the court would have kept records.

That the law courts seem not to have kept records is significant. Archaeological context by itself suggests that the function of the preserved trial texts is related to the needs of the proprietor of the archive and not of the court in which these proceedings took place. This, in turn, weakens the presumption that the texts accurately describe the legal system of Nuzi. There is no obvious reason why the archive's proprietors should have wished to preserve such accurate description.

If the function of the trial records does not necessarily relate to the needs of the court per se, then we should seek the function of these documents in the archival, that is the conceptual, context of the records with which they were found. I have explored this issue elsewhere (Maidman 1979). Here it will suffice to say that both contracts and trial records alike serve the interest of the archive's proprietor. Both categories of text constitute evidence favoring the proprietor in case the issue at stake should ever become an issue at law or an issue at law again.

We have already noted that one or both of the contending parties are frequently called upon to produce supporting documentation in a case. Sometimes, a party succeeds in doing so. In a few cases, as already noted above, we possess not only the trial record describing this procedure but the document itself that was produced by the litigant.

According to the contents of the archives, then, the primary function of the tablet is to establish proof of a contractual relationship. Thus, identification of the parties involved, their relationship to property, definition of that property, and perhaps the circumstances in which that relationship came about, are the crucial points to be delineated in a private archival text, whether that text is a contract *or* a trial text. In a sense, the trial text should merely be a special type of contract. It is a text in which the circumstances establishing title are adversarial, in a courtroom, rather than cooperative, through an agreement voluntarily reached.[1] Therefore, it is not only the archaeological context of the trial texts which points to the function of these documents. The contents of the texts point in the same direction—private interest.

This motivation, saving records for potential future need, explains a stark characteristic of these archives. The proprietor of the archive is never described as losing a case, even where several dozen trial records may be preserved.[2] Not that he necessarily never lost a case, but why should he bother saving a trial record of a lost cause? Leave *that* to one's adversary! And for that matter, why bother recording the details, the precise realities, of the court proceedings? The archive owner is interested in evidence, not in precision. Once again, the private tablet owner is certainly not interested in providing us with evidence of legal history. The relevant evidence for the winner would consist in the outline of the case—more or less detailed, as suits the winner—written on a piece of clay and sealed by the very judges who tried the case. Their sealings guarantee that the case was indeed substantially as described.[3]

To be sure, some of our trial texts are quite detailed. These are the documents that enable us to reconstruct the workings of Nuzi's courts

1. Finkelstein (1968: 588-89) already recognized formal and functional connections between Mesopotamian contracts and trial records. Yet he there overstated the value of the Nuzi trial records for the reconstruction of courtroom activity.

2. Exceptionally, a trial memorandum (*taḫsiltu*) will often lack a verdict. For further details and examples, see Maidman (1976a: 134 with notes). Yet this type of text is preserved in private archives. Perhaps a clue to the preservation of this type of text lies in its name. It might represent a temporary memorandum, useful pending an outcome of a case. The issue requires systematic study.

3. This function probably lies behind a germane *terminus technicus*. At Nuzi, the genre of trial texts appears to bear a specific name, 'tablet of victory', *ṭuppi ša lē'ûti*. See *EN* 9/1 432:20; 448:9; and the reading in *CAD* L (162b) of *P-S* 71:15.

as sketched above. But there are other trial texts as well, texts which appear no less useful or valid than any others. One of these latter (*G* 37) may be quoted in its entirety:

> Akiya son of Unap-še took Wullu son of Puḫi-šenni to court before judges over .2 homers of land. Wullu won the case. The judges sentenced Akiya to (pay) two homers of barley and two bunches of straw to Wullu (Seal impressions of Niḫriya, Uthiya, Lâ-qêpu and others).[1]

There is not much description in this text. But, if we follow the posited function of these documents, not much description is needed. Trial records of property cases must, as stated above, identify principal parties and their relationship to the property, define the property, declare ownership, and be officially sealed. Nothing more. Explicit evidence of court procedure is not necessary. Its presumed presence may even lead to scholarly misunderstanding. Text no. 6 provides a case in point. Detail appears to be present and evidence from the contending parties is supposedly quoted. But even a superficial glance at the text reveals the procedure to be either inane or insane. An accusation is levelled (6:7-11) and the defendant immediately concedes his accuser's point: 'Yes, indeed!' (*annimi*; 6:14). Text no. 5 provides just as stark an example (5:5-17).[2]

This is no accurate record of trial procedure at all! It presents no initial conflict of claims, no contradiction. It merely sets the stage for the next round of legal conflict by establishing the winner of the last round. And this is why some of our documents appear inane, as indeed they would be if they were meant to have served as accurate reflections of legal processes. This is also why some texts are very short, recording as they do only the facts of trial, principal parties and issues, and victory. And, finally, this is why losers readily and immediately admit guilt and defeat, often employing the very words of the victors.

Thus, the trial records from Nuzi supply, when all is said and done, not transcripts of trial proceedings or even summaries of what happened in a given trial. They are not, strictly speaking, even court records. They give a partial, almost accidental picture of court procedure and legal detail. This picture must often be distorted. This

---

1. See also, e.g., *HSS*, V, 45, 50; *JEN* 713.
2. Such a seemingly nonsensical sequence of accusation and admission is common in the Nuzi trial records.

kind of record demands to be treated with caution by the legal historian. He may not, as legal historians have in the past, presume to be looking at law and legal procedure through transparent text descriptions. The texts are anything but transparent.

On the other hand, the trial records constitute a relatively straightforward primary source of data for the nature and workings of private economic establishments and of the difficulties they were liable to run into. That is, these texts find their most natural, most communicative context, not in the company of all other Nuzi trial texts, but, quite literally, 'at home', surrounded by all the other documents from the archive together with which they were stored in antiquity.

4. *Trial Records: A Sampling of their Potential for Socio-Economic History*

The pattern of legally excavated Nuzi private archives, as already noted, is substantially clear and easily identified. They consist of contracts, trial records and other documents, all united by repeated mention of a common purchaser or lender or producer or victor at law. This 'star' of the show will have been a proprietor of the archive; and the archive's documents will have protected his interests. Precisely the same pattern of text distribution and archival profile are discernible in the illicitly excavated texts from Nuzi. That is to say, but for our ignorance of the archaeological context of groups of texts such as those of the British Museum, we would, when reading these texts, have no doubt that they came from a series of discrete private archives from Nuzi. Much additional circumstantial evidence—both internal/textual and archaeological[1]—buttresses this deduction. It is on the basis of this evaluation that I believe our British Museum trial texts, combined with texts of other genres, can be most illuminating by elucidating elements of Nuzi's socio-economic history. I offer here several examples of the benefits for historical reconstruction of juxtaposing Nuzi texts as archival artifacts.

One of the 'hidden' archives illegally excavated turns out to be that of Urḫi-tešup son of Tarmiya. Two of our texts (nos. 5 and 6) depict him as victor in two trials, both involving Šêlebu son of Abu-ṭâbu as loser. In the former case, Urḫi-tešup son of Tarmiya had extended a long-

---

1.   Maidman 1976b: 129-31.

term loan of tin to Šêlebu son of Abu-ṭâbu. As the court's award makes clear, the interest on the loan was a typical 50 per cent.[1] In the latter case, Urḫi-tešup had again loaned tin to this same Šêlebu. This time, the interest consisted of the labor of a female slave, this labor rendered for as long as the loan remained outstanding.

Given the reasoning enunciated above, these two texts should be part of a larger pattern of economic activity on the part of Urḫi-tešup, a pattern which may be discerned in other texts. In other words, these two trial texts should be an integral part of a significantly larger corpus of material. The pattern in fact obtains and includes at least the following three elements. First, Urḫi-tešup son of Tarmiya had multiple, profitable dealings with Šêlebu son of Abu-ṭâbu. Secondly, his activity seems to have been weighted towards finance, that is, making loans, rather than, say, toward acquiring real estate or producing bricks. Finally, and most curiously, he seems to have had peculiarly free access to tin, a commodity not commonly traded at Nuzi.[2]

These three elements are present in other texts dealing with Urḫi-tešup son of Tarmiya as are other data which flesh out the dimensions of his economic prowess. Regarding Šêlebu son of Abu-ṭâbu, this seemingly hapless individual reappears in text no. 7 where he and another individual sell agricultural real estate to Urḫi-tešup son of Tarmiya in return for mobilia. Incidentally, the formulation of this contract as an adoption is a guise, mere legalistic jargon, and need not detain us here. It is a sale, pure and simple.

Text no. 8 is a fragmentary text where Šêlebu son of Abu-ṭâbu makes a declaration. It is probable that he declares he has paid something. The payee appears to have been, once again, Urḫi-tešup son of Tarmiya. Such repeated transactions between a creditor and a single, ever poorer debtor are not unusual in the Nuzi corpus.

As noted above, the two trials reveal a second pattern as well. In both texts, Urḫi-tešup son of Tarmiya is described as having loaned commodities. Three other texts describe similar activity. Text no. 9 is a barley loan where the interest rate is, as in no. 5, 50 per cent. Text

---

1. Owen 1970: 38-42.
2. Thus, regarding text no. 5, Carlo Zaccagnini comments (personal communication): '[This is a] unique occurrence—at least as far as I know—of capital in *tin* for a trade venture'. Capital, in these contexts, typically takes the form of copper or, less frequently, silver. See Zaccagnini (1977: 185-88).

no. 10 involves the loan of a garment. Here the interest due is payable in tin. Text no. 11 is a third loan. This time tin is loaned and possibly the use of a garment and something else is due as interest.

Thus Urḫi-tešup's dealings in movable goods include slaves (no. 6), barley (no. 9), possibly finished textiles (nos. 10 and 11), and, conspicuously frequently, tin (nos. 5, 6, 10, and 11). This third characteristic of Urḫi-tešup son of Tarmiya, his use of tin, is attested as well in a published British Museum text (*G* 52). There, Urḫi-tešup son of Tarmiya purchases a female and pays for her with barley, sheep and tin.

Although tin is not rare at Nuzi (it is worth only about 1/180 the equivalent weight of silver [Eichler 1973: 15]), it is unusual that so many transactions from a single archive involve the movement of this metal. The relative ubiquity of the metal in Urḫi-tešup's texts may imply that he had a special connection to tin, perhaps in the capacity of merchant or commercial investor. Text no. 5 suggests precisely this activity; Urḫi-tešup son of Tarmiya invests capital for mercantile purposes. Although he could have performed this function as agent for the municipal government, the same text suggests that he invested, at least in this case, as a private individual. (Urḫi-tešup son of Tarmiya is also attested in one text [*JEN* 794:21] as a witness to a contract. This too may suggest a certain independent economic standing.)

If the identification of Urḫi-tešup son of Tarmiya as a merchant is correct, then perhaps another published text (*HSS*, XV, 167), from the main mound of Nuzi, becomes germane to this dossier. There, one man in one locality is described as delivering to a second man in a different place a great quantity of military and other goods—including tin. In this case, it appears that the deliverer is acting as a government agent. This deliverer is named Urḫi-tešup son of Tarmi-tešup, not Tarmiya. The name 'Tarmiya' may easily serve, at Nuzi, as a hypocoristicon, a nickname, for Tarmi-tešup.[1] If this last text is pertinent, that is, if this piece of guesswork pans out, the owner of this archive would have engaged in a lively private economic enterprise based on the surplus he would have accumulated both as a government merchant and, perhaps at the same time, as a private investor as well.

However, guesswork it is and I would be loath to ground any

1. For example, Tarmiya son of Eḫli-tešup (*JEN* 148:18; 695:16) is Tarmi-tešup son of Eḫli-tešup (*JEN* 104:21; 146:27).

meaningful conclusion on such speculation. But even ignoring the possibility that Urḫi-tešup son of Tarmiya is a government merchant of some sort, it emerges clearly that his economic life was active, that it involved accumulation of mobilia and real property, and that, if only modestly, he seems to have prospered during his career.

It also transpires that his gains were accompanied by some minor legal difficulties. One of the sources of his wealth, Šêlebu son of Abu-ṭâbu, resisted, at least twice, repayment of interest on outstanding loans. And it is here, in this type of context, that the trial texts assume their real life significance. They are seen as part of the pattern of ongoing economic activity by an individual and, to judge from the rest of his texts, a not terribly bothersome or important part of that activity.

5. Conclusions

I conclude by summing up my findings and noting some of their implications. The function of the Nuzi trial texts is indeed court related. These texts do permit us to reconstruct, in part, courtroom activities at Nuzi. Such documents, however, are not institutional records detailing with precision legal proceedings. The function of these texts is to prove a legal status quo, a status quo of benefit to him who possessed those documents.[1] The records owe their existence to economic self-interest, not to some abstract notion of justice. It may further be added that neither do they owe their existence to the administrative needs of the justice system.

As these texts cannot divulge important aspects of law and legal procedure at Nuzi, we may now enumerate some of those aspects, although the list is hardly exhaustive.

First, on the small scale of court procedure, our trial records give us no real notion of argumentation or of the court procedure involved in the presentation of evidence. This is perhaps the most conspicuous area of our ignorance in the wake of these tablets.

Secondly, we achieve through the Nuzi trial texts no real insight

---

1.   Such documents can benefit the proprietor whether or not his own name appears in them, so long as the texts are stored in his archive. For this phenomenon to be of use to the historian, knowledge of the archaeological provenience of the texts is, of course, necessary. See further, Maidman (1979: 183) on the significance of such 'background' documentation to current activity.

into the reasons for many disputes. For example, cases of trespass or illegal occupation of land are very common among the trial texts. This seems to have been an ongoing, perhaps endemic, problem for Nuzi landowners. Yet the grounds for these cases are virtually ignored in the trial texts. Certainly, the circumstances surrounding such trespass would have emerged during the course of a trial. This silence is particularly to be regretted since our resulting ignorance affects social historians as well as legal scholars.

The loss is demonstrable, not merely surmised. It so happens that other data—mostly epigraphical—suggest an increasing impoverishment of the rural peasantry during the century and a half bracketed by the Nuzi texts.[1] A local economy marked by substantial small freeholds gradually gives place, it seems, to fewer and larger estates, privately owned by a few and productively worked by the families of the former freeholders, that is, the vendors of real estate. With this knowledge in mind, the trials for trespass, it emerges, often represent cases where vendors of land, still present on that land, claim legal title to that land. One may deduce that that title was asserted in practical terms by withholding annual produce from the purchaser, that is, the landlord.

Similarly, the particular trial texts we possess deprive us, by reason of their peculiar archaeological provenience, of any knowledge of the degree (if any) to which the peasantry successfully resisted progressive encroachment by relatively few powerful families. Any success of the small peasants would also have been recorded. But the records of the small peasants too would have been preserved in their homes. Their dwellings would have been small-scale affairs located away from town. And small-scale buildings away from town are precisely what financially strapped archaeologists usually avoid. Indeed, they did avoid such complexes in the region of Nuzi during the excavations of the 1920s and 1930s.

In these three areas, then—courtroom argumentation, the background to disputes, and the degree of legal success enjoyed by the small peasantry—the very nature of the Nuzi trial records precludes illumination. Our tablets, for all their apparent detail, fail to deliver us the minutiae which could reveal the real world of the court and its role in the social dynamic of ancient Nuzi. We must clearly recognize that the Nuzi trial records are, first of all, private archival records

---

1. See most recently the summary statement of Wilhelm on this subject (1989: 48).

that the Nuzi trial records are, first of all, private archival records serving private interests. Context and content converge on this point. And, therefore, we must also clearly recognize that these records are chiefly valuable for the light they shed on the life of the community outside—not inside—the courtroom.

6. *The Texts*

The 11 Nuzi texts presented here are published with the kind permission of the acting keeper of Western Asiatic Antiquities, Mr T. Mitchell, and the Trustees of the British Museum. In addition to my own examination of the tablets, some of these texts were collated by C.B.F. Walker of the British Museum (texts nos. 1-2, 4-6, 11) and Grant Frame of the Royal Inscriptions of Mesopotamia (University of Toronto; texts nos. 5, 8, 10-11). I am grateful to both of them for their help. Many of the collations presented here stem from their efforts. I wish also to thank Alan Millard for making available to me preliminary copies and notes to some of the texts treated here, and the Social Sciences and Humanities Research Council of Canada for their support. The Council's generosity made possible my visit to the British Museum to study the unpublished Nuzi texts.

In the transliterations and translations, series of vertically placed dots will occasionally be seen. These represent completely destroyed lines of text.

The text transliterations, translations, comments and notes are followed by copies of broken signs (represented in the transliterations by 'x') where such copies might prove useful. Unusual sign forms (represented in the transliteration by [sign]!) are also copied.

Text 1   (= *BM* 26221; 98-5.14-39)

obverse
1. [^{m}*Tar-mi-ya*] DUMU *Ar-ta-še-en-ni*
2. *it-[ti* ^{m}*H]a-ši-ip-til-la*
3. [AŠ] *di-ni^{r}a?-na^{1}pa-ni* $^{LÚ.MEŠ}$DI.KU$_5$ [*i-te-lu-(ma)*]
4. *u[m?-ma?* x x x x (x) ^{m}]*Tar-mi-ya*
5. x [   ] *ša* LU [   ]
6. x [   ] x ŠE x [   ]
7. x [   ]

9. x [   ]-*ma*
10. x [   ]
11. [   ]-ZI
12. [   ] x(-)*um-mi-šu*
13. [   ] x-*šu*
14. [   ] AD DU PA-*mi*
15. [   ] x-*ya*
16. [   ] *šu-ma*
17. [   ] x *la* SUM-*nu-mi*
18. [ᵐ*Ḫa-ši-i]p-til-la*
19. [   ] IGI. MEŠ GIŠ
20. [   ] x MEŠ- *šu*
21. [   ] x *ya-nu*
22. [   ] x *ma-an-za-tuḫ-lu*
23. [   ] x-*nu-ku* ᵐ*Um-pí-ya*
24. [x] x x *šu-nu-ti*
25. *ša* ᵐ*Ḫa-ši-ip-til-la*
26. *iq-ta-bu-ú* DINGIR. MEŠ
reverse
27. ᶠ*Ku-un-tù-ya*
28. *i-ši-šu-ú-mi iš-tu* DINGIR. MEŠ
29. ᵐ*Ḫa-ši-ip-til-la it-tù-ra*
30. AŠ *di-ni* ᵐ*Tar-mi-ya il-te-e-ma*
31. *ù* DI.KU₅.MEŠ *a-na* 1 GUD
32. ᵐ*Ḫa-ši-ip-til-la*
33. *ù* ᵐ*Zi-ké it-ta-du-uš*
34. *ù* ᵐ*It-ḫi-til-la* ᴸᵁ*in-ka₄-rù*
35. ᵐ *Ḫa-ši-ip-til-la iš-tap-ru!-uš*
36. UZU.MEŠ *ḫu-šu-un-na at-ta-din*
37. *ša še-el-we-ni*-WA
38. ŠU ᵐ*Ḫa-ši-ip-til-la* DUB.SAR

39. ᴺᴬ⁴ KIŠIB ᵐ*Ti-ri-i-ú* DUMU *Mu-šu-ya*
    (seal impression)
40. ᴺᴬ⁴ KIŠIB ᵐ*Šúk-ri-ya* DUMU *A-kip*-LUGAL
    (seal impression)
upper edge
41. ᴺᴬ⁴ KIŠIB ᵐ*A-ku-še-en-[ni]*
    (seal impression)

42. DUMU *Ḫa-am-pí-*KU
left edge
43. ᴺᴬ₄ KIŠIB ᵐ*Ta-i-še-en-ni* ᴺᴬ₄ KIŠIB ᵐ‹*Pa›-i-šar-ri* DUMU *Ta-a-x*
     (seal impression)   (seal impression)
44. DUMU *Wa-an-ti₄-ya*

Translation
   (1-3) Tarmiya son of Artašenni [took] to court, before judges, Ḫašip-
tilla.
   (4-24) (no context:) Thus? (spoke)...Tarmiya...[Ḫašip?]-tilla...
his mother?...they did not give...Ḫašip-tilla...witnesses?...there
are none...bailiff(s)...Umpiya...them?
   (24-29) [The judges] addressed Ḫašip-tilla: 'Lift the gods against
(the woman) Kuntuya'. But Ḫašip-tilla turned back from the gods.
   (30-33) So Tarmiya won the case and the judges sentenced Ḫašip-
tilla and Zike to (pay) one ox.
   (34-37) Itḫi-tilla, the court official, sent Ḫašip-tilla. He (!) gave the
flesh...
   (38) Hand of Ḫašip-tilla, the scribe.
   (39-44) Seal impression of Tiriu son of Mušuya (seal impression);
seal impression of Šukriya son of Akip-šarri (seal impression); seal
impression of Aku-šenni (seal impression) son of ḪampiKU; seal
impression of Tai-šenni (seal impression) son of Wantiya; seal
impression of ‹Pa›i-šarri son of Ta-x (seal impression).

Comments
Texts nos. 1 and 2 perhaps deal with the same, or at least related,
events. The scribe and sealers of these texts are probably the same
(1:38-44 // 2:28-33). In both, a woman, Kuntuya, succeeds: in the
former text, she is vindicated (1:26-29); in the latter, she wins the case
(2:23-24).

Notes to the Lines
1-3: For the restorations of these lines, cf. 29-30. A patronymic is
expected after 'Ḫašip-tilla'.
19-28: Cf. the vaguely similar *P-S* 73:19-27.
19: GIŠ. *sic.* This sign is unexpected here.
22: For the connection of bailiffs and the procedure of 'lifting the
gods' (26-28), see Frymer-Kensky (1981: 127).

24-29: For the interpretation and legal implications of clauses such as this one, see Frymer-Kensky (1981: 120-31).

25: *ša. sic. a-na* is expected.

34: $^{L\acute{U}}in$-ka_4-*rù*. For the use of this term as applying to a court official, see *CAD*, I/J, p. 53a and, already, Oppenheim (1938: 47).

36-37: These lines are unclear to me.

38: The scribe, Ḫašip-tilla, identified here is not to be confused with the like-named loser of this case.

39: *Mu*. The sign is clear. Yet note text 2:32 where the same sealer's patronymic is given as *Ku-šu-ya*. Both 'Kušuya' and 'Mušuya' are attested Nuzi PN's. See also below, next note.

42: *Ḫa-am-pi*-KU. Cf. text 2:31, where this patronymic appears as *Ḫa-am-pí*-LU. Neither 'Ḫampiku' nor 'Ḫampilu' is otherwise attested at Nuzi. 'Ḫampizi' is well attested but KU (or KU! = LU) = *zì* is most unlikely in these texts. See also above, immediately preceding note.

43: ^{m}‹*Pa*›. The first sign is written over an erasure. For the restoration of *Pa*, see text 2:33. It appears that the scribe omitted the determinative, began to write PA, and, realizing his mistake, erased that sign, replaced it by DIŠ, and then forgot the PA.

Text 2   (=*BM* 102360)

obverse

1. [   ] *la?* ^{m}*Ḫa-ma-an-na*
2. [   ]⌐*A*⌐ *-ri-ya*
3. [$^{?}$*Ku?-un?*]-⌐*t*⌐*ù-ya-ma* ^{m}*Bal-ṭù-UD-ŠI*
4. [   ] *x-nu-mi*
5. [   ] x

.
.

6. [*i*] *š-tu*
7. [   ] x
8. [   ]-*mi*
9. [   ]⌐*a*⌐*!+na pa-ni* DI.KU₅.MEŠ
10. [   ] x
11. [   ]-⌐*e*⌐
12. [   ]-*x-ú-mi*
13. [   ] x

14. [ᵐ   ]-*al-te-šup*
15. [   ] x
16. [   ] ŠI
17. [   ] x *ša*
18. [*uš?/ul?-t]e?-ri-ib-šu-mi*
lower edge
19. [   ] x x x
20. [*i]m?-*⌐ta⌐ !?-nu-ú-mi*
reverse
21. ⌐*ki*⌐-*i-me-e a-wa-ti-šu*
22. *ši-na-ap-šu-um-ma*
23. DÙ-*uš* AŠ *di-ni* ᶠ*Ku-un-tù-ya*
24. *il-te-e-ma ù* DI.KU₅.MEŠ
25. *a-na* 1 GUD ᵐ*Bal-ṭù*-UD-ŠI *a+na*
26. ᶠ*Ku-un-*⌐*t*⌐*ù-ya*
27. *it-ta-d*⌐*u*⌐-*uš*
28. ŠU ᵐ*Ha-ši-ip-til-la* DUB.SAR

---

29. ᴺᴬ⁴ KIŠIB ᵐ*Ta-i-še-en-ni* DUMU *Wa-an-ti₄-ya*
     (seal impression)
30. ᴺᴬ⁴ KIŠIB ᵐ*A-ku-še-en-ni*
     (seal impression)
31. DUMU Ha-am-pí-*LU*
upper edge
     (seal impression)
32. ⌐ᴺᴬ⁴ KIŠIB ᵐ*Ti-ri*⌐-*ú* DUMU *Ku-šu-ya*
left edge; facing obverse
33. ⁽ᴺ⁾ᴬ⁴ KIŠIB ᵐ*Pa-i-šar-ri*   ᴺᴬ⁴ KIŠIB ᵐ*Šúk-ri-ya*
     (seal impression)   (seal impression)

Translation

(1-20) (no context):...Hamanna...Ariya...and [...]-tuya, Baltu-UD-ŠI...from...before   the   judges...-al-tešup...he brought? him/it"...they testified?'.

(21-27) Since his testimony was invalid?, (the woman) Kuntuya won the case and the judges sentenced Baltu-UD-ŠI to (pay) one ox to (the woman) Kuntuya.

(28) Hand of Ḫasip-tilla, the scribe.

(29-33) Seal impression of Tai-šenni son of Wantiya (seal impression); seal impression of Aku-šenni (seal impression) son of ḪampiLU; (seal impression) seal impression of Tiriu son of Kušuya; seal impression of Pai-šarri (seal impression); seal impression of Šukriya (seal impression).

Comments
This text has possibly one missing line between lines 5 and 6.

This tablet has recently been published by Katarzyna Grosz (1988: 159-60; translation, 145). My readings differ from hers at some points and supplement hers at others. Grosz also omits what are here identified as lines 5, 7, 10, 13, 15-16. For these reasons, it is felt that a new publication of this text here is warranted.

For further on this text, see comment to text no. 1.

Notes to the Lines
3: [ˤ?*Ku?-un?*]. For this possible restoration cf. 23, 26.
4: *mi*. Not *ma* as Grosz reads [1988: 159; all further references to Grosz in these notes are to this page).
14: *a*. Cf. Grosz.
19: For the remaining traces, see Grosz.
20: [*i]m?-*⌐*ta*⌐!? The traces noted by Grosz are more precisely rendered below, under 'Collations'.
22-23: *ši-na-ap-šu-um-ma* DÙ-*uš*. This phrase is attested here and in *JEN* 668:37 (partially restored); *HSS*, IX, 8:31; *EN*, 9/1, 396:20; 434:50, 52 and, possibly, *SMN* 2480 and 3500 (both are unpublished and unavailable to me; the latter is cited by Hayden [1962: 136]).

In at least three of those cases (*EN* 9/1, 396 is partially broken at a crucial point but most likely agrees with the other three texts), the phrase is applied to the testimony (*awatu*) of a litigant or of witnesses on behalf of a litigant. It is something negative, resulting in legal defeat for that litigant. Accordingly, a general meaning of 'lie' or 'perjure' or 'recant testimony' (for this last possibility, see the next paragraph) probably approaches the semantic field of the phrase, if the grammatical subject is the litigant (or his witnesses). Or, if *awatu* be the subject, then the meaning might be that the testimony itself was somehow impeached, discredited, or otherwise invalidated. Hayden's translation, 'to change one's testimony' (1962: 136, 138; cf. 109), does not capture the negative consequences apparently implicit in the phrase.

The term, *šinapšumma*, is to be linked to Hurrian *šinapši-*. The latter describes a cultic structure in Hittite texts (Haas and Wilhelm 1974: 36-38, including previous literature; especially 36 note 4 for the Nuzi material). Haas and Wilhelm (1974: 38) tentatively translate the term by 'absolution' (*Entsühnung*). In light of the somewhat less ambiguous Nuzi evidence, perhaps 'repentance' ('recant testimony') might better apply to the Hittite material.

30: *še*. Although Grosz reads *le*! for ŠE, *še* is to be preferred. Cf. text 1:41.

31: *Ḫa-am-pí*-LU. See above, note to text 1:42. Grosz's reading, *zu*, for the last sign is incorrect. (Her restoration of ^{NA_4} KIŠIB ^{m} at the start of this line is also to be rejected.)

32: *Ku*. On the initial element of the patronymic, see above, note to text 1:39.

Text 3   (= *BM* 26242; 98-5.14-60)

obverse

1. ^{m}*E-ez-zi* ÈR *ša* ^{m}*Šur-ki-til-la*
2. *it-ti* ^{m}*Ta-ú-uk-ka₄-an-ni* DUMU *Ak-ku-le-en-ni*
3. AŠ *di-ni a-na pa-ni* DI.KU₅.MEŠ *i-te-lu-ma*
4. *um-ma* ^{m}*E-ez-zi-ma* 1 ANŠE ⌐E⌐? DI BA
5. *ù* ^{m}*Ta-ú-uk-kà-an-ni*
6. *i-na* MURUB₄ NUMUN.MEŠ *ša* ^{m} ⌐*Šur-ki*⌐*til-*⌐*l*⌐[*a* x?]
7. *i-re-e'-e ù a-na* x [x x x]
8. *ù* DI.KU₅MEŠ *sí-li-*⌐*ku*⌐*-[uḫ/u'-lu* x?]
9. *ša* ^{m}*E-ez-zi i-te-e[r?-šu?]*
10. *ù ú-bi-la* ^{m}*A!?-ti-*[x x x x] x
11. ^{m}ÈR-*ya* DUMU *Ú-z*⌐*i*⌐*pu* [x? x? x?]
12. 2 $^{LÚ.MEŠ}$*sí-l i-ku-uḫ/u'* -[*lu* x? x?]
13. *ša* ^{m} ⌐*E*⌐-*ez-zi a-na p*⌐*a-ni*⌐[DI.KU₅MEŠ]
14. *im-ta-nu* ⌐*u*⌐*m-ma* ⌐*šu*⌐?-[*nu?-ma?*]
15. ANŠE ^{m}*Ta-ú-u[k-kà/ka₄-an-ni* x x]
16. ⌐*i*⌐-*na* MURUB₄ NUM[UN x x x x x x]

.

.

.

reverse

.

.

.

17. [*it?*]-ᵀ*ta?-du₄?-uᵀš*
18. ŠU ᵐ*Ši-la-ḫi-te-šup* DUB.SAR
19. ᵀN˹A₄ KIŠIB ᵐ*A-kap-tùk-ké*
(seal impression)
20. [ᴺ] ᵀA₄˥ KIŠIB ᵐ*Ur-ḫi-ya*
(seal impression)
21. [ᴺ] ᵀA₄˥ KIŠIB ᵐ*Ša-ti-ki-in-tar*
(seal impression)
upper edge
22. ᴺA₄ KIŠIB ᵐ*A-mur-ra-bi*
(seal impression)
left edge; facing obverse
(seal imp.) | (seal imp.) | (seal imp.)
23. [NA₄ (KIŠIB) ᵐ] x x [NA₄ (KIŠIB) ᵐ NA₄ (KIŠIB) ᵐ]-*x-te-šup*

Translation
    (1-3) Ezzi slave of Šurki-tilla took to court, before judges, Taukkanni son of Akkul-enni.
    (4-7) Thus Ezzi: 'Taukkanni grazed one... donkey in the middle of the seed (store) of Šurki-tilla and for/to...'
    (8-14) Then the judges requested witnesses of Ezzi. He brought (them). A?ti-..., Wardiya son of Uzipu; [these?] two witnesses of Ezzi testified before [the judges].
    (14-16) Thus they? (i.e. the witnesses): 'Taukkanni [grazed?] a donkey in the middle of the seed (store) [of Šurki-tilla]...

.

.

.

    (17) ... they sentenced? him.
    (18) Hand of Šilaḫi-tešup, the scribe.
    (19-23) Seal impression of Akap-tukke (seal impression); seal impression of Urḫiya (seal impression); seal impression of Šati-kintar (seal impression); seal impression of Amurrabi (seal impression); (seal impression) [seal impression? of]...; (seal impression) [seal impression? of...]; (seal impression) [seal impression? of]... -x-

Comments

The end of the obverse (1-3 lines), the lower edge, and the start of the reverse (1-3 lines) are absent.

Notes to the Lines

4: ⌐E⌐? DI BA. For the first sign, see below, 'Collations'. I do not understand this qualifier. Cf. line 15.

Text 4   (= *BM* 102373)

obverse

.
.
.

1. *m[i?- / u[l?*   ]
2. *e-x-[*   ]
3. *um-ma* ᵐ [   ]
4. *ul* AK-[   ]
5. *a-na* ᵐDINGIR-*ni-š[u*   ]
6. *ši-bu-ti-ka₄* MEŠ [   ]
7. KAxGIŠ *ša* 2 x x [   ]
8. ⌐N⌐I IN ZI ID KA x [   ]
9. ANŠE DI NI TI *i+n[a*   ]
10. *ul aš-ri-iq-m[i?*   ]
11. *ši-bu-ti-šu a-na pa-[ni*   ]
12. ᵐ*Be-la-aḫ-ḫe-šu* [   ]
lower edge
13. ᵐTI-*ḫu-ú-še-en-n[i*   ]
14. ᵐᵈXXX-LUGAL DUMU x-KI [   ]
15. ᵐ*A-kip-ti-la* DUMU AN [   ]
reverse
16. AM? A RI IL LI x x [   ]
17. *x-ḫa-li-tu₄* AŠ? [   ]
18. *an-nu-ut-tu₄* [   ]
19. *ša* ᵐDINGIR-*n[i?-šu?*   ]
20. *i-[*   ]

.
.
.

left edge; facing obverse
21. [D]I.KU₅⌐N⌐[A₄]   ⌐NA₄⌐ ⁽ᵐ?⁾ E-⌐ni⌐-ya
   (seal impression)   (seal impression)

Translation

.

.

.

(1-2) (no context)
(3-4) Thus (Mr). . . (:) 'I did not. . .
(5-6) (Thus the judges said?) to Ila-nîšū(: '). . . your witnesses. . . '
(7-10) '. . . of two. . . a x-donkey. . . I did not steal. . . '
(11-19) His witnesses, [he brought?] before [the judges?:] Bêl-
aḫḫēšu [son of ?. . .], Tiḫu?-šenni [son of ?. . .], Sin-šarri son
of. . . ,Akip-tilla son of. . . , these are [the witnesses of?] Ila-n[îšū?].
   (20) (no context)

.

.

.

(21) Seal impression of Eniya, the judge (seal impression); seal
impression of. . . (seal impression).

Comments
Although this text is clearly a record of a trial involving theft of
mobilia (see lines 3, 6, 9, 10, 11ff., 21), more precise context is
elusive for several reasons. First, only a small part of the text is
preserved. Secondly, and more frustrating, much of what is preserved
makes no sense at present (see lines 7-9, 14, 16-17 [if these last two
lines do not mask PN's]). And finally, the scribe appears to employ a
series of idiosyncratic spellings (TI-ḫu-ú-še-en-ni [l. 13] for *Teḫup-
šenni?; -ti-la [l. 15] for -til-la; an-nu-ut-tu₄ [l. 18] for an-nu-tu₄; failure to supply the male determinative before names of men [lines 16?,
17?, 21?]).

Notes to the Lines
9: ANŠE. Less likely, TUM.
10: m[i?]. Or, as in line 1, u[l].

Text 5   (= *BM* 17604; 94-10-13, 8)

obverse

1. [ᵐ*Ur-ḫi-te-šup*] DUMU *Tar-mi-ya*
2. [*it-ti* ᵐ*Še]-le-bu* DUMU *A-[bu-uṭ-ṭá-bi*]
3. [*i-na*] ⌐*di*⌐-*ni a-na pa-ni* DI.KU₅.MEŠ
4. *ša* URU *Ta-ku*-WA ⌐*i*⌐-*te-lu*-⌐*ú*⌐
5. *um-ma* ᵐ*Ur-ḫi-te-šup-ma*
6. 1 GUN AN.NA.MEŠ *iš-tu* 15 MU-*im*
7. ᵐ*Še-le-bu* DUMU! *A-bu-uṭ-ṭá-bi*
8. *a-na* DAM.GÀ⌐R⌐ [*i*]-*na* KASKAL-*ni me-me-li*
9. *a-šar ya-[ši] il-te-qè* 2 GUN 10 MA.NA AN.NA ⌐*a*⌐?-[*na* MÁ]Š?-
                    ṭ⌐*a*? *ša*⌐? AN.NA?.M[EŠ]?
                    :*a-šar* ᵐ[*Še-le-bu*] *el-te-qè-mi*
10. *ù* DI.KU₅.MEŠ [ᵐ]*Še-le-bu iš-ta-lu-uš*
11. *um-ma* ᵐ*Še-[le]-bu-ma a-an-ni-mi*
12. 1 GUN AN.NA *a-na* DAM.GÀR
13. *i-na* KASKAL-*ni me*-⌐*me!-li*⌐*x? a-na* 15 MU.MEŠ
14. *a-šar* ᵐ*Ur-ḫi-te-šup el-te-qè-mi*
15. *ù a-na* [MÁŠ-*ta*?] *ša* AN.NA.MEŠ
16. *ša-a-šu* [2] GUN 10 MA.NA AN.NA. MEŠ
17. *a-na* ᵐ*Ur-ḫi-te-šup at-ta-din*
18. *ù* DI.KU₅.MEŠ [*ni*?-*sà*?-]*ak-ka₄-mu-um-ma*
19. *i-te-ep-[šu(-uš*?) 1+]1 GUN 10 MA.NA AN.NA.MEŠ
20. *ša-a-šu* [MÁŠ?-*ta*? *ša*?]
21. ᵐ[*Še]-le-bu* [x? *a-na* ᵐ*Ur-ḫi*]-*te-šup*
22. *it-ta-[ad?-nu*?   ]
23. x x x x [x?] AN.NA [   ]
24. [   ]-*ma*

lower edge

25. [   ] x x [   ] x [   ]

reverse

26. *ù* DI.KU₅.MEŠ *ki-i* EME-*šu-ma*
27. *ša* ᵐ*Še-le-bu*
28. *a-na* 5 GUN 20 MA.NA AN.NA.MEŠ
29. *a-na* MÁŠ-*ta-šu ša* DAM.GÀR-*ru-ti*
30. ᵐ*Še-le-bu*
31. *a-na* ᵐ*Ur-ḫi-te-šup*
32. *it-ta*-⌐*du-uš*⌐

33. ^{NA}₄ KIŠIB x [   ]-*li*
34. (seal impression)   (seal impression) ^m? *A-ri-ik-ka₄-ni*
35. ^{NA}₄ KIŠIB ^m[   ]
36. (seal impression) (seal impression) [^{NA}₄? KIŠIB? ^m] *Tup-ki-til-la*
37. [DUMU?] x x x [   ] x-*ya*
     (seal impression)?
upper edge
38. [DUMU?   ] x [x?] x [x?]

Translation

(1-4) [Urḫi-tešup] son of Tarmiya took to court, before judges of the town of Taku, Šêlebu son of Abu-ṭâbu.

(5-9) Thus Urḫi-tešup: 'Fifteen years ago, Šêlebu son of Abu-ṭâbu took from me one talent of tin for (purposes of) commerce for a venture for profit. Now I have taken (back only) two talents, ten minas of tin as? interest? on the tin? from [Šêlebu]'.

(10) Then the judges interrogated Šêlebu.

(11-17) Thus Šêlebu: 'Yes, indeed. I did take from Urḫi-tešup one talent of tin for (purposes of) commerce for a venture for profit for fifteen years and, as [interest?] on that tin, I gave to Urḫi-tešup [two] talents, ten minas of tin'.

(18-25) Then the judges made an [ac]counting?. Those two talents, ten minas of tin, [the interest? which?] Šêlebu gave back to Urḫi-tešup,... tin...

(26-32) Then the judges, in consequence of Šêlebu's declaration, sentenced Šêlebu (to pay) five talents, twenty minas of tin as the (appropriate additional) commercial interest.

(33-38) Seal impression of x-...-li (seal impression); (seal impression) Arik-kani; seal impression of... (seal impression) [son? of?]... -ya; (seal impression) [seal? impression? of?] Tupki-tilla; ([seal impression?]) [seal? impression? of?... son? of?]...

Comments

Grant Frame informs me that there is possibly one line missing between lines 24 and 25 and another one possibly missing after line 37.

Notes to the Lines

8: DAM.GÀ⌐R⌐ This spelling apparently represents *tamkārutu*, not *tamkāru*. Cf. the fuller form in line 29. That the spelling is deliberate and not careless is proved by the same spelling in line 12.

8: *me-me-li*. Cf. also *me-[me]-li*, line 13 and the note to that line. The interpretation of these signs is problematic. However, it seems most likely that this context should be linked to *HSS*, IX, 154. There, a merchant is said to have taken goods with the object of turning a profit [line 3] *ana nēmeli*). Later, he is to bring *me-me-el-šu* (line 6) to the owner of those goods. (*HSS*, IX, 154 is not available for collation: it could not be located. I thank Piotr Steinkeller of Harvard University for attempting to find this tablet for me.) Clearly, *me-me-el-šu* means 'his profit' and is to be related to *ana nēmeli* of the same text. *AHw* (1959–1981: 776b) seems to consider this spelling an error for *né-me-el-šu*, a position also adopted by Zaccagnini (1977: 180). *CAD* (1958–, N/II: 160a) renders the word *me-me-el-šu* without comment and translates it, 'profit'. However, *CAD*'s failure to recognize a lemma, *mēmelu*, suggests that this dictionary, like *AHw* and Zaccagnini, considers *me-me-el-šu* an error for *né-me-el-šu*.

Now in the present text, it is unlikely that *me-me-li* is an accidental spelling error; the same spelling very probably appears in line 13. One must presume that a word, **mēmelu*, is meant to be represented. Perhaps, then, *me-me-el-šu* in *HSS*, IX, 154:6 is no error at all. And, if it is no error there and if the two texts contain the same word, then the meaning here must certainly be that which is clearly present there, i.e., 'profit'. In short, **mēmelu* appears to be a byform of *nēmelu*.

(Cf. Berkooz [1937: 52] who cites *HSS*, IX, 154 as demonstrating an n›m phonetic shift in Nuzi Akkadian. However, he musters no other examples for such a shift and none is known to me from either the lexicon or the onomasticon.)

In the context of the foregoing, we should perhaps render the relevant phrases in lines 8, 13 as a 'venture for profit'. Cf. already *CAD*'s translation (1958–, N/II: 160a) of *ana nēmeli* in *HSS*, IX, 154:3: '(a business venture for) profit'. A difficulty in this interpretation here is the presence of KASKAL-*ni* (lines 8, 13) where KASKAL (that is *status constructus*) is expected. However, '*ni*' may here be a frozen form automatically following KASKAL rather than a true phonetic complement.

On the notion of *nēmelu* in the Nuzi texts, see Zaccagnini (1977: 179-80, 187).

9: Everything on this line after *ilteqe* appears to have been a scribal afterthought. The clause extends onto the reverse and continues with a greatly indented 'half-line' before line 10.

9: ⌈a⌉?-[na]. The trace is a single vertical wedge. For the restoration, cf. line 15.

9: MÁ]Š?-t⌈a? ša⌉? AN.NA?.M[EŠ]? Cf. the presumably parallel passage, lines 15-16. Note also line 29.

13: me-⌈me!-li⌉. Walker (personal communication) doubts that the second sign is ME (see 'Collations'). However, cf. the parallel passage, line 8.

15: [MÁŠ?-ta?]. Cf. line 29.

18: [ni?-sà?]. For this restoration, cf. the *CAD* (1958–, N/II: 227b *sub* 'g)').

33-38: In these lines, the interpretation of the relation of text and seal impressions, as implied in the translation, is very tentative.

37: As noted above, Frame suggests that traces of a line between lines 37 and 38 might survive on this badly abraded surface. In light of line 38, perhaps this space was once occupied by a seal impression.

Text 6   (=*BM* 80178; Bu. 91-5-9, 297)

obverse

1. ᵐU[r-ḫi-te]-š⌈up⌉DU[MU *Ta]r-mi-y[a]*
2. ⌈i⌉t-ti ᵐ[Še-le-b]u
3. DU[MU] *A-bu-uṭ-*⌈ṭ⌉*á-bi*
4. *i-na* ⌈di⌉-ni ⌈a⌉-na pa-ni
5. DI.KU₅.MEŠ *ša* URU *Ta-ku*-WA
6. *i-*⌈t⌉*e-*⌈l⌉*u-ma um-ma* ᵐ*Ur-ḫi-te-šup-ma*
7. ⌈GEME₂⌉ᶠⁱŠa-šu-ri* ᵐ*Še-le-bu*
8. ⌈a⌉-na ti₄-de₄-en-nu-ti ki-i AN.NA.ME[Š]
9. *a-na ya-ši it-ta-din* GEME₂ *ša-a-šu*
10. ⌈ù⌉ᵐ⌈Še-l⌉*e-bu-ma iš-tu*
11. É-y⌈a il⌉-te-qè DI.KU₅.MEŠ
12. ᵐŠ⌈e-le-b⌉u iš-ta-lu-uš
13. *um-[m]a* ᵐ[Še]-⌈le⌉-bu-ma
14. *a-an-ni-mi* 1 GEME₂ ᶠŠa-šu-ri
15. *a-na t i₄-[de₄]-en-nu-ti*
16. *ki-i* AN.NA.MEŠ *a-na* ᵐ*Ur-ḫi-te-šup*
17. *a*⌈t⌉-ta-din ù a-na-ku-ma
18. *el-te-qè-mi*

19. *ù iš-tu* É-*ya*
lower edge
20. *i[ḫ]-ta-li-iq*
21. ᵐ*U[r]-ḫi-te-šup*
22. ⌜*ki-i*⌝ EME-*šu-ma*
reverse
23. ⌜*ša*⌝ [ᵐ*Š]e-le-bu*
24. *i-nadi-ni il-te-e-ma*
25. *[i]š-t*⌜*u*⌝ UD-*mi an-ni-im*
26. ᵐ*Še-le-bu aš-šu-um* GEME₂
27. ⌜*fš*⌝*a-šu-ri*
28. ⌜*i*⌝-*[na* EGͳIR⌝-*ki*
29. ⌜*ša*⌝! ᵐ⌜*Ur*⌝-*ḫi-te-šup*
30. *la* ⌜*i*⌝-*[š]a-as-sí*

---

31. ŠU ᵐ AḪ-*ḫi-ya*
32. D⌜U⌝MU *Šúk* -*ri-ya*
33. ᴺ⌜ᴬ⌝₄ KIŠ⌝IB *Ni-i[ḫ-ri]te-šup*
   (seal impression)   (seal impression)
34.   ᴺᴬ₄ KIŠIB ᵐ*Šúk-ri-ya*
upper edge
35. ᴺ ᴬ₄ KIŠIB ᵐ*Tù-ra-ri*
   (seal impression)
left edge; facing obverse
36. ᴺᴬ₄ KIŠIB ᵐ*A-ri-ik-ka₄-ni*
37. (seal impression)   ᴺᴬ₄ KIŠIB ᵐ⌜*Tup?-ki*⌝?-*[til?]-*⌜*la*⌝?
                                      (seal impression)

Translation

(1-6) Urḫi-tešup son of Tarmiya took to court, before judges of the town of Taku, Šêlebu son of Abu-ṭâbu.

(6-11) Thus Urḫi-tešup: '(In exchange) for an antichretic loan of tin, Šêlebu gave to me the female slave, Šašuri. Then, Šêlebu took that female slave from my house'.

(11-12) The judges interrogated Šêlebu.

(13-20) Thus Šêlebu: 'Yes, indeed. (In exchange) for an antichretic loan of tin, I did give to Urḫi-tešup one female slave, Šašuri. And I did take her (back) and she has disappeared from my house'.

(21-30) Urḫi-tešup won the case in consequence of Šêlebu's declaration. Furthermore, from this day forward, Šêlebu shall not

hail Urḫi-tešup into court over the female slave, Šašuri.
(31-32) The hand of Aḫḫiya son of Šukriya.

(33-37) Seal impression of Niḫri-tešup (seal impression); (seal impression) seal impression of Šukriya; seal impression of Turari (seal impression); seal impression of Arik-kani (seal impression); seal impression of Tupki-tilla? (seal impression).

Notes to the Lines

20: *i[ḫ]-ta-li-iq*. *ḫalāqu* in the Nuzi texts denotes disappearance. The notion of escape is represented by *abātu, na'butu (nābutu)*. This distinction is treated in more detail in my forthcoming article, '"The Land of the Kassites": The View from Nuzi'.

28: EG]⌐ IR⌐-*ki*. *šu* has been erased after this word.

29: ⌐*ša*⌐!. The traces actually look more like ⌐*i*⌐-*na*. Either one, however, would be a mistake since no word at all is expected at this point. Cf. *JEN* 137:16; 149:17-18; etc.

The scribe, having erased *šu* in line 28 (see immediately preceding note), evidently forgot to erase *ša* in the next line.

Text 7   (= *BM* 102356)

obverse

1. *ṭup-pí ma-ru-ti š[a]*
2. ᵐ*Še-le-bu* DUMU *A-bu-[uṭ-ṭá-bi]*
3. *ù ša* ᵐ*Ni-iḫ-ri-y[a* DUMU KI?.MIN?]
4. 2 ŠEŠ.MEŠ *an-nu-ti* x [   ]
5. ᵐ*Ur-ḫi-te-šup* DUMU *Tar-m[i-ya]*
6. *a-na ma-ru-ti i-te-[ep-šu-uš]*
7. 17 ANŠE A.ŠÀ *i-na mi-i[n-da-ti* (GAL) *ša* É.GAL]-*lì*
8. *i-na mi-ṣí-ir-šu* [   ]
9. *i-na su-ta-an* x [   ]
10. *i-na il-ta-an* [   ]
11. ⌐*i-na*⌐ *e-le-en m[i-iṣ?-ri?*   ]
12. *i-n*⌐*a šu-p*⌐*a-al mi-[iṣ?-ri?*   ]
13. ᵐ*Še-le-bu [ù* ᵐ*Ni-iḫ-ri-ya ki-ma* ḪA.LA-*šu a-na]*
14. ᵐ*Ur-ḫi-te-šu[p it-ta-ad-nu]*
15. *ù* ᵐ*Ur-ḫi-[te-šup* x ANŠE? ŠE?.MEŠ]
16. *ki-ma* NÍG.B[A(-*šu*) *a-na* ᵐ*Še-le-bu]*
17. *ù a-na* ᵐ[*Ni-iḫ-ri-ya it-ta-din]*

18. ⌜*šum*⌝-*ma* A.Š[À *pa-qí-ra-na i-ra-aš-ši*]
19. [ᵐ*Še-l]e-[bu ù* ᵐ*Ni-iḫ-ri-ya*]

.

.

.

reverse

.

.

.

20. ⌜*a*⌝? [   ]
21. ⌜*i*⌝? [   ]
22. *š[a i-na bi₄-ri-šu-nu* KI.BAL-*tu₄*]
23. 1 [MA.NA KÙ.BABBAR 1 MA.NA KÙ.GI *ú-ma-al-la]*
24. IGI [   ]
25. IGI [   ]
26. IGI x [   ]
27. IGI x [   ]
28. IGI x [   ]
29. IGI x [   ]
30. ⌜I⌝GI x [   ]
31. ⌜IGI⌝ [   ]
32. IG[I   ]
33. IGI [   ]
34. IGI x [   ]
35. IGI *Ka*-[   ]
36. IGI *Ni*-[   ]
37. IGI *A*-RI-[   ]
38. IGI *Ḫa-ši-ip*-[   ]
39. *i-na ur-k[i šu?-du?-ti? šá?-ṭi?-ir?]*
upper edge

40. NA₄ ᵐ*Tar-mi-ya*		N⌜A₄⌝ᵐ [ ]
41. NA₄ ᵐ(sic) DUB.SAR	(seal imp.)	[ ] x [ ]

42. NA₄ ᵐ*Ni-iḫ-ri-ya*		EN [A.ŠÀ]
(seal impression)		(seal imp.)
left edge; facing obverse		
(seal imp.)	(seal imp.)	(seal imp.)

43. [NA₄ ᵐ]x-a-a NA₄ ᵐIt-ḫ-til-la NA₄ᵐNi-iḫ-ri-te-šup ᴸᵁna-gi₅-rù
          (seal impression)
43. (cont'd.)   NA₄ ᵐŠe-le-bu EN A.ŠÀ

Translation

(1-6) Tablet of adoption of Šêlebu son of Abu-ṭâbu and of Niḫriya [son of ditto?]. These two brothers... adopted Urḫi-tešup son of Tarmiya.

(7-14) Šêlebu [and Niḫriya gave to] Urḫi-tešup [as his inheritance share] a field, 17 homers by the [large?] standard of the palace. Within its boundary [is...]. It is south of..., north of..., east of the border? of..., west of the border? of...

(15-17) And Urḫi-tešup [gave x homers? of barley?] as [his?] gift [to Šêlebu] and [to Niḫriya].

(18-21?) Should the field [have claimants, Šêlebu and Niḫriya shall clear (that field) (and give it to Urḫi-tešup)].

(22-23) Which[ever (party) amongst them abrogates (this contract) shall pay] one [mina of silver and one mina of gold].

(24-38) Before...; before... ; before... ; before... ; before;...; before... ; before... ; before... ; before... ; before... ; before...; before Ka-...; before Ni-...; before A-RI-...; before Ḫašip-...

(39) [Written?] af[ter the proclamation?]

(40-43) Seal impression of Tarmiya; seal impression of the scribe (seal impression); seal impression of... (seal impression); seal impression of Niḫriya, owner of [the field] (seal impression); (seal impression) [seal impression of] x-aya; (seal impression) seal impression of Itḫi-tilla; (seal impression) seal impression of Niḫri-tešup, the herald; (seal impression) seal impression of Šêlebu, owner of the field.

Comments

The genre of contract of which this text is an example is well known. Restorations of broken passages, therefore, although conjectural *senso strictu*, are based on common and frequently attested formulas. Individual words, forms and spellings may vary, but the basic content is assured.

Notes to the Lines

2: *A-bu-*[*uṭ-ṭá-bí*]. The restoration of the patronymic follows 5:7; 6:2-3;

and 8:1-2. In those three texts, as in this one, Šêlebu has dealings with Urḫi-tešup son of Tarmiya.

3: [KI?.MIN?]. This restoration is based on the asserted fraternity of Šêlebu and Niḫriya in line 4. However, that fraternity could as easily consist only of their shared legal status vis-à-vis Urḫi-tešup son of Tarmiya.

4: x. The trace is a single horizontal wedge head.

7: *li.* Although this sign on the reverse fits well the context of line 7, Frame perceives it to be a continuation of line 6.

9: x. The trace is part of one horizontal wedge.

11-12: The restoration of *miṣri* in these two lines is based on a common Nuzi formula for describing the location of real estate. For examples, see *CAD* (1958–, M/II; 113b-114a).

18-19: This clear title clause would have continued on the next line(s) with *ú-za-ak-ku-ú (ù a-na* ᵐ*Ur-ḫi-te-šup i-na-an-di-nu)* or the like. It is possible that this conclusion is partially preserved in lines 20-21: (20) ⌈*a*⌉*-[na* ᵐ*Ur-ḫi-te-šup]* (21) ⌈*i*⌉*-[na-an-di-nu].* ⌈*a*⌉? appears as two adjacent vertical wedges and ⌈*i*⌉? as three horizontal wedges, one on top of the other.

However, it is also possible that lines 20 and 21 (and any totally lost line[s]) could contain the so-called *ilku* clause whereby the vendors undertake continued responsible for this real estate impost.

20-21: See the note immediately above.

26-30: The traces on these lines are minimal: line 26—one *Winkelhaken*; line 27—one vertical resting on another (possibly *z[a]* or *ḫ[a]*]; line 28—one *Winkelhaken*; line 29—two small *Winkelhaken*'s, one above the other; line 30—one *Winkelhaken*.

34: x. The trace is a single horizontal wedge.

39: The restoration of this line is quite tentative. If correct, it would be a very unusual, perhaps unique, version of the *šūdûtu* clause.

40-41: It is possible that Tarmiya is the scribe. At any rate, there is but one impression for these 'two' sealers.

41: ᵐ· *sic.*

43: x. The trace looks like PA with the wedge heads cut off.

Text 8   (= *BM* 95353; 190-10-12, 1006)

obverse
1.EME-*šu* ᵐ*Še!* ⌈ *le*⌉*-[bu]*

2. DUMU *A-bu-uṭ-ṭ[á!-bi]*
3. *a-na pa-ni* L[Ú.MEŠ]
4. *an-nu-tù* DIŠ x [   ]
5. ⌈*a*⌉-*na* ᵐ*Ur-[ḫi?-te?-šup?*]
6. [*ṭ]ù?-up-[pa?-tù?*   ]
7. [   ] x [   ]
.
.
.

reverse
.
.
.

8. [ᴺᴬ₄]⌈ KIŠIB ᵐ⌉ x [   ]
9. (seal impression)   ᴺᴬ₄ KIŠib ᵐ x[   ]
10. ᴺᴬ₄ KIŠIB ᵐ*I-sa-a-a*
upper edge
   (seal impression) | (blank)
left edge; facing reverse
   (seal impression)   [?   ]
11. ᴺᴬ₄ KIŠIB ᵐ [   ]

Translation

(1-4) Declaration of Šêlebu son of Abu-ṭâbu before these men.

(4-7) ... to Ur[ḫi-tešup?], tablets?...

(8-11) Seal impression of...; (seal impression) seal impression of...; seal impression of Isaya (seal impression); (seal impression) seal impression of...

Notes to the Lines

3: This line seems too short to permit an additional restoration of [*ši-bu-tù*] or of [DI.KU₅.MEŠ]. (The latter is less likely in any case since there are too many sealers here for a typical bench present at a declaration.)

4: x. The trace is the head only of a vertical wedge.

5: [*ḫi?-te?-šup?*]. The proposed restoration is based on the strong links of Šêlebu son of Abu-ṭâbu to Urḫi-tešup son of Tarmiya established by texts nos. 5, 6, and 7.

6: This restoration is a guess.

Text 9 (= *BM* 26290; 98-5.14-108)

obverse
1. *li-ša-an-šu ša*
2. ^mDINGIR-*a-a* DUMU *Šum-m[i-*   ]
3. *a-na pa-ni* ^{LÚ}IGI.MEŠ *a[n?-nu?-ti?*]
4. *ki-am iq-ta-bi*
5. 10 ANŠE ŠE.M EŠ *ša* ^m*Ur-ḫi-t[e-šup*]
6. DUMU *Tar-mi-ya a-n a* UR₅. RA [*el]- t e-qè-mi*
7. *i-naur- ki* EBUR *it- ti* [MÁŠ-*(ti-)šu*]
8. 15 ⌜AN⌝ŠE ŠE.MEŠ ^mDINGIR-*a-a*
9. *i-na* URU *Ta-ku-*WA
10. *a-na* ^m*Ur-ḫi-te-šup*
11. *ú-ta-ar*
lower edge
12. ^{NA₄} DUB.SAR
     (seal impression)
13. ^{NA₄} ^mDINGIR-*a-a*
     (seal impression)
reverse
14. IGI *Te-ḫi-ip-til-la* DUMU *Še-eš-ki-ya*
15. IGI *A-ta-a-a* DUMU *Ú-ru!-um-pa*
16. IGI *En-na-ma-ti* DUMU *Ip-šá-ḫa-lu*
17. IGI ⌜*Ḫ*⌝*a -na-a-a* DUMU *Eḫ-li -te-šup*
18. IGI *Ḫa -ši-ip-til-la* DUB.SAR
19. ^{NA₄} ^m*Te-ḫi-ip-til-la*
     (seal impression)
20. ^{NA₄} ^m*A-ta-[a-a]*
upper edge
     (seal impression)
left edge; facing obverse
     (seal impression)
21. NA₄ ^m*Ḫa-na-a-a*

Translation
   (1-4) Declaration of Ilaya son of Šummi-... before witnesses; thus
he spoke:
   (5-11) 'I have taken on loan 10 homers of barley of Urḫi-tešup son

of Tarmiya; after the harvest, I shall return (it) at the town of Taku to Urḫi-tešup with [its interest], (a total of) 15 homers of barley.'

(12-13) Seal impression of the scribe (seal impression); seal impression of Ilaya (seal impression).

(14-18) Before Teḫip-tilla son of Šeškiya; before Ataya son of Urumpa; before Enna-mati son of Ipša-ḫalu; before Ḫanaya son of Eḫli-tešup; before Ḫašip-tilla, the scribe.

(19-21) Seal impression of Teḫip-tilla (seal impression); seal impression of Ataya (seal impression); (seal impression) seal impression of Ḫanaya.

Notes to the Lines
7: [MÁŠ-*(ti-)šu*]. Or the like. The restoration is based on standard language in the Nuzi loan texts. For examples, see *CAD* (1958–, Ṣ: 161a) and, especially, Owen (1970: 65ff.).
12-13: These lines on the lower edge, together with their accompanying seal impressions, are written upside down with respect to the rest of the tablet. One presumes that these lines were written last of all.

Text 10   (= *BM* 95220 + 95223 + 95438; 1901-10-12,
                    873 + 1901-10-12, 226 + 1901-10-12, 1091)

obverse

.

.

.

1. ⌜*i*⌝*q-t[a?-bi*?] 1 TÚG SIG₅-*qú* 6 MA.NA]
2. *šu-qú-u[l-ta-šu ša* TÚG]
3. 15 *am-m[a-ti] m[u-ra-ak-šu]*
4. *ù* 5 *am-m[a]-ti ru-pu-u[s-sú]*
5. TÚG *an-nu-ú a-šar* ᵐ*Ur-ḫi-te-šup*
6. DUMU *Tar-mi-ya a-na* UR₅.RA
7. ⌜*e*⌝*l-te-qè-mi i-na* EGIR-*ki*
8. EBUR!?-*ti*!? TÚG *an-nu-ú qa-du* MÁŠ-*ti* [(?)]
9. MÁŠ-*ti-šu ša* TÚG *an-nu-ú*
10. 2 MA.NA 30 GÍN AN.NA.MEŠ
11. TÚG! *an-nu-ú* ⌜*i*⌝*t-ti* AN.[N]A.MEŠ x x
12. *i-na* ITI-*ḫi še-ḫa-l[i ša]* ⌜ᵈ⌝IM

13. *a-n⌐a ᵐUr⌐-[ḫi]-⌐te-šup⌐ [ú-ta]-⌐ar⌐*

14. *um-ma* [	]
15. DUMU *Na-x-*[	]
16. *a-šar* [	]
17. *a-na* [	]
18. *i-na* [	]
19. *mu-x* [	]
20. *a-*[	]
21. x [	]

.

.

.

reverse

.

.

.

22. DUMU *T[ù?-*	]
23. IGI *U[r-*	]
24. DUMU *A-*[	]
25. [I] ⌐G⌐[I	]

.

.

.

Translation

(1)... he spoke?:

(1-13) [One piece of fine cloth], the weight [of the cloth is 6 minas], its length, 15 cubits, its width, 5 cubits. I have taken this garment on loan from Urḫi-tešup son of Tarmiya. After the harvest!?, this garment together with the interest (on it)—the interest on this garment is 2 minas, 30 sheqels tin—this garment with... tin, in the month of šeḫali ša Tešup, I shall return to Urḫi-tešup'.

(14-21) (no context:) Thus... son of Na-... from...to/as... in...

(22-25) [Before...] son of Tu?-...; before Ur-... son of A-...; before [... son of...].

Comments

If the restoration of the first word of line 1 is correct, the text may well be a declaration before witnesses or judges.

The left edge of the tablet is blank.

Notes to the Lines

1-2: The restoration of these lines is based on a somewhat standard pattern in Nuzi textile texts (Zaccagnini 1981; cf. the brief observation in *CAD* 1958–, M/II: 217a). Thus, for example, cloth is frequently attested as measuring 15 x 5 cubits (so here, lines 3-5). The weight of cloth of these dimensions is often 6 minas (so restored here in line 2).

The particular restorations are made following *HSS*, V, 36: 5, 8-10 (cf. Zaccagnini 1981: 351), a text with close syntactic analogues to the relevant surviving portion of the present text. Although the restorations are plausible, they are, of course, not certain.

1: *t [a*?]. The heads of two parallel horizontal wedges survive.

5: TUG *an-nu-ú*. The meaning, 'this garment', is self-evident. The interpretation of this phrase in Maidman (1986: 276) is to be corrected accordingly.

14-21: These lines might represent the statement (*umma* [line 14]) by the borrower (...son of Na-... [line 15]) that he had actually received the cloth from (*ašar* [line 16]) Urḫi-tešup on (*ana* [line 17]) loan, to be returned after (*ina*... [line 18]) the harvest...

15: x. The trace appears as an initial, single *Winkelhaken*.

19: x. The trace is a single vertical wedge.

Text 11 (= *BM* 102359)

obverse

1. EME-*šu ša* ^{m}*U*⌜*r*⌝*-ḫi-ya*
2. DUMU *Ar-te-šup* ⌜*a-n*⌝*[a p]a-ni* $^{\text{LÚ.MEŠ}}$
3. *ši-bu-tù*^{MEŠ} *an-n[u-t]ù*
4. *iq-ta-bi* 1 GUN [A]N.NA.MEŠ
5. *a-šar* ^{m}*Ur-ḫi-te-šup*
6. DUMU *Tar-mi-ya el-te-q[è]*
7. *ù a-na-ku ki-i* AN.NA.ME[Š] ⌜*an*⌝*-nu-ú*
8. *tu-sí-iḫ-ḫu-ur-šu*
9. ⌜*i*⌝*š?-tu* É *ú-ru-ḫul-še*
10. ⌜*i?-na*⌝? URU DINGIR.MEŠ *ša* ^{m}*Ur-ḫi-te-šup*

11. x x AK? *ù* ^m*Ur-ḫi-te-šup*
12. [x x]-*šu ù lu-bu-ul-ta-šu*
13. [*a?-na?* ^m]⌐*Ur*⌐-*ḫi-ya i-na* MU.MU *i-na-an-din*
14. [*tu-sí]-iḫ-ḫu-ur-šu*
15. [*ša?* ^m*U]r-ḫi-te-šup* ^m*Ur-ḫi-ya*
16. [x x x] ⌐*ù*⌐ ^m*Ur-ḫi-ya*
17. [   ] *x-ni ša* [^m]*Ur-ḫi-te-šup*
18. [   ]⌐*i*⌐-*/ e -pu-uš*
19. [*ù ki?]-me-e* 1 GUN AN.NA.MEŠ
20. ⌐*k*⌐*[i?-i? ṭu]p?-pí [an?]-ni-im*
21. ^m*U[r-ḫi?-ya? x]* ^m*Ur-ḫi-te-šup*
22. [x x x] RI [x? *t]u-sí-iḫ-ḫu-ur-šu*
23. [^m*Ur]-ḫi-te-šup*

lower edge

24. [   ] x
25. [   ] x

reverse

26. [   ]x QA?

.

.

.

27. [-R]U
28. [*ṭu]p-pu an-nu-ú*
29. [*i-na* EGIR-*ki šu]-du-ti*
30. [*i-na*   ] x *ša* URU-*Ta-ku*-WA
31. [*ša₁₀??-ṭì??-ir??* IGI *A-kam]-mu-uš-ni* DUMU *Tar-mi-ya*
32. [IGI *Ip-š]á-ḫa-lu* DUMU *Eḫ-li-te-šup*
33. [IGI *x]-x-wa-al*-TI-*e*
34. [DUMU ^d]IM-LUGAL
35. [IGI] *Wa-an-t[i-i]š-še* DUMU *Ti-wi-ir-ra*
36. IGI *Be-la-[a]*-⌐*a*⌐ DUMU *A-ri-iḫ-ḫa-ma-an-na*
37. IGI *Šúk*-⌐*ri*⌐-*ya* DUMU *A-kip*-LUGAL
38. ^{LÚ}*ma-ṣ*⌐*a*⌐*r* KÁ.GAL
39. IGI AḪ-*ḫi-ya* DUMU⌐*Šúk*⌐-*ri-ya*

| 40 DUB.SAR | NA₄ ^m*Šú[k-r]i-ya* |
| (seal impression) | (seal impression) |

41. ^{NA₄} KIŠ[IB ^m]*Wa-an-ti-iš-še*

upper edge

42. ^{NA₄} [KIŠ]IB ^m*Be-la-a-a*

43. (seal impression) | ^{NA_4} KIŠIB ^{m}A-[ka]m-mu-uš-ni
  (seal impression)
left edge; facing obv.; last three lines are actually on the obv.
44. [^{NA_4} KIŠIB ^{m}x]-x-wa-al-TI-e
45. ^{NA_4} KIŠIB ^{m}Ip-šá-ḫa-lu

  (seal impression) (seal impression)
46. [^{m}Ur-ḫi]-te-⌈šup⌉qa-an-na-šu
47. [?] a-na pa-ni $^{LÚ.MEŠ}$
48. [ši-bu-tù^{MEŠ}i]m-ta-šar

Translation

(1-4) Declaration of Urḫiya son of Ar-tešup; he spoke (as follows) before these witnesses:

(5-11) 'I have taken one talent of tin from Urḫi-tešup son of Tarmiya. And I, for this tin, shall [give? (to him)] his substitute?/replacement? from the *uruḫulše*-house in? the town of Āl-ilāni of? Urḫi-tešup'.

(11-13) And Urḫi-tešup shall give (back?) [to?] Urḫiya his... and his apparel after some years.

(14-18) Urḫiya [shall...] Urḫi-tešup's substitute?/replacement? and Urḫiya shall... fashion? the... of Urḫi-tešup.

(19-23) [And?] for the one talent of tin [as? per?] this? tablet?, Urḫiya?...? Urḫi-tešup...Urḫi-tešup's substitute?/replacement?...

(24-28: no context)

(28-31) This tablet [was written? after] the proclamation [in the...] of the town of Taku.

(31-40) [Before] Akam-mušni son of Tarmiya; [before] Ipša-ḫalu son of Eḫli-tešup; [before] ...-walte? [son of] Adad-šarri; [before] Wantiš-še son of Tiwirra; before Bêlaya son of Ariḫ-ḫamanna; before Šukriya son of Akip-šarri, the gatekeeper; before AḪḫiya son of Šukriya, the scribe.

(40-45) (seal impression) Seal impression of Wantiš-še; seal impression of Šukriya (seal impression); seal impression of Bêlaya (seal impression); seal impression of Akam-mušni (seal impression); [seal impression of]...-walte? (seal impression); seal impression of Ipša-ḫalu (seal impression).

(46-48) Urḫi-tešup pressed his hem (onto this clay)... ? in front of these [witness]es?.

Comments

According to this text, Urḫiya son of Ar-tešup obtains tin for a period
of time from Urḫi-tešup son of Tarmiya in exchange for goods. The
nuances of this transaction are, unfortunately, elusive due to lacunae
and to the presence of rare, if not unique, key technical terms. (On
these, see further below, notes to lines 8 and 9.) The poor understanding of this text is reflected in the very tentative and choppy
translation.

C.B.F. Walker notes that possibly two lines are lost between lines
26 and 27.

Notes to the Lines

8-13: The very syntax of these lines is not secure.

8: *tu-sí-iḫ-ḫu-ur-šu*. The word reappears in lines 14, 22. Neither
*tusiḫḫuru nor any word close to it is known to me. Since it appears,
on the basis of lines 7-8, to represent a *quid pro quo* for the tin,
'substitute' or 'replacement' might well be in the semantic range of
this term. If so, then the contents of this counterpart to the tin would
be the unknown item and the apparel mentioned in line 12.

9: *ú-ru-ḫul-še*. This term, like the previous one, is unknown to me.
One is tempted, both because of a certain resemblance of form and
because of appropriateness of context (both features are striking), to
see in this word a form of *uriḫul(lu)*, '*Ersatzzahlung für nicht getane
Arbeit*' (*AHw* 1959–1981: 1430a). The fullest discussion of this term
remains that of Eichler (1973: 22-25). To the references noted in
AHw (1959–1981: 1430a) may be added IM 70972:12 (Fadhil 1972:
93-94; Deller 1978: 300) and *JENu* 1124: 20 (unpublished).

Still, one may not assume an identity of these two terms. The second
vowel here, /u/, is nowhere else attested for *uriḫul(lu)*. Furthermore,
the last syllable, *-še*, makes no apparent sense unless one assumes the
scribe to have transformed the common pronominal suffix *-šu* into a
frozen form, /šV/.

11: x x AK?. A verb is expected here, with *anāku* (line 7) as subject.

13: [*a?-na?*]. Perhaps *ša* should be restored here. The resulting translation would be 'And Urḫi-tešup shall give (back?) Urḫiya['s]. . . and
apparel after some years'.

16: [x x x]. *ú-ta-ar*, '(Urḫiya) shall return. . .', might be appropriate
here.

30: x. The trace is a final vertical wedge.

31: The verb seems to be required at the start of this line. However, most usually, the witness list begins with a new line, not in a line concluding a prior clause.

COLLATIONS

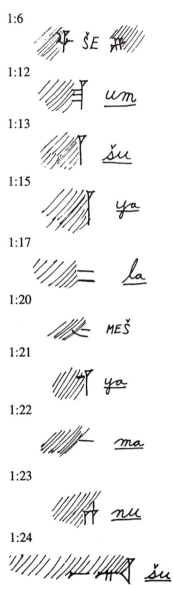

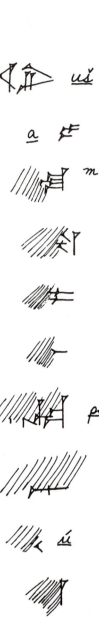

2:15

2:17

 ša

2:18

 *ri*

2:20

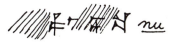 *nu*

3:4

 DI

3:7

na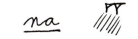

3:9

te

3:10

m

3:14

ma

3:16

MURUB₄

3:17

 uš

3:23

3:23   (=FIRST TWO TRACES)

te

4:1

4:2

e

4:7

2

4:8

KA

4:14

KI

4:16

A

4:16

LI

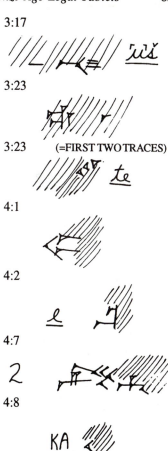

4:17

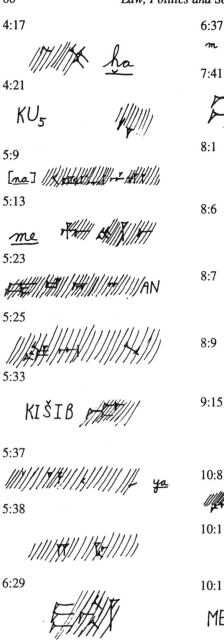

ha

4:21

KU₅

5:9

[*na*]

5:13

me

5:23

AN

5:25

5:33

KIŠIB

5:37

ya

5:38

6:29

6:37

m

7:41

(=LAST TRACE)

8:1

m

8:6

 *up*

8:7

8:9

m

9:15

ú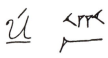

10:8

 TÚG

10:11

 *an*

10:11

MEŠ

10:21

10:22

11:9

11:11

11:17

11:18

11:20

11:24

11:25

11:26

11:33

BIBLIOGRAPHY

Berkooz, M.
1937   *The Nuzi Dialect of Akkadian: Orthography and Phonology* (Language Dissertations, 23; Philadelphia: Linguistic Society of America/ University of Pennsylvania).

Deller, K.
1978   Review of B.L. Eichler, *Indenture at Nuzi*, in *Die Welt des Orients* 9: 297-305.

Donbaz, V., and M. Kalaç
1981   'Two Tablets from Nuzi Housed in Istanbul', *Zeitschrift für Assyriologie und vorderasiatische Archäologie* 81: 205-14.

Eichler, B.L.
1973   *Indenture at Nuzi: The Personal Tidennūtu Contract and its Mesopotamian Analogues* (Yale Near Eastern Researches, 5; New Haven: Yale University).

Fadhil, A.
1972   'Rechtsurkunden und administrative Texte aus Kurruhanni' (unpublished Master's thesis, Heidelberg).

Finkelstein, J.J.
1968   'Law, Law in the Ancient Orient' (Hebrew), in B. Mazar *et al.* (eds.), *Encyclopaedia Biblica*, V (Jerusalem: Bialik Institute): cols. 588-614.

Frymer-Kensky, T.
1971   'Suprarational Legal Procedures in Elam and Nuzi', in D.I. Owen and M.A. Morrison (eds.), *Studies on the Civilization and Culture of Nuzi and the Hurrians*, I (*in Honor of Ernest R. Lacheman*) (Winona Lake, IN: Eisenbrauns): 115-31.

Gadd, C.J.
1926   'Tablets from Kirkuk', *Revue d'assyriologie et d'archéologie orientale* 23: 49-161.

Grosz, K.
1988   *The Archive of the Wullu Family* (Carsten Niebuhr Institute Publications, 5; Copenhagen: University of Copenhagen).

Haas, V., and G. Wilhelm
1974   *Hurritische und luwische Riten aus Kizzuwatna: Hurritische Studien*, I (Alter Orient und Altes Testament Sonderreihe, 3; Kevelaer: Butzon & Bercker).

Hayden, R.E.
1962   *Court Procedure at Nuzu* (dissertation, Brandeis).

Lacheman, E.R.
1976   'Tablets from Arraphe and Nuzi in the Iraq Museum', *Sumer* 32: 113-48.

Lacheman, E.R. *et al.*
1987   'Texts in the Harvard Semitic Museum: Excavations at Nuzi 9/1', in D.I. Owen and M.A. Morrison (eds.), *Studies on the Civilization and*

Culture of Nuzi and the Hurrians, II (Winona Lake, IN: Eisenbrauns): 355-702.

Liebesny, H.
1941 'Evidence in Nuzi Legal Procedure', *JAOS* 61: 130-42.
1943 'The Administration of Justice in Nuzi', *JAOS* 63: 128-44.

Maidman, M.P.
1976 *A Socio-Economic Analysis of a Nuzi Family Archive* (dissertation, Pennsylvania).
1976b 'The Tehip-tilla Family of Nuzi: A Genealogical Reconstruction', *JCS* 28: 127-55.
1979 'A Nuzi Private Archive: Morphological Considerations', *Assur* 1: 179-86.
1986 'The Nuzi Texts of the British Museum', *Zeitschrift für Assyriologie und vorderasiatische Archäologie* 76: 254-88.
forthcoming Review of J.N. Postgate, *The Archive of Urad-Šerūa and His Family*, *BO*.

Oppenheim, L.
1938 'Bemerkungen zur neueren amerikanischen Nuzi-Literatur, I', *Wiener Zeitschrift für die Kunde des Morgenlandes* 45: 38-48.

Owen, D.I.
1970 *The Loan Documents from Nuzu* (dissertation, Brandeis).

Pfeiffer, R.H., and E.A. Speiser
1936 *One Hundred New Selected Nuzi Texts* (Annual of the American Schools of Oriental Research, 16; New Haven: American Schools of Oriental Research).

Wilhelm, G.
1989 *The Hurrians* (trans. J. Barnes; Warminster: Aris & Philips).

Zaccagnini, C.
1977 'The Merchant at Nuzi', *Iraq* 39: 171-89.
1981 'A Note on Nuzi Textiles', in D.I. Owen and M.A. Morrison (eds.), *Studies on the Civilization and Culture of Nuzi and the Hurrians*, I (*in Honor of Ernest R. Lacheman*) (Winona Lake, IN: Eisenbrauns): 349-61.

THE ROLE OF LAW IN EARLY ISRAELITE SOCIETY

Robert R. Wilson

Introduction

Throughout much of its history, critical biblical scholarship on Israelite law has focused most of its attention on the literary form of the biblical laws and on the ways in which the contents of the laws were related to other ancient Near Eastern law codes. As a result, much progress has been made in the literary analysis of the legal material (beginning with the pioneering work of Alt), and the whole Near Eastern view of law is much better understood. Much work remains to be done, but at least there has been demonstrable progress.

However, considerably less attention has been paid to the relationship of law to the other major institutions of ancient Israelite society. The one major exception has been the work of George Mendenhall, who in two famous articles explored the relation between law and covenant (Mendenhall 1954a; 1954b). After analyzing ancient Near Eastern treaties, particularly the Hittite suzerainty treaties, Mendenhall suggested that the groups composing early Israel were bound together by a covenant having a form similar to that of the Hittite treaties. A standard part of the Near Eastern treaties was the list of obligations that the maker of the treaty imposed on the vassal. In the case of Israel's covenant, the obligations were expressed in the laws that were given to the people at Sinai. Because the covenant in Israel was with Yahweh, the laws were thought to have divine sanction. For Mendenhall, covenant is both a religious and a political institution, and the covenant laws therefore have both religious and political dimensions.

Mendenhall's attempt to link law to other social institutions was quickly amplified by other scholars, and law was soon being related to other spheres of Israelite society as well. Most of the scholarly attention was focused on the functions of law within the religious sphere. Since covenant was such a fundamental religious concept, scholars felt that it must have left traces in many of Israel's religious institutions. It did not take scholars long to find these traces. For example, some writers argued that the prophets based their indictments on the laws which were part of the covenant. Attempts were made to locate specific prophetic references to the various Israelite law codes. Furthermore, for some scholars the presence of legal language in the prophets indicated that they were engaged in formally indicting the people for covenant breaking. Some writers even went so far as to isolate a peculiar prophetic lawsuit pattern within the prophetic literature. Prophets were then seen as legal agents of the covenant, who pursued their activities in cultic settings where trials were held for covenant breakers (Wilson 1973: 119-20).

To be sure, the various elaborations of Mendenhall's work did provide a detailed social setting for Israelite law, but they also went far beyond the available evidence. A firm link between law and prophecy is in fact difficult to establish. The prophets almost never mention the covenant, and their use of legal language is normally metaphorical. The few lawsuit oracles that scholars have been able to isolate have turned out to be distressingly dissimilar. There is no evidence for formal cultic trials for covenant breaking, much less any evidence that prophets participated in such trials. It is not even clear that the prophets based their indictments on specific biblical laws, and only occasionally is it possible to argue that an extant biblical law is being cited in a prophetic text. In short, in spite of all of the activity inspired by Mendenhall's work, many basic questions about Israel's law remain to be answered. The nature of the legal process is still unclear. Little is known about the court system or the mechanisms of law enforcement. The relationship between law and custom has yet to be fully explored. Links between law and other social institutions remain to be studied in detail. In general, the relation of law to its social matrix is still imperfectly understood. To put the matter more bluntly, we still do not know how law worked in ancient Israel.

After this litany of problems, it is heartening to note that scholars are now taking up the question of the sociological dimensions of law with renewed vigor. In the past few years, several articles on the general subject of law and society have been written, and specific studies are beginning to appear (Wilson 1983a; 1983b; McKeating; Bellefontaine). There now seems to be a trend toward recognizing the importance of exploring the social dimensions of biblical law, and we can undoubtedly expect more studies in this area in the future (Niehr).

However, while these new studies may shed light on Israelite law, the inclusion of sociological concerns within the field of legal research makes the task of the investigator doubly difficult. Not only must the researcher study law and its development, but the social structure of ancient Israel must also be reconstructed, and then the two must be related to each other. If there is little scholarly agreement on the nature and history of Israel's law, there is even less agreement on the structure and development of Israelite society. Still, the magnitude and difficulty of the task should not forestall scholarly attempts to undertake it. I will therefore devote the remainder of this discussion to an exploration of a few of the major issues that must be tackled before a sociology of Israelite law can be written. In doing this, I do not mean to imply that I have answers to the questions that I am raising, but I think that it is important that the questions be faced.

However, before beginning a survey of major issues in the study of law and society, it is first necessary to highlight a major methodological problem that plagues all areas of the investigation. Evidence on the subject of the sociological dimensions of law is sparse, and in some areas of investigation it is virtually nonexistent. Comparative Near Eastern material is sometimes helpful, but here the evidence is limited as well, particularly on the subject of dispute settlement and court structure. Modern anthropological evidence can be employed, but its genuine comparability and relevance must be clearly demonstrated. Because of this lack of evidence, every exploration of the social dimensions of law must inevitably involve a great deal of speculation and reconstruction. This sort of approach is unavoidable if anything is to be said on the subject at all, but the tentative quality of the research means that the researcher must constantly review what has been done and revise previous work in the light of new evidence and insights. With these methodological warnings in mind, I will now turn to a survey of some major problems that require further investigation. For the sake of convenience, the survey can be broken down into three historical periods: the premonarchical period, the monarchical period, and the postexilic period. Certain problems, such as the basic structure of the court system, persist in all three periods, but each period has its own peculiar problems as well.

The Premonarchical Period

In the premonarchical period, the nature of the judicial system remains highly controverted, and it is not even generally agreed that any of the existing biblical laws actually go back to this period. Furthermore, there is no general agreement on the nature of Israelite society before the monarchy, although there have been several recent attempts to use modern anthropological evidence to reconstruct the premonarchical social structure. Such a reconstruction would be important for the study of the legal system because if the nature of the society could be determined more precisely, it might be possible to make a few more deductions about the function of law within the society. George Mendenhall seems to have had this approach in mind when he talked about a group of traditional tribes bound together into a league by the covenant. All political power was ceded to Yahweh, who was understood as Israel's only ruler (Mendenhall 1954b; 1962). The difficulty with this view is that it leaves unanswered most of the basic questions about the legal system. The notion of God's kingship may be an attractive theological construct, but it says nothing about how the society actually operated. There are no references to the human agents of God's rule, and there is no indication of how judicial authority was exercised.

The weaknesses in Mendenhall's reconstruction were recognized by Norman Gottwald, who drew on anthropological evidence to describe more clearly the way in which the social system actually operated. What biblical scholars usually identify as a tribal system of government was, Gottwald argued, more closely connected with what anthropologists have called lineage-based societies. Such societies are ordered on the principle of real or fictive kinship and have been extensively studied by anthropologists, particularly by the British functionalists (Gottwald 1979: 293-341).

The fundamental description of a lineage was given by A.R. Radcliffe-Brown and was further amplified by his students, E.E. Evans-Pritchard and Meyer Fortes. Building on suggestions made by Durkheim, Radcliffe-Brown portrayed lineages as societies in which the metaphor of kinship is applied throughout the social structure, regardless of the actual blood ties between the individuals involved. The basic social unit in the lineage is the nuclear family (two or more children of the same parent). Individual nuclear families can, in turn, be related to each other through a common ancestor, and these interrelated nuclear families would form a larger lineage. This larger lineage could then be related to other lineages of the same size through a common ancestor, and the process could continue until all members of the society had been included. Radcliffe-Brown further noted that because lineages use the nuclear family as their model, they are characterized by segmentation. All of the children of the same parent are on the same genealogical level with each other, as are two or more lineages that claim descent from the same ancestor. These lineages, which are segments of a larger lineage, are theoretically equal to each other and, at least to outsiders, appear as a harmonious social unit. Radcliffe-Brown called lineage-based social systems segmentary societies and argued that they are driven by a desire for social stability and unity. The interlocking web of social relationships, given expression in a comprehensive lineage genealogy, has to be maintained at all costs in order for the society to survive, and all parts of the social system, including the judicial system, are oriented toward that end (Radcliffe-Brown 1965; Evans-Pritchard 1964).

After a careful study of the biblical evidence on the various social units in early Israelite society, Gottwald concluded that the early Israelite tribes were in fact large lineages that were unified through a common ancestor, Jacob/Israel. Following Radcliffe-Brown, Gottwald further argued that each tribe, each sub-tribal lineage, and ultimately each individual, were equal to all others on the same level of the social structure. Thus, for Gottwald, governance in early Israel is best understood as a form of primitive democracy in which social equals made collegial decisions about the future of their own groups. The unity of the society was preserved by the allegiance of all Israelites to one God, and this unity was celebrated in the cult. Although Gottwald does not comment on the legal system per se, he presumably would treat it in the same way that he does the political system. Legal decisions would have been rendered after group discussions in which all members participated as equals, and verdicts would have been enforced by group consensus (Gottwald 1979: 489-663).

In several earlier studies I also used the lineage model to describe early Israelite society and then drew from this model some implications for our understanding of the legal system (Wilson 1983a; 1983b; 1984: 30-53). However, in addition to the ground covered by Gottwald, I also noted that although lineages appear to outsiders as egalitarian social units characterized by an emphasis on social unity, they are in fact expressions of inequality and exhibit tendencies toward disunity. The use of a genealogical metaphor to describe lineages means that lineage members are related to each other only by being related to someone who is above them in the social system. This hierarchical dimension of lineages encourages the exercise of power by individuals and groups that are highly placed in the lineage and has the potential to create resentment and a desire for a new social position on the part of those who occupy lower positions. Lineages thus always contain the seeds of instability and are likely to be in a constant state of flux as individuals and groups seek to adjust their social positions. Lineage legal systems function most efficiently at their lowest levels, where living individuals, the lineage heads, have the power to enforce decisions that are in accord with the society's customary law.

Resolution of judicial disputes is more difficult to achieve when large lineages are involved, for in this case the distant ancestor unifying the lineages is likely to be deceased or even fictitious. In such cases legal solutions must be found through negotiation among the living lineage heads.

Since the early work of Gottwald, a number of scholars have employed the lineage model to describe early Israelite society, but the usefulness of the model has also been challenged, most recently and sharply by J.W. Rogerson (1986: 17-26). Rogerson rightly points out the social complexity and diversity exhibited by lineage-based societies, noting that they vary greatly in size and in the way that they organize social and political interaction. The basis for social integration varies from society to society, as does the way in which they choose leaders and allow them to exercise power. Although early Israelite groups do indeed exhibit some of the characteristics of lineages, they also differ from typical lineages, particularly in the way in which authority is exercised within the family. According to Rogerson, in lineage-based societies parental authority is weak, even within the nuclear family, because of the degree to which social cohesion depends on social consensus. The pressure towards social stability also complicates succession and inheritance, and fosters the notion of equality within the family. In neither of these instances is the situation in Israel similar to that found in lineage-based societies. In Israel parental authority was strong, if not absolute, and succession and inheritance regularly led to inequalities in the possession of power and property. Rogerson therefore concludes that early Israel resembled a segmentary state more than it did a lineage-based society.

Rogerson's criticisms provide a healthy corrective to the work of scholars such as Gottwald who attempt to couple the lineage model with a notion of primitive democracy in early Israel. At the same time, it is important that the alleged differences between lineage-based societies and early Israelite groups are not overemphasized. There is very little biblical evidence on marriage and inheritance patterns in premonarchical Israel, and even the stories that purport to deal with this period may in fact reflect later social practices. In the same way, little is known about family structure and authority, and it may be that the strongly authoritarian family attested in some texts is a retrojection from a later period. It is important to note also that in lineage-based societies the authority of the lineage head is weak primarily when the individual seeks to enforce something contrary to the norms of the society as a whole. Thus lineage heads have difficulty avoiding the punishment of obvious wrongs or imposing strictures regarded by the society as unfair or unusual. Conversely, when lineage heads are enforcing commonly held community norms and standards, their power is much greater.

In spite of Rogerson's cautions, then, it still appears that some sort of lineage model is the most appropriate one to use in understanding Israel before the rise of the monarchy. As far as the legal system is concerned, this means that laws were most easily enforced at the lowest levels of the hierarchy of lineages, where living individuals were in a position to impose justice and to assure obedience to social norms. In cases of disputes between larger lineages, where no living individual existed to play this authoritarian role, justice would have been more difficult to impose, and the resolution of disputes would have depended more heavily on achieving group consensus through compromise.

It is not precisely clear when this lineage-based judicial system began to break down. As Rogerson correctly notes, the appearance of the judges—if in fact they actually played a role in the judicial system—would have created a situation in which tensions might arise between the customary judicial systems of the lineages and the judicial interests of the judges themselves (Rogerson 1986: 23-24). However, until more is known about the functions of these figures, it is not possible to say any more on this question.

The Monarchical Period

In the monarchical period a number of changes took place in Israelite society, and these changes all had an impact on the nature of the judicial system. First, the tendency toward centralized leadership that may have begun in the period of the judges was strengthened considerably during the reigns of David and Solomon. There is much scholarly disagreement over the reliability of the narratives that deal with this period, but it is probably safe to assume that as the monarchy grew stronger it attempted to exercise more control over the judicial system, although the precise extent of that control is unclear. In the Davidic period the royal administration of justice may have consisted primarily of the king's ability to govern the royal court and the army directly (Whitelam 1979: 71-166). However, by the Solomonic period centralized control of local administration and economic affairs seems to have become a reality, and with this growth in royal power it is likely that a system of national laws and courts was also set in place. Centralized control of the judicial system is presumed by Deut. 17.2-13 and 2 Chron. 19.4-11, although both of these texts are tendentious and probably reflect later judicial practice. Whatever the details of the central judicial system, its existence would have opened the door for conflicts with the older lineage legal systems, and these conflicts probably continued throughout the monarchical period (note 1 Kgs 21).

The second change in the Israelite social system during the monarchical period was the new role played by other nations in Israel's national life. Both in Ephraim and Judah the people were at various times subject to foreign governments, most notably the Assyrians and Babylonians. These foreign powers were in a position to influence the development of local Israelite law and to create legal conflict by imposing foreign laws that differed from those observed in Israel, but the extent to which they did so remains a highly controversial issue that requires additional study.

Thirdly, the monarchical period witnessed the growth of centralized priesthoods both in Judah and in Ephraim. A detailed history of these priesthoods remains to be written, but it is clear that their very existence led to the creation of a body of religious law which was totally under the control of the priests. It is normally assumed that before the exile this religious law was thoroughly integrated into the civil law coming from traditional sources and from the monarchy, but this assumption may not in fact be correct. There may always have existed religious laws which dealt with technical matters of the cult and which were of concern only to religious specialists. If so, these religious laws would have had a history quite different from that of the civil law.

Finally, during the monarchical period prophecy began to flourish in a way that it did not in Israel's early history. Although prophecy is certainly not the creation of the monarchy, as some have claimed, prophetic activity seems to have been at home in the royal courts, and prophets took an active role in shaping religious, political and social life. Because prophets by definition derive their authority directly from God rather than from a particular set of laws, they always have the potential to create legal conflict and to move the society toward the violation of law (see, for example, 1 Kgs 18). The prophets were thus a destabilizing factor within the monarchical judicial system, and their role in this respect deserves far more attention than it has been given.

The Postexilic Period

In the postexilic period several of the tendencies of the monarchical period became more prominent and made a lasting impact on the legal system. Foreign powers played an increasingly large role in governing the Israelite state. First the Persians, and then the Greeks and Romans put their stamp on Israel's civil law, although the extent of this influence cannot be studied until a fairly late period. Increasing foreign domination must have also caused intensified conflict within the judicial system as foreign law and local law clashed in the administration of justice. However, at the same time the postexilic period saw the decline of prophecy and a rise in the power of a unified priesthood. This means that for practical purposes the destabilizing tendencies of prophecy ceased to be major factors in the judicial system, but that more attention was given to religious law that was not greatly influenced by outside forces. In the Persian period a distinction seems to have been made between religious law, which was under the control of the priests, and secular law, which was under the control of the foreign ruler (2 Chron. 19.4-11). The nature of the interaction between these two legal systems requires further study, but the distinction itself is significant, for it allowed the religious community to survive in the context of a number of different political states. In the end it was the priestly law, given final form in the Torah, that gave the Israelite legal system its distinctive stamp and shaped Jewish communities for generations to come.

BIBLIOGRAPHY

Alt, A.
     1966   'The Origins of Israelite Law', in *Essays on Old Testament History and
                  Religion* (trans. R.A. Wilson; Oxford: Blackwell; German edn, 1934): 79-
                  132.
Bellefontaine, E.
     1987   'Customary Law and Chieftainship: Judicial Aspects of 2 Samuel 14.4-
                  21', *JSOT* 38: 42-72.
Evans-Pritchard, E.E.
     1964   'Social Anthropology', in *Social Anthropology and Other Essays* (New
                  York: Free Press): 1-134.
Gottwald, N.K.
     1979   *The Tribes of Yahweh* (Maryknoll, NY: Orbis Books).
McKeating, H.
     1979   'Sanctions against Adultery in Ancient Israelite Society, with Some
                  Reflections on Methodology in the Study of Old Testament Ethics', *JSOT*
                  11: 57-72.
Mendenhall, G.E.
     1954a   'Ancient Oriental and Biblical Law', *BA* 17: 26-46.
     1954b   'Covenant Forms in Israelite Tradition', *BA* 17: 50-76.
     1962   'The Hebrew Conquest of Palestine', *BA* 25: 66-87.

Niehr, H.
  1987   *Rechtsprechung in Israel* (Stuttgart: Katholisches Bibelwerk).
Radcliffe-Brown, A.R.
  1965   'On the Concept of Function in Social Science', in *Structure and Function in Primitive Society* (New York: Free Press): 178-87.
Rogerson, J. W.
  1986   'Was Early Israel a Segmentary Society?', *JSOT* 36: 17-26.
Whitelam, K.W.
  1979   *The Just King: Monarchical Judicial Authority in Ancient Israel* (Sheffield: JSOT Press).
Wilson, R.R.
  1973   'Form-Critical Investigation of the Prophetic Literature: The Present Situation', in *Society of Biblical Literature Seminar Papers* I (Chico, CA: Scholars Press): 100-21.
  1983a   'Enforcing the Covenant: The Mechanisms of Judicial Authority in Early Israel', in H.B. Huffmon *et al.* (eds.), *The Quest for the Kingdom of God: Essays in Honor of George E. Mendenhall* (Winona Lake, IN: Eisenbrauns).
  1983b   'Israel's Judicial System in the Pre-exilic Period', *JQR* 74: 229-48.
  1984   *Sociological Approaches to the Old Testament* (Philadelphia: Fortress Press).

Virginia Hunter

An aspect of Athenian life that has intrigued scholars in recent years is the bond of women to their natal kin. Cheryl Cox (1988), for example, has examined brother/sister ties, while Margaret Visser (1986) has devoted an article to the natal versus the conjugal family in Greek and Roman myths about women.[1] The perception of this bond is not new: it was one of the major themes of a seminal article published in 1944 by Hans Julius Wolff under the title 'Marriage Law and Family Organization in Ancient Athens'. There Wolff noted that in Athenian law 'the woman's separation from her original family never became complete' (1944: 47). In matters of property relations, for example, she remained a 'member of her original family' (1944: 53). More recently, David Schaps, in his study of women's economic rights in Greece (1979: 95), has commented on the 'legal and social paternalism' prevalent in Athens, noting the dependence of a woman on her natal family, including the protection afforded by her brother. He believes that this paternalism derives from the 'patriarchal family structure' (1979: 92). Schaps's explanation of what he calls 'paternalism' is vague, but it does serve to underscore the fact that no one has attempted to explain either theoretically or structurally the place of women, especially married women, in the natal family and in the kinship structure.

---

1. See also Hunter (1989: 298) and Foxhall (1989: 39), who notes that women had 'a foot in two households'. Cf. Seaford (1990) for examples of conflicting loyalty to husband and natal kin in Euripides.

Athenian Kinship and the Law

It is widely recognized that the principle of Athenian kinship was bilateral, with an Athenian's kindred comprising relatives on both the father's and the mother's side (Broadbent 1968: 233; Littman 1979: 5-7; Humphreys 1986: 58-59; Just 1989: 83-85). These are his or her cognates. In addition, at the centre of this bilateral group was a nucleus of agnatic kin, or those who traced their relationship through males. Studies of Athenian kinship have, however, tended to downplay the significance of agnation, noting that the agnatic group was not, like the Romans *gens*, a lineage, where descent was traced unilineally to a distant male ancestor and where membership conferred on agnates distinct rights and obligations. Rather than the lineage, the central institution of Athenian society was the household (Humphreys 1978: 194-97). The conclusion of a recent study (Humphreys 1986: 89) bears out this view, indicating that 'the material from Attic forensic speeches in no way suggests that agnates had a particular obligation to support each other in court'. On the contrary, the study found, there was a slight tendency for kin on the mother's side to be more supportive than those on the father's. Such a conclusion is significant, in that it reveals the kind and extent of kin interaction in an important area of Athenian public life. But based as it is on only one context, witnessing in the law courts, it underestimates the strong hold of agnatic kinship not only in Athenian law but in Athenian family practice and ideology.[1]

It is my contention that agnation was still lively among Athenians, bonding patrikin to one another. Paradoxically, agnation also cemented the ties of a woman to her natal kin, thus serving to strengthen the bonds with matrikin noted in the above study. In order to prove this contention, I shall begin by considering the *anchisteia* and some of its peculiarities.

The *anchisteia* was the structure of bilateral kindred, extending on both the mother's and the father's side to the children of first cousins (Harrison 1968: 143; Broadbent 1968: 231-35; MacDowell 1978: 98-108; 1989: 17; Just 1989: 85-89).[2] As embodied in the law, the

---

1. Goody (1983: 226) suggests a number of other contexts in which kinship is used or reckoned, such as, 'membership of a kin group', 'succession to office' and 'the inheritance of property'. Cf. Humphreys' remarks about context (1986: 90-91).

2. The *anchisteia* extended first to the descendants of ego's father and then to those of his grandfather before admitting kin on the mother's side. Is. 11.1-2 refers

anchisteia was effective in two broad areas: homicide and intestate succession. For the law designated both those kin who were entitled, indeed, bound, to prosecute the murderer of one of their number and those who had rights of succession and inheritance when a man died without a will. The latter included the parallel right, or the obligation, as the case may be, to marry an inheriting daughter or *epikleros*. For the purposes of this paper, two features of the *anchisteia* are noteworthy. First, agnates take precedence. In the case of homicide, while the bilateral kindred of the deceased are responsible for initiating a homicide case by proclamation in the agora, close agnates alone, father, brother(s), and son(s) may grant pardon and a return from exile to the killer (Dem. 43.57; Dem. 47.72). Only if there are no surviving close blood relatives in the male line, does this duty fall to the bilateral kindred of the deceased (*IG* I^2 115.11-32; MacDowell 1963: 18 and 117-20; Broadbent 1968: 128-34; Gagarin 1981: 48-58).[1] Similarly, in the case of inheritance, agnates precede, beginning with the deceased's brother(s), then his sister(s), and moving from his siblings and their children to his first cousin(s) once removed. It is only after agnates have been considered that even a uterine half-brother is allowed to claim an inheritance. Following a uterine half-brother or half-sister, kindred on the mother's side may claim. This principle holds, *mutatis mutandis*, for claiming the hand of an *epikleros*.

to degrees of relationship, the closest being brothers and the sons of brothers, followed by sisters and their children, and then cousins on the father's side and their offspring. The same passage specifies that this order of succession also prevailed on the mother's side. For a comprehensive statement of the law, see Dem. 43.51, where it is laid down in addition that in the same degree of relationship males took precedence over females. Cf. Dem. 43.78, Dem. 44.62 and Is. 7.20. Based on the claims of one of the protagonists in Isaeus 11 (Theopompus), some scholars have interpreted the children of cousins to include second cousins, thus extending the *anchisteia* to descendants of ego's great-grandfather (Miles 1950; Harrison 1968: 143; Thompson 1976: 1-7). This view, however, has not found general acceptance. See, for example, Wyse (1904: 673), Davies (1971: 79), and MacDowell (1978: 106-107).

1. Gagarin (1981: 55) interprets lines 20–23 of *IG* I^2 115 to imply that 'the duty to prosecute lay with the agnate relatives, but the other relatives and phratry members were to assist them'. This is entirely possible and, if so, suggests that the involvement of agnates was even more pronounced. Cf. MacDowell (1963: 18), who lists some of the individuals who did in fact take the initiative in homicide cases. These include a son (Ant. 1), a father (Ant. 3) and a brother (Ant. 6). Whatever the law permitted, clearly it was usual for the closest relatives to initiate a homicide case.

The second point to be observed is that females in this structure inherit. In the absence of brothers, the sisters of the deceased precede his uncles and his cousins, and even any uterine half-brother. In other words, based on their place in the kinship structure, sisters inherit, though they may in fact be married and in the *kyrieia* of a husband. And here I am not concerned with what happened to that inheritance after a woman received it, that is, whether her husband as *kyrios* managed it or whether it eventually devolved to her son. What I would stress is that women inherit under Athenian law and that they do so as sisters (or as cousins) because they have, or retain, agnatic ties to their natal family. Where practice is concerned, the Attic lawsuits provide a number of significant examples of women holding property inherited from a brother or even a cousin (Is. 7.31; Is. 11.9 and 49). Such women are also found claiming or contesting an inheritance in court (Is. 3.3; Is. 11.17). Not only did the court recognize such claims but speakers refer to the women who brought them as active disputants, as if they were *sui iuris*, though in each instance a *kyrios* was present in court as a woman's representative. Following this principle, if a sister was deceased, her children inherited, brother preceding sister. In other words, if a deceased man had no brothers, but only a sister, and she too was dead, her son—or even her daughter—would inherit his property. The very fact of such female inheritance suggests that, whatever the nature of the *kyrieia* in Athenian family life, in no sense did it approximate Roman *patria potestas*. That power, reflected in marriage with *manus*, severed a woman from her agnatic kin, making her a full member of her husband's descent group with rights of inheritance as if she were his daughter (Watson 1971: 22; Hallett 1984: 124-25; Crook 1986: 59-61). Athenian women had no such rights in their husband's *oikos*. Rather, they retained rights of inheritance, albeit limited ones, in their natal family. These rights were strong enough to descend to their children as well, even though the latter were members of an entirely different *oikos* and in their father's *kyrieia*.

Family Practice: Adoption

So far I have considered law. But what about practice? Here I shall look at adoption, in particular, those instances of adoption that were the result of deliberate choice made either through a will or *inter*

vivos.[1] For in the absence of a son, an Athenian had the right to designate as his heir a person of his choice (Is. 2.13; 3.68; 9.13; and 10.2).
Whom did Athenians adopt? And what was the attitude of Athenians
both to adoption itself and to those actually adopted? For an answer to
these questions, I shall turn for the most part to the lawsuits, some few
in the Demosthenic corpus, but primarily those composed by Isaeus,
11 of whose 12 orations deal with wills and adoptions. In total, I have
found 17 instances where a man exercised his choice in the matter of
adoption (see Table 2). Those adopted include four agnatic relatives (a
first cousin, a first cousin once removed, a collateral relative whose
identity is unclear, and a brother), five children of sisters (two sons,
two daughters and one grandson), three relatives on the mother's side
(one each of a uterine half-brother and half-sister and the son of a
uterine half-sister), and finally two affines, two stepsons, and one
friend.[2] Of 17 cases, in other words, while only four adoptees are
agnates proper, five others are the children of sisters, who, I have
suggested, retain formal rights of inheritance based on agnatic

---

1. Gernet (1955) is seminal on wills and adoption. I have also benefitted from
Harrison (1968: 82-96), MacDowell (1978: 99-101) and Thompson (1981).

2. My list of adoptions derives in the first instance from Gernet (1955: 129). He
counted 27, from which I have subtracted his nos. 3, 9, 16, and 19. Gernet no. 3
(Is. 2.10) is not an adoption but a contemplated adoption of a brother's son. It did
not take place. Gernet no. 9 (Is. 7.6) is purely conjectural: there is no mention of
either a will or an adoption. As Wyse observes (1904: 555): 'It is improbable that
Eupolis pretended to have been made his brother's son. . .' Gernet no. 16 (Is.
11.8) is in fact the same as his no. 22. According to Hagnias's will, if anything
happened to Gernet no. 15 (my no. 7), Hagnias's uterine half-brother Glaucon was
to be his heir. At Dem. 43.4 (Gernet no. 22) both Glaucon and his brother Glaucus
claim to be Hagnias's heirs under a will which they themselves produced. The will
was declared spurious by the court. For further complexities, see Davies (1971: 83).
Gernet no. 19 (Isoc. 19.12) does not involve an Athenian adoption. I have, on the
other hand, added to Gernet's list the adoption of Leocrates I by Archiades (Dem.
44.19 and 46), my no. 9, and the adoption of Diocles by his stepfather (Is. 8.40-
41), my no. 15. See below, page 108, n. 1, for further additions to Gernet's list.
My no. 4 (Gernet no. 14) deserves comment. Aristarchus II had been adopted
posthumously by his paternal grandfather, thus leaving his own house and ending
his relationship as a brother to Xenaenetus II. In effect, he became the adoptive uncle
of his brother and so, while still an agnate, was legally no longer Xenaenetus's
brother. In challenging his will, the speaker of Isaeus 10 does not argue, as he
might, that an adopted son had no right to make a will (Dem. 44.64 and 67-68; Wyse
1904: 650).

affiliation. The latter are the largest single group.

What might influence an Athenian's choice in adopting a son or daughter? Isaeus 2 is revealing in this regard. The case involves the estate of Menecles, who had adopted as his heir the brother of his second wife. The latter is defending his rights as an adopted son against the challenge of Menecles' own brother. One explanation he offers for his adoptive father's choice of himself is that his brother had only one son, whom Menecles considered it wrong to ask for in adoption (10-11). At the same time, he had no other relatives from whose families he might have chosen a son. The speaker then proceeds to set out the order of potential adoptees. After a brother's son, a sister's son is to be preferred, then the son of a male or a female cousin (21; cf. Is. 3.72). In other words, the ideal order of adoption followed the *anchisteia*, designating as first choice the blood relatives closest to the adopter in the male line, or agnates. Indeed, when a man chose a more distant relative or a friend, it was thought to be the result of some hostility harboured against his close relatives. Such a situation actually did arise in Isaeus 7, *On the Estate of Apollodorus*. Apollodorus was an orphan who, as a child, had been cheated by his paternal uncle and guardian. In time, finding himself childless, he adopted as his heir the son of his uterine half-sister. After his death, a female cousin, the daughter of this same uncle, and so a close agnate, claimed the estate as next-of-kin. One of the justifications offered by the speaker for Apollodorus's choice of himself as his adopted son is that his uncle refused to leave his wealth to his nearest relatives because of the injuries he had suffered at their hands (7.4). Nor was it unusual for adoption, especially testamentary adoption, to incur the hostility, and so the opposition, of close kin. For as one speaker states: 'All blood relatives think they have the right to dispute the succession of a son adopted by will' (Is. 3.61). Hence, a common theme running through Isaeus's orations is the opposition of *genos* and *dosis*, kinship versus bequest, as one individual contests the right of another to succeed to the deceased's estate. In other words, a deeply ingrained negative attitude to adoption encouraged Athenians to challenge a deceased relative's choice of a son.[1]

---

1. Although the opposition of kinship and bequest is omnipresent in Isaeus's orations, it is strongly articulated at 1.41, 3.61, 4.15-16 and 22, 5.14-16, and 9.23-25 and 34. Further indications of a negative attitude to adoption are found at Is. 3.72-73 and 4.18 and 26 and Dem. 44.63.

Among the 17 cases noted above, ten were contested. A sister's sons, for example, challenged the right of a collateral relative to inherit their uncle's fortune (Isaeus 1); a brother of the deceased challenged the adoption *inter vivos* of his wife's brother (Isaeus 2); a paternal cousin opposed a friend (Isaeus 4); and paternal half-brothers contested the adoption of a sister's son (Isaeus 6). These challenges are in themselves instructive, for they indicate that though legally an Athenian had the right to choose as his successor anyone he wished, in practice his choices seem to have been rather limited. As a strategy of heirship, adoption was, ideally, based on the principles underlying intestate succession. Consequently, if an adoption veered too far from these principles, it might well face a challenge in the courts. In fact, such challenges confronted not only relatively distant connections like affines or uterine half-brothers but also close blood relatives whose claims were formally weaker than other *anchisteis*.

How did individuals who adopted balance the competing claims of obligation to close kin and personal inclination? One way was to emphasize the ties of adopter and adoptee, including not only the bonds of kinship but close acquaintanceship and deep affection such as to convince the adopter he would leave his estate to a responsible and loving heir. Unfortunately, such a justification, which may after all only amount to rhetoric on the part of an adoptee defending his position, could work both ways. In Isaeus 1, two nephews contest the will of their maternal uncle, explaining away his choice of a collateral relative. They themselves, they point, out were not only his closest kin as a sister's sons but their uncle had loved them dearly, taking care of them as orphans (12-14). They allege that he had even intended to adopt them. In a word, they were their uncle's natural heirs. Clearly, the best policy to follow in adopting a son was to designate an individual whose claims could not be contested. And this meant not only following one's own inclinations but respecting popular mentality about the relative legitimacy of heirs. In the best of all worlds, this was a close blood relative who also commanded the respect and affection of the adopter. The thread, however, that runs through all these cases is the conjunction of rights and obligations. Under the laws of intestate succession, close agnates or those with agnatic ties like sisters and their children could expect to inherit. Very reasonably, since they stood to inherit, they might expect to be chosen as adopted heirs. In such a case, the obligation they assumed in preserving the house of a deceased relative would balance the inheritance that was theirs by right.

The notion of obligation serves to introduce a series of adoptions, 11 in all, that are not the result of a will or a deliberate choice on the part of the deceased (see Table 2).[1] The majority (six) concern the posthumous adoption of an *epikleros*'s son into the house of his maternal grandfather. In fact, whether such an adoption took place or not, the son (or sons) of an *epikleros* inherited his grandfather's estate when he reached his majority. That right devolved upon him through his mother, who was an inheriting daughter. Before that time, however, it was expected that his father would have him adopted into the house of his wife's father. An example is the transfer of Euboulides III by his father Sositheus into the house of his maternal grandfather. (Euboulides' mother was Phylomache, the only child of Euboulides II.) Sositheus himself, as speaker of Demosthenes 43, declares that it had been his intention to preserve his father-in-law's house, thus fulfilling the wish of the latter that a son of his daughter be adopted into his *oikos* (11-12). In other words, the *epikleros* had unique rights of inheritance and the concomitant obligation to provide an heir for her father's house.[2] Some such principle also operated in the case of sisters who inherited, for they were under a strong obligation, on receiving an inheritance from a brother, to provide a son as heir to his estate posthumously. For example, Is. 7.31-32 records an attack made on two sisters who inherited their brother's

1. To Gernet's list I have added the adoption of Macartatus by his mother's brother (Is. 11.49-50), my no. 26, and that of Leostratus and his successors by Archiades (Dem. 44.20-23), my no. 28. It is unclear whether Archimachus, my no. 21, is the maternal grandfather of the anonymous witness (Dem. 43.37). Both Gernet (no. 24) and Wyse (1904: 617) assume so. Gernet (no. 26) also assumes that Aeschylus is the maternal grandfather of Charidemus (Dem. 58.31), my no. 22. Davies (1971: 6), however, believes that Aeschylus is his guardian. There are a series of adoptions that follow that of no. 28 (Dem. 44), as each adopted son returned to his own *oikos*, leaving a son in his place down to Leocares, the second great, great grandson of Archiades's sister, and the brother of the preceding adoptee. There were in all four adoptions including nos. 9 and 28 before a challenge was made to their legality. I have not included the final two replacements on my list. In a sense, all are the same adoption. See Gernet (1957: 125-30).

2. Seminal on the *epikleros* is Gernet (1921). I have also consulted Harrison (1968: 132-38), Karnezis (1972), Schaps (1979: 25-47) and Just (1989: 95-98). Both Asheri (1963) and Lane Fox (1985) discuss the institution of the *epikleros* in the context of the general rules of inheritance.

fortune but who failed to give up a son for adoption. They were considered indifferent to their brother's childlessness and condemned for allowing his house to die out. On the other hand, the opposite occurs at Is. 11.49, where the speaker's brother-in-law had died leaving his sister heir to his property. At that point, he states, he was persuaded by his wife to allow one of their two sons to be adopted into the house of Macartatus, his brother-in-law. In other words, on the analogy of an inheriting daughter or *epikleros*, an inheriting sister might, indeed seems obliged to, produce an heir for her brother. In both cases the inheritance rights of women were tied to obligations to their natal kin.

Women and their Natal Kin

We have returned to the bond of women to their natal kin. How close such ties were, the lawsuits once again document. A law cited by Demosthenes (46.18), for example, lists those relatives entitled to give a woman's hand in marriage (marriage, that is, by *engye*, a valid betrothal, which alone permitted her to produce legitimate children). The list includes her father, followed by her homopatric brother, and then her paternal grandfather—her closest agnates.[1] These have been called her 'natural *kyrioi*' (Karnezis 1976: 91). In fact, one of this group, being her original *kyrios*, retained that role not only up to the time of her marriage but even after a marriage had taken place. In that capacity he could encourage or assist a daughter or sister to divorce and remarry (Dem. 41.4; Is. 8.36; Menander, *Epitrepontes* 655-60 and 714-21; Harrison 1968: 109; Karnezis 1976: 92-99). In general, women were but slowly assimilated to their conjugal family, roots being established with the birth of a child, especially a son. Before that time, if a wife died, her dowry reverted to her family of origin (Is. 3.36; Harrison 1968: 56). Indeed, until a woman was past the age of child-bearing, her dowry belonged in some sense to her natal family. Hence, a young widow without children would return with her dowry to her kin. Even after she had borne children, for the most part, she still returned, with or without her children, to her

---

1. The law next contemplates the case in which a woman, heiress or otherwise, has none of these relatives. See Harrison (1968: 19-21 and 109-11) for some of the problems involved. A woman's *kyrios* could, if absent, delegate his power, as will become clear from our discussion of Menander's *Aspis*, below.

family of origin. At that point, her father or her brother should move to recover her dowry (Is. 3.8-9). It was the duty of her *kyrios* to remarry the widow (Dem. 40.6-7; Is. 8.8; Is. 9.27). In the meantime, the widow resided in his house, often with her children (Lys. 3.6-7; Lys. 19.9 and 32-33). In other words, the widow remained a member of her natal family and was ensured of the protection of her kin and of a place in her family of origin (Hunter 1989).

In his essay, 'Marriage Law and Family Organization', Wolff (1944: 50) points out that 'along with her function in her husband's family, the woman had the task of bringing forth heirs for her own family, who might carry it on if no sons or descendants of sons or close agnates capable of doing so were available'. We have already seen evidence of this obligation in the case of the *epikleros*. But sisters too were under a similar obligation and expected to offer a son as heir to a dead brother. How strong was this obligation? Was a sister who inherited also an *epikleros*? Up to now, the weight of scholarly opinion has been against such a view (Wyse 1904: 655-56; Gernet 1921: 346-47; Harrison 1968: 137-38). For while Isaeus 6 (46 and 51) seems to suggest that a sister could be claimed as an *epikleros* to her brother, the case is complicated by the fact that the deceased's property had never been separated from that of his father. Hence, the woman claimed, the widow of Chaereas might reasonably be considered *epikleros* to her father, not her brother. Or this is the conclusion of Harrison (1968: 138), who states: 'On the whole it seems likely that if a man died without issue, but was survived by a sister, that sister was regarded as heiress to her father rather than her brother'. This view has recently been challenged by MacDowell (1982) in an essay examining Menander's *Aspis*. In this play, MacDowell finds evidence allowing him to clarify a number of points of family law previously open to conjecture. The play itself is worth considering as an illustration of the role of agnates in both law and life. It tells of an orphaned girl living with her brother, Cleostratus, who is also her *kyrios*. On departing for military service, Cleostratus transfers his *kyrieia* to a paternal uncle. In time, the latter, believing his nephew to be dead, is ready to marry his niece to his own stepson (133-36). But the niece/sister, it transpires, has become an *epikleros* and is so claimed by an older paternal uncle, Smicrines (138-43, 182-87). What the *epikleros* inherits in this case is her brother's fortune, comprised of booty won on his campaign. While one might have expected a sister to inherit in her own right, in fact this is not the case. Smicrines himself makes this very clear when he refuses to take the booty and leave the *epikleros* to marry a younger man. For if she has a son, he points out, the property will be his (269-73). In other words, and this is MacDowell's point (48), her brother's fortune is not hers at all but remains with her only until she has a son to inherit it. The *Aspis*, in other words, provides an example of a sister who is *epikleros* to her brother and not her father.[1]

This is an important new point and one I believe MacDowell is correct in inferring from the text. What is equally significant is the fact that a sister does not inherit in her own right. As we have already seen, a sister is like a daughter in inheriting only in the absence of males in the same degree of relationship. The rule is precisely the same for the two. What we did not know before is that she is also like a daughter in being claimable by an agnate. Either way, whether she is *epikleros* to her brother or her father, a woman who inherits ensures that the *oikos* of her father is continued. This rule explains the social pressure on sisters who already had sons (and so technically were not *epikleroi*) to give one of their sons in adoption to a brother after his death. Such a duty was surely deeply embedded in the mentality of the Athenians.

Agnatic Kinship: The Patrilineal Bias

The explanation of the bond of Athenian women to their natal kin lies, I believe, in the very nature of the kinship structure, which we have characterized as bilateral with strong agnatic elements. In suggesting this hypothesis, I am following those anthropologists who have studied bilateral systems and who have noted that not all are 'pure' but that some fall between 'pure' bilateralism and 'pure' unilineality. In this case, there can be a proclivity to agnation, referred to as an agnatic or patrilateral bias (Fox 1967: 153; Gulliver 1971: 12, 283 and 307; Goody 1983: 238). Such a bias may hold in only one or some areas of

---

1. This might explain and validate the claim of the speaker of Isaeus 10 that his mother was an *epikleros* after the death of her brother, who was too young to make a will and so adopt an heir (10.4, 12, 19 and 21). He speaks of his mother's *kleros* (10.15, 17 and 23) and her paternal estate (10.24-25), calling her *kyria* (10.23). Hitherto scholars have been uncertain 'whether the woman was to be regarded as succeeding to her father or to her brother' (Harrison 1968: 311). I am not impressed by the arguments adduced against MacDowell by Brown (1983).

social life, but in those areas agnatic kin have rights and privileges in preference to cognates. This, as we have seen above, holds true for Athenian society in matters of succession and inheritance, where the preference for agnates was strong and significant and carried over into family practice.[1]

The notion of agnation has itself undergone transformation since Sir Henry Maine propounded its traditional definition in his study of ancient law (1907: 154). Agnates, Maine defined as all cognates who trace their connection exclusively through males or 'all who remain after the descendants of women have been excluded'. In addition, he explained agnation as founded in the authority of the father or *patria potestas*, concluding that this is the reason why a woman's descendants are outside the limits of kinship. 'If she married, her children fell under the Patria Potestas, not of her Father, but of her Husband, and thus were lost to her own family' (155). Basing himself as he did on the principles of the Roman family, Maine produced a model that exactly fits a strict patrilineal system like the Roman one. It fits, for example, Chinese lineage, where the rules of patrilineal descent and patrilocal marriage were so strict that lineages lost virtually all control over their own sisters and daughters. Instead, they gained an analogous control over incoming wives and daughters-in-law. Or as Freedman (1958: 134) points out: 'Having few ritual and virtually no economic ties with her own agnates, the married woman was forced to cast her interests fully within the group of which she was a member by marriage'. In such a system, brothers alone inherit and widows remain members of the conjugal family. But agnatic ties need not correspond to Maine's model. This is the view of modern anthropologists, who have reconsidered *patria potestas* and its applicability to all forms of patriliny. For instance, I.M. Lewis's study (1965) of the descent principle and the loyalties created by it provides ethnographic data to show that in certain patrilineal societies women are not absorbed into their husband's family by marriage but retain affiliation to their natal kin. In some instances, a woman's life both before and after marriage is primarily the responsibility of her own kin. In these societies 'women, although of markedly inferior status to men, have yet strong patrilineal rights and obligations. Such cases resemble matrilineal societies in that the sibling bond is strong between the

---

1. Just (1989: 87) acknowledges 'a patrilateral bias in the order of succession'. For wider ramifications of such a bias, see Foxhall (1989: 40-43).

sexes to the corresponding detriment of the marriage tie' (1965: 104). A correlate of this type of patriliny is, he suggests, the existence of strong matrilateral ties.

In Athens, of course, we are not dealing with a pure unilineal system. Nonetheless, patriliny was deeply rooted enough that agnaticism suffused the structures of the family and kinship. In order to elaborate this statement, we must first distinguish between kinship and descent. The principle of Athenian descent was patrilineal, succession passing from father to son, while in practice Athenians routinely followed their own name by that of their father, demotics notwithstanding. In addition, every Athenian was a member of a phratry or patrilineal clan (Dem. 57.24; Flower 1985: 234; Humphreys 1986: 59). Phratries were active in Athenian life, holding property and being associated with cults and sacrifices. More importantly, they controlled the entrance of new members to the citizen body. A father introduced his children to his phratry at the annual festival of the Apaturia, thus establishing a semi-official record of their 'citizenship' (Dem. 39.4; Dem. 57.46 and 54; Is. 3.76; Is. 8.19). Similarly, a man introduced his wife to his phratry by offering his *phrateres* a wedding-feast and thus ensuring the legitimacy of their union (Dem. 57.43; Is. 3.76; Is. 8.18-20). On the basis of such functions, Davies (1977: 110) has characterized the phratries in the classical period as 'first and foremost a mechanism for buttressing descent and legitimacy'.[1] A subdivision of the phratry was the *genos*, an aristocratic patriclan (Humphreys 1986: 89). Not everyone belonged to a *genos*, for originally it was an elite group within a phratry (Andrewes 1961). Like the phratry, it was recruited patrilineally. It also held property and was linked to cults and sacrifices. Like the phratry too it buttressed legitimacy. The *genos* of the Brytidae, for example, refused to accept Phrastor's son, the grandson of Neaera, challenging him to take an oath that his wife, Neaera's daughter, was an Athenian woman and one duly betrothed to

---

1. An adopted son was also introduced to his adoptive father's phratry, whereupon the *phrateres* voted on his admission (Is. 2.14; Is. 7.15-17). In addition, the phratry was involved in homicide procedures, its members sharing in the prosecution with the deceased's bilateral kin and affines (*IG* I^2 115.21-23). On phratries, in addition to Davies (1977), I have consulted Andrewes (1961), Schmitt (1977), Humphreys (1978: 94-97; 1985: 342-43), Flower (1985), and Golden (1985).

him by law (Dem. 59.59-61).[1] Phratries and *gene* offered a structured relationship and a place of association for agnates, indicating that the principle of descent as well as the descent group itself was still vital in Athenian life.

Such descent groups as existed were not, however, constituted of lineages, but of households, an institution that is itself significant in a study of agnation. To an Athenian, the preservation of his house was of deep, almost obsessive, concern, an attitude reinforced at the level of the state by institutions such as the epiclerate and adoption. The state might well be concerned, for as an association of theoretical equals, Athenian society rested on the continuation of individual households. In the classical period, the house approximated what Goody (1983: 238) calls a *lignage*, not a lineage proper, but an agnatic line of filiation, recruited patrilineally and dedicated to the preservation of landed property. Where women are concerned, Hughes (1978: 284) has argued that the dowry as an institution strengthened the patrilineal or agnatic house. For generally, it 'drew attention away from the conjugal bond to focus it instead on the relations between the couple and the wife's kinsmen, whose rights toward children of the marriage the dowry guaranteed'. If this was so in general, in Athens even greater leverage existed to draw attention away from the conjugal to the natal family. A father could, as we have seen, end his daughter's marriage. Moreover, when a daughter was widowed, a father (or a brother, for that matter) not only required the return of the dowry, but often effected in addition the return and remarriage of his daughter. Perhaps most significant of all was the right of the natal family to

1. Roussel (1976) is important for both phratry and *genos*. He rejects the notion of the latter as a segment of a tribal organization with a continuity from the pre-Solonic to the classical era. Also consulted on *gene* were Hignett (1952: 61-67), Bourriot (1976), and Smith (1985). Other institutions in which patrifiliation was the rule are the deme and tribe, although neither is a descent group in the anthropological sense. Patronymics were also employed in a number of contexts. For example, the phratry list *IG* II^2 1244 gives 20 names with patronymics, while *IG* II^2 1245 adds 'patronymic and demotic spasmodically' (Andrewes 1961: 9). Of the more than 50 names of *gene* that are known, most are patronymics, referring to the ancestor of the *genos*, e.g., the Eteoboutadae, Boutes, the Eumolpidae, Eumolpus, the Alcmeonidae, Alcmeon, etc. For the *genos* was a group of families who believed they were 'descended from a single ancestor, who was always a hero or a god' (Hignett 1952: 63). Finally, certain 'houses' used a patronymic referring to their founder, examples being the Pisistratidae and the Bouselidae (Hignett 1952: 63).

expect an inheriting daughter, or a sister, to produce an heir for its line. The last especially kept alive the affiliation and responsibilities of a woman to her own kin. Anthropologists have debated the effects of this affiliation. Some believe that a lineage is strengthened by its ability to absorb incoming wives, Rome and China being examples. Others take precisely the opposite view, convinced that a lineage is strengthened by the fact that its women do not lose their affiliation to it at marriage (Lewis 1965: 101-106; Goody 1983: 225).[1] I would agree with the latter, for it is clear that, in the absence of lineages, the agnatic family derived some of its strengths from retaining daughters as members with continuing responsibilities. In particular, the right of the natal family to the reproductive powers of its daughters offered it a significant strategy of heirship.

Conclusions

To speak of an agnatic bias is to underestimate the vitality of patriliny in Athenian society. As a principle of descent it was fundamental, while descent groups were themselves still active at a number of levels. Hence every Athenian belonged to one or more corporate groups, while being simultaneously at the centre of a personal grouping of bilateral kindred. Even where kindred were concerned, law gave precedence to agnates, and generally family practice followed.

It is beyond the scope of this paper to speculate as to the origins of the Athenian kinship structure. Perhaps in pre-Solonian times Athens was already a patrilineal society of the type that retained its women as affiliated members. Or the kinship structure may have acquired its

---

1. Abu-Lughod's study (1986) of Bedouin social life offers many parallels with Athenian family practice. For example, a woman may consider herself an outsider in her husband's home even after twenty years of marriage. For women derive their identification from their natal family. In fact, in any dispute with her husband's family, a woman is expected to side with her own kin. The latter, in addition, protect her from abuse in marriage. 'When angry, she packs a few of her possessions in a bundle and heads off toward her family's camp. And in case of divorce, she can return home, where she is entitled to support. But because she is identified with her kin, her behavior affects their honor and reputation, just as theirs affects hers. Her kin, not her husband, are ultimately responsible for her and are entitled to sanction all her wrongdoings, including adultery' (54-55). This study makes it clear that women's patrilineal affiliation has a profound effect on their position in the family and on the way they live their daily lives.

distinctive features in an evolution from strict patriliny to bilaterality, gradually extending limited rights and responsibilities to females. Either is possible. Nor is it unusual for a structure of bilateral kindred to co-exist with descent groups (Fox 1967: 168). What is clear is that bilateral kinship is at least as old as Draco. Furthermore, the rules of intestate succession and the institution of the epiclerate are archaic, adjustments to each being attributed to Solon (Plutarch, *Solon* 20-22; wills and adoption, Gernet 1955; the epiclerate, Gernet 1955: 133). Both intestate succession and the epiclerate gave precedence to agnates; both offered limited rights and responsibilities to women based on their membership in the agnatic family. The epiclerate, moreover, explicitly encouraged endogamy among agnates, revealing a weak adherence to the incest prohibition among Athenians (Gernet 1921: 377-78; 1968: 348-49; Vernant, 1974: 73-74). Endogamy among both agnates and cognates continued to characterize Athenian marriage patterns in the classical era (Thompson 1967; Littman 1979: 20-24). Whatever the functions of these institutions in the pre-Solonian era, with the consolidation of the state they became integral to the preservation of the *oikos*, the primary unit of Athenian society. As a concomitant, whatever the role of women in the kinship structure before the advent of the state, it was now securely linked to the reproduction of that basic unit and with it the social structure (Vernant 1974: 62-64).

The distinctions I have drawn in respect of kinship help to explain the mass of empirical data documenting the fact that Athenian women were not totally absorbed into the conjugal family but retained strong links to their siblings and agnates, among whom they had distinct rights and responsibilities, some of them incorporated in the Athenian legal structure. Paradoxically, it was agnation, rooted in the kinship structure itself, that produced these links as well as rights and obligations. Structurally, it is obvious why ties with matrikin would be strong. Given the mortality rate, there was a good chance that wives as widows would return to their family of origin with their dowry and often with their children. Then a father or brother was required to exercise his responsibility. Given too the problem of heirship, there was some chance that a maternal uncle might consider adopting one of his sister's sons.[1] All of this surely served to draw affines into the

---

1. Bremmer (1983) has documented the strong relationship of a mother's brother with her son in both mythology and history.

kinds of strong alliances we know existed. But there is also an emotional factor often overlooked. Matrikin must have provided a welcome emotional relief for agnates, whose squabbles over property, wills, and adoptions produced, as we have seen, deep tensions and conflict among even close blood relatives.

Table 1: Adoptions by Will or *Inter Vivos*

	No.	Oration	Deceased	Adopted Child	Manner	Contested by Agnates
	1	Isaeus 1 (Gernet no. 1)	Cleonymus	a collateral relative	will	sister's sons
	2	Isaeus 5 (Gernet no. 6)	Dicaeogenes II	paternal cousin (son of father's sister)	will	sisters and their children
	3	Isaeus 9 (Gernet no. 12)	Astyphilus	first cousin once removed (son of father's first cousin)	will	uterine half-brother
	4	Isaeus 10 (Gernet no. 14)	Aristarchus II	brother/ adoptive nephew	will	son of sister by adoption
	5	Isaeus 3 (Gernet no. 4)	Pyrrhus	a sister's son	will	no contest
	6	Isaeus 6 (Gernet no. 7)	Philoctemon	a sister's son	will	putative half-brothers
Children of sisters	7	Isaeus 11 (Gernet no. 15)	Hagnias	a sister's daughter	will	no contest
	8	Isaeus 11 (Gernet no. 17)	Theophon	a sister's daughter	will	no contest
	9	Dem. 44	Archiades	great nephew (a sister's grandson)	will or inter vivos*	brother's grandson
	10	Isaeus 7 (Gernet no. 10)	Apollodorus	uterine half-sister	will	no contest
Relatives on the mother's side	11	Isaeus 7 (Gernet no. 11)	Apollodorus	son of uterine half-sister	*inter vivos*	first cousin (daughter of father's brother)
	12	Isaeus 11 (Gernet nos. 16 and 22)	Hagnias	uterine half-brother or half-brothers (Dem. 43)	will	first cousin (son of father's sister)
Affines	13	Isaeus 2 (Gernet no. 2)	Menecles	brother of second wife	*inter vivos*	brother
	14	Dem. 41 (Gernet no. 20)	Polyeuctus	brother of wife	*inter vivos*	no contest
Stepsons	15	Isaeus 8	stepfather (of Diocles)	stepson	will	no contest
	16	Plutarch** (Gernet no. 18)	Isocrates	stepson	*inter vivos*	no contest
Friends	17	Isaeus 4 (Gernet no. 5)	Nicostratus	fellow mercenary	will	first cousins (sons of father's brother) and others

* Davies (1971: 195)

** *Lives of the Ten Orators*, 839B

Table 2: Athenian Posthumous Adoptions

	No.	Oration	Deceased	Adopted Child	Comments
	18	Isaeus 10 (Gernet no. 13)	Xenaenetus I	Cyronides	possibly *inter vivos**
	19	Dem. 42 (Gernet no. 21)	Philostratus	Phaenippus	
	20	Dem. 43 (Gernet no. 23)	Euboulides II	Euboulides III	
Sons of epikleroi	21	Dem. 43 (Gernet no. 24)	Archimachus	name unknown	
	22	Dem. 58 (Gernet no. 26)	Aeschylus	Charidemus	
	23	Plutarch** (Gernet no. 27)	Lycophron	Lycophron	*inter vivos*
	24	Isaeus 6 (Gernet no. 8)	Philoctemon and Ergamenes	putative half-brothers, sons of Euctemon	
	25	Isaeus 10 (Gernet no. 14)	Aristarchus I	Aristarchus II, grandson (son of son)	
Other posthumous Adoptions	26	Isaeus 11 (Dem. 43)	Macartatus	Macartatus, sister's son	
	27	Dem. 43 (Gernet no. 25)	Macartatus	sister's grandson, son of Macartatus (above, no. 26)	
	28	Dem. 44	Archiades	Leostratus, sister's great grandson, son of adoptive son, Leocrates (above, no. 9)	

*   Wyse (1904: 655)

** *Lives of the Ten Orators*, 843A

BIBLIOGRAPHY

Abu-Lughod, L.
1986   *Veiled Sentiments: Honor and Poetry in a Bedouin Society* (Berkeley: University of California Press).

Andrewes, A.
1961   'Philochoros on Phratries', *JHS* 81: 1-15.

Asheri, D.
1963   'Laws of Inheritance, Distribution of Land and Political Constitutions in Ancient Greece', *Historia* 12: 1-21.

Bourriot, F.
1976   *Recherches sur la nature du génos: étude d'histoire sociale Athénienne—*

périodes archaïque et classique (2 vols.; Lille: Université Lille).

Bremmer, J.
1983 'The importance of the Maternal Uncle and Grandfather in Archaic and Classical Greece and Early Byzantium', *ZPE* 50: 173-86.

Broadbent, M.
1968 *Studies in Greek Genealogy* (Leiden: Brill).

Brown, P.G.McC.
1983 'Menander's Dramatic Technique and the Law of Athens', *CQ* 33: 412-20.

Cox, C.A.
1988 'Sibling Relationships in Classical Athens: Brother-Sister Ties', *Journal of Family History* 13: 377-95.

Crook, J.A.
1986 'Women in Roman Succession', in B. Rawson (ed.), *The Family in Ancient Rome: New Perspectives* (Ithaca, NY: Cornell University Press): 58-82.

Davies, J.K.
1971 *Athenian Propertied Families 600–300 BC* (Oxford: Clarendon Press).
1977 'Athenian Citizenship: The Descent Group and the Alternatives', *The Classical Journal* 73: 105-21.

Flower, M.A.
1985 '*IG* II^2 2344 and the Size of Phratries in Classical Athens', *CQ* 35: 232-35.

Fox, R.
1967 *Kinship and Marriage: An Anthropological Perspective* (Harmondsworth: Penguin Books).

Foxhall, L.
1989 'Household, Gender and Property in Classical Athens', *CQ* 39: 22-44.

Freedman, M.
1958 *Lineage Organization in Southeastern China* (London: Athlone Press).

Gagarin, M.
1981 *Drakon and Early Athenian Homicide Law* (New Haven: Yale University Press).

Gernet, L.
1921 'Sur l'épiclérat', *Revue des études grecques* 34: 337-79.
1955 'La loi de Solon sur le "testament"', in *Droit et société dans la Grèce ancienne* (Paris: University Press): 121-49 = *Revue des études grecques* 33 (1920): 123-68, 249-90.
1957 (ed.), *Démosthène: Plaidoyers Civils*, II (Paris: Les Belles Lettres).
1968 'Mariages de Tyrans', in *Anthropologie de la Grèce antique* (Paris: François Maspero): 344-59 = *Homage à Lucien Febvre* (Paris, 1953): 41-53.

Golden, M.
1985 'Donatus and Athenian Phratries', *CQ* 35: 9-13.

Goody, J.
1983 *The Development of the Family and Marriage in Europe* (Cambridge: Cambridge University Press).

Gulliver, P.H.
1971 *Neighbours and Networks: The Idiom of Kinship in Social Action among*

the *Ndendeuli of Tanzania* (Berkeley: University of California Press).

Hallett, J.P.
1984   *Fathers and Daughters in Roman Society: Women and the Elite Family* (Princeton: Princeton University Press).

Harrison, A.R.W.
1968   *The Law of Athens*, I (Oxford: Clarendon Press)

Hignett, C.
1952   *A History of the Athenian Constitution to the End of the Fifth Century BC* (Oxford: Clarendon Press).

Hughes, D.O.
1978   'From Brideprice to Dowry in Mediterranean Europe', *Journal of Family History* 3: 262-96.

Humphreys, S.C.
1978   *Anthropology and the Greeks* (London: Routledge & Kegan Paul).
1985   'Social Relations on Stage: Witnesses in Classical Athens', *History and Anthropology* 1: 313-69.
1986   'Kinship Patterns in the Athenian Courts', *GRBS* 27: 57-91.

Hunter, V.
1989   'The Athenian Widow and her Kin', *Journal of Family History* 14: 291-311.

Just, R.
1989   *Women in Athenian Law and Life* (London: Routledge & Kegan Paul).

Karnezis, J.E.
1972   *The Epikleros (Heiress): A Contribution to the Interpretation of the Attic Orators and to a Study of the Private Life of Classical Athens* (Athens: n.p.).
1976   *Solonian Guardianship Laws of Classical Athens and the Senatus Consultum (Dig. 23, 2, 59)* (Athens: n.p.).

Lane Fox, R.
1985   'Aspects of Inheritance in the Greek World', in P.A. Cartledge and F.D. Harvey (eds.), *Crux: Essays in Greek History Presented to G.E.M. de Ste. Croix* (London: Gerald Duckworth): 208-32.

Lewis, I.M.
1965   'Problems in the Comparative Study of Unilineal Descent', in *The Relevance of Models for Social Anthropology* (ASA Monographs, 1; London: Tavistock Publications): 87-112.

Littman, R.J.
1979   'Kinship in Athens', *Ancient Society* 10: 5-31.

MacDowell, D.M.
1963   *Athenian Homicide Law in the Age of the Orators* (Manchester: Manchester University Press).
1978   *The Law in Classical Athens* (Ithaca, NY: Cornell University Press).
1982   'Love versus the Law: An Essay on Menander's *Aspis*', *Greece and Rome* 29: 42-52.
1989   'The *Oikos* in Athenian Law', *CQ* 39: 10-21.

Maine, Sir H.
1907   *Ancient Law* (London: John Murray, 10th edn).

Miles, J.C.
1950   'The Attic Law of Intestate Succession (Demosthenes, *Contra Macart.*

51)', *Hermathena* 75: 69-77.

Roussel, D.
1976   *Tribu et cité: Études sur les groupes sociaux dans les cités grecques aux époques archaïque et classique* (Paris: Les Belles Lettres).

Schaps, D.M.
1979   *Economic Rights of Women in Ancient Greece* (Edinburgh: Edinburgh University Press).

Schmitt, P.
1977   'Athéna Apatouria et la ceinture', *Annales ESC* 32: 1059-72.

Seaford, R.
1990   'The Structural Problems of Marriage in Euripides', in A. Powell (ed.), *Euripides, Women, and Sexuality* (London: Routledge): 151-76.

Smith, R.C.
1985   'The Clans of Athens', *Classical Views* 29 NS 4: 51-61.

Thompson, W.E.
1967   'The Marriage of First Cousins in Athenian Society', *Phoenix* 21: 273-82.
1976   *De Hagniae Hereditate: An Athenian Inheritance Case* (Leiden: Brill).
1981   'Athenian Attitudes toward Wills', *Prudentia* 13: 13-23.

Vernant, J.-P.
1974   'Le mariage', in *Mythe et société en Grèce ancienne* (Paris: François Maspero): 57-81.

Visser, M.
1986   'Medea: Daughter, Sister, Wife and Mother: Natal Family versus Conjugal Family in Greek and Roman Myths about Women', in M. Cropp, E. Fantham and S.E. Scully (eds.), *Greek Tragedy and its Legacy: Essays Presented to D.J. Conacher* (Calgary: Calgary University Press): 149-65.

Watson, A.
1971   *Roman Private Law around 200 BC* (Edinburgh: Edinburgh University Press).

Wolff, H.J.
1944   'Marriage Law and Family Organization in Ancient Athens', *Traditio* 2: 43-95.

Wyse, W.
1904   *The Speeches of Isaeus* (Cambridge: Cambridge University Press).

SOME IMPLICATIONS OF ARISTOTLE'S CONCEPTION OF AUTHORITY*

Marguerite Deslauriers

Aristotle does not develop an explicit conception of authority in his
Politics. He does express views about the aim of the state, the different
sorts of constitutions which can bind people in a political union, the
relative merits of these constitutions, as well as views about the citizen
per se and the citizen relative to the constitution, about law, justice
and revolution, and about the relation between the establishment of
laws and the administration of law. But he offers no account of the
mechanism or the justification of authority. That is, he does not tell us
in so many words how governments act authoritatively, nor does he
tell us why the citizen in a state should feel obliged to obey either the
established law or those who rule.

At the same time, it is clear that the absence of a developed concept
of authority in his political works is not owing to a cynicism about the
possibility of rule without coercive measures. On the contrary,
Aristotle claims that a government which exercises power only in the
coercive sense, a government which can impose social controls only
by the use of force, is not really a government at all, and not worthy
of discussion in a treatise on political theory (*Pol.* 7.2.1324b22-28).
So the search for some concept of authority implicit in Aristotle's
political theory should not be fruitless; whatever he opposes to
coercion to explain the functioning of legitimate government will be

*   Earlier versions of this paper were presented to the members of the Seminar
in Advanced Research at York University in January, and to the members of the
Department of Philosophy at McGill University in April 1988. I am grateful to those
who participated for their questions and comments. I would like to thank also
Karen Wendling, who read the paper in preparation and pointed out several unclear
expressions which I have tried to amend.

the basis for his views on political authority.

The concept of the city, polis, as natural, which one finds in Book 1 of the *Politics*, serves as this basis, since Aristotle claims that it is precisely insofar as the structure of a city conforms to that specified by nature that its government can operate without coercion. But to say that Aristotle considered the authority of the state to be natural, without specifying the sense of 'natural' intended, can only be a preliminary answer to the question. The first task, then, is to examine this notion of the state as natural to see how it functions to explain the operation and the justification of political authority. To supplement this examination it will be instructive to look at cases which Aristotle viewed as failures or surrenders of authority. I shall look at three such cases, one from each of the three spheres of practical inquiry distinguished by Aristotle. The first is the problem of *akrasia* or weakness of will in the individual, the second is the claim that the *bouleutikon* of women is *akyros* or without authority in relation to their husbands, and the third is the claim that some constitutions, in particular the oligarchical, suffer from *akrasia* and that this is what makes them illegitimate, since it impels them to the use of force.

In the course of this investigation I shall argue for two conclusions. First, that the concept of authority which emerges from Aristotle's understanding of the state as natural, and from these cases of failure or surrender of authority, includes a sense in which authority is strictly conventional. That is, the nature of the ultimate constituents of the state—people—is such that it is precisely natural for them sometimes to agree to designate authority by convention. Secondly, that Aristotle's views on the relations between ruler and ruled in each of the three spheres of practical inquiry inform his views on these same relations in the other spheres. For example, the received opinion that Aristotle modelled his ideas about politics on his understanding of the household, rather than on the individual (and that this distinguishes him from Plato) is misleading (Arendt 1958: 85-86). First of all, Aristotle, outside of Book 1 of the *Politics*, is more wont to compare the state to the individual than to the household or to any particular relation in the household; and secondly, when such comparisons between the state and the household *are* made they suggest that it was his views on politics which influenced his understanding of the structure of the household, rather than that he imposed the household model on the larger sphere.

I shall begin with a few remarks about the nature of authority. First, it is important to distinguish authority from other means of obtaining obedience, and particularly to distinguish it from power and persuasion. If, for example, a police officer should want a reluctant citizen to return home quietly, she might tell him that if he does not he will be confined, or that it is in his best interests to return home. Either of these measures might in fact obtain obedience, but neither of them is an example of the exercise of authority. In the first case, the police officer has threatened coercive action, and in the second she has tried to persuade the citizen to do as she instructs by offering him a reason why he might want to do what she wants him to do. To exercise authority I must give you a reason for obeying my command which is independent of the content of the command itself (for example, because I said so). In this sense obeying authority is like doing something because one has promised to do it, rather than because one has a reason for performing that particular action. One has a formal reason sufficient for one's action, whatever material reasons one might also have.[1] Any account of authority must, then, offer the citizens of a state a reason for obeying the commands of a government, independent of the particular reasons they may have for performing particular actions.

It is a feature of political authority that it is not necessarily founded on expertise. In other words, political authority is practical rather than theoretical; it offers people a reason for their actions, but this reason is not necessarily accompanied by any claim to expertise on the part of the authority. It might turn out that, in fact, in most circumstances, to have authority one must have some kind of expertise. This seems to be the view of Aristotle, for although he allows that in the case of masters and slaves in the household, 'The master is not called a master because he has knowledge, but because he is of a certain character' (1.7.1255b20-22),[2] it is not clear that he can give any account of character which does not involve some kind of special knowledge, and perhaps even theoretical knowledge. This is important because it

1. I am indebted to Leslie Green for allowing me to read in manuscript his book, *The Authority of the State*, from which I have drawn the distinction between authority on the one hand, and coercion and persuasion on the other (Green 1988: 71-75).
2. This and all subsequent translations of Aristotle are from Barnes 1984.

suggests that Aristotle is committed to a view of authority according to which one must have some special acquaintance with the aim of the state in order to have legitimate authority in the state.[1]

Another feature of political authority is that it can inhere in a variety of items, for example, in laws, or constitutions, or governments, or persons. Most philosophical discussion is concerned with the authority of laws because, 'the most important locus of authority in the state is law, for it claims to bind many persons, to regulate their most vital interests, and to do so with supremacy over all other mechanisms of social control' (Green 1985: 329). At the same time, it is often remarked that the authority of laws stems from the authority of the governments which enact those laws; and in Aristotle's case, the authority of governments is a function of the authority of the constitution which they embody: 'The goodness or badness, justice or injustice of laws varies of necessity with the constitutions of states' (3.11.1282b8-10). So I shall treat the question about authority in Aristotle as, fundamentally, a question about the authority of constitutions and governments, though of course certain things will follow about the authority of laws.

Aristotle's Remarks on Natural Law and Justice

Outside of the *Politics* Aristotle makes a few remarks which suggest that he held something like a theory of natural law (by which I mean the view that there is a set of laws fixed in the nature of things or in the mind of some divinity, such that the role of positive law is to replicate as closely as possible those laws [Allen 1980: 111]). On this view, law-making is a question of discovery rather than invention.

Of the precedents for such a view available to Aristotle, the most famous is found in Sophocles' *Antigone*:

> For me it was not Zeus who made that order.
> Nor did that Justice who lives with the gods below
> mark out such laws to hold among mankind.
> Nor did I think your orders were so strong
> that you, a mortal man, could over-run
> the gods' unwritten and unfailing laws.

1. For an argument that authority does always involve expertise, see Bell 1971. That Aristotle and others understood legitimate political authority to involve a certain kind of expertise is argued by Hintikka 1967.

Not now, nor yesterday's, they always live,
and no one knows their origin in time.
(ll. 450-57)

Aristotle himself draws a distinction between two kinds of law in his *Rhetoric*, where he quotes from this same speech in the *Antigone*, and says, 'By the two kinds of law I mean particular law and universal law. Particular law is that which each community lays down and applies to its own members... universal law is the law of nature' (1.13.1373b4-11). But Aristotle does not mean to commit himself to the suggestion that divine law establishes certain immutable laws for the conduct of mankind, and that the task for mankind is therefore to discover and establish those immutable laws.

The evidence for this is in Book 5 of the *Nicomachean Ethics*, where he draws a similar distinction to that in the *Rhetoric*, a distinction between 'natural' (*physikon*) justice and 'legal' (*nomikon*) justice, where the former is characterized as being everywhere the same and the latter as differing from place to place (5.7.1134b18-21). The claim is not that certain actions are always and everywhere just or unjust; Aristotle allows that even natural justice is changeable, at least for those who are not gods (5.7.1134b24-35). This contrast between the justice appropriate to gods and that appropriate to mortals is interesting for two reasons. First, because it makes clear that when Aristotle speaks of 'nature' or the 'natural' in his ethical and political works as well as in his physical works, the term is relative to some species or kind. In this case, then, the justice that is natural to gods is different from that natural to mortals. And, secondly, because mortals are changeable, the justice that is natural to them will itself be susceptible to change. In other words, the difference between universal law and natural justice on the one hand and particular law and legal justice on the other is *not* that between immutable and mutable, but between the sort of law and justice appropriate to the nature of people (which will be determined by an investigation of that nature and will be subject to change and variation to the extent that that nature changes and is varied) and that which is strictly conventional.[1]

---

1. Joachim Ritter has argued persuasively that on Aristotle's view universal, natural justice is not opposed to particular, legal justice: 'un "juste par nature" ne peut exister, selon Aristote, separé et en soi, mais seulement dans la multiplicité de ce qui, dans la cité est consideré comme juste"' (Ritter 1969: 437).

The State as Natural

In the *Politics* Aristotle's arguments for the naturalness of the polis depend on the analogies he sets up between the polis and both the individual and the household. I shall look first at these analogies, and then at the claims that people, households and states are natural.

The analogy of polis to the individual is developed in the *Politics* in two ways. Aristotle speaks both of the soul ruling the body and of one part of the soul (*nous*) ruling the other part (*oreksis*), and speaks of this arrangement as natural (*kata physin*) as opposed to hurtful (*blaberon*) (1.5.1254b2-10). He sometimes compares the person as a whole, soul and body, to the city as a whole; and sometimes compares the soul itself to the constitution and the class of citizens. In the latter case, Aristotle distinguishes rational and irrational faculties of the soul, leaving aside the body altogether, and distinguishes the councillors from the warriors in a city, while leaving aside the labouring class as external to the city per se. 'As in other natural compounds the conditions of a composite whole are not necessarily organic parts of it, so in a state or in any other combination forming a unity not everything is a part which is a necessary condition' (7.8.1328a21-25). From this general argument Aristotle concludes that, 'farmers, artisans, and labourers of all kinds are necessary to the existence of states, but the parts of the state are warriors and councillors' (7.9.1329a35-38).

Aristotle justifies the exclusion of these classes from the state and their relegation to conditions necessary for the state by showing that the state does not exist for their sake, but rather they exist for the sake of the state. In like manner, he argues that the soul does not exist for the body, but the body for the sake of the soul.[1]

Whether Aristotle compares the city to the person as a whole or only to the soul, the analogy he develops is structural; the parts of a city are said to resemble the parts of the individual person or the

---

1. The city/person comparison in Aristotle most often takes one of two forms: (1) a comparison of virtues, where a city is said to have or to lack virtues in just the way and for just the reasons that a person does (4.11.1295a35-40; 5.9.1310a18-19; 7.1.1323b32-36), and (2) a comparison in terms of health, where both a person and a city are said to be 'doing well' or 'doing badly' in virtue of the maintenance or destruction of certain properties (5.3.1302b35–1303a2; 5.9.1309b21-31; 6.6.1320b33–1321a1).

person's soul. The analogy between city and household, on the other hand, is functional rather than structural. Aristotle claims that household and state both function to supply the needs of people and to make them self-sufficient (1.2.1252b27–1253a1); and his comparison of the various domestic relations with the forms of constitutions is a comparison of functions determined by roles (1.12.1259a37–1259b17).

Both the analogies between the city and the individual or the household, and the claim that household and city are 'natural', depend on the idea of an end or aim common to individual, household and city. Aristotle claims, 'the end of individuals and of states is the same...' (7.15.1334a11-12). 'A city, too, like an individual, has a work to do...' (7.4.1326a13). 'The active life will be the best, both for every city collectively, and for individuals' (7.3.1325b15-16). Not only, then, do city and person each have a task, but they have the same task, on a different scale—to provide a good life: 'the state comes into existence, originating in the bare needs of life, and continuing in existence for the sake of a good life. And therefore, if the earlier forms of society are natural, so is the state, for it is the end of them, and the nature of a thing is its end' (1.2.1252b27-32).[1]

The naturalness of the city depends, then, on whether the societies which constitute it are natural, and whether living in a city is the ultimate aim of each level of social organization prior to the city, that is, of households and villages. Aristotle treats the first of these as a matter for empirical investigation. The naturalness of households and villages depends only on the naturalness of people's desires to form these societies. Now, while it is not always the case, it is the case for the most part, says Aristotle, that people are inclined to form societies and that they do indeed form societies unless somehow impeded (1.2.1253a2-5). That their ultimate aim in so doing is to form cities Aristotle demonstrates with a standard argument about wholes and parts—the material parts of a thing exist for the sake of the whole, the whole does not exist for the sake of the material parts. So, for example, a hand exists for the sake of a whole person, but a person does not exist for the sake of their hand; and households and villages exist for the sake of forming cities/states (1.2.1253a19-25).

This, then, is Aristotle's argument for the naturalness of the city:

1. For a general account of Aristotle's notion of the state as a natural entity, see Bradley 1880.

households and villages are natural because they arise out of certain desires natural to people; the aim of anything natural is itself natural; the city is the aim of villages and households.

Of course, not all cities are natural, but only those which conform to a structure, a constitution, which Aristotle considers natural. The natural constitution of a city is one which mirrors the structure of the soul of the virtuous individual; this is where the analogy between city and individual becomes important. As I have said above, there are two implications of Aristotle's notion of authority which will emerge from the following three case studies of failure or surrender of authority. First, that the sense in which Aristotle understands authority as natural is not a sense which excludes conventional designations of authority; and secondly that Aristotle models his understanding of the family and his understanding of the state on one another.

Three Cases of Inoperative Authority

a. *Authority in the Oikia*

Aristotle's *oikia* includes three sorts of ruler/ruled relations. The male head of the household is said to rule over slaves, children and women, but in different ways, according to the state of the deliberative faculty (*to bouleutikon*) of those ruled. His authority over slaves is due to the complete absence of such a faculty in those who are by nature slaves; his authority over children is due to the imperfection or immaturity of their deliberative faculty; and his authority over his wife stems from the character of her deliberative faculty as *akyros* (1.13.1260a12-14). Notice that Aristotle's argument must be that this failure of the deliberative faculty in women does not simply deprive them of authority over themselves but makes them subject to the authority of their husbands. But what does Aristotle mean by *akyros*? And why does the *akyros* character of the *bouleutikon* of women subject them to the rule of men? To answer the first question is to answer the second.

This is the one occurrence of the term *akyros* in the *Politics*. It occurs in nine other passages in the corpus, twice in the *Rhetoric* (1376b12; 1376b27), once in the *Nicomachean Ethics* (1151b15), three times in the zoological works (*G.A.* 772b27; 778a1; *M.A.* 698b7) and three times in the *Constitution of Athens* (45.3.4; 68.3.4; 68.4.11). In the *Rhetoric* it is contracts or business arrangements which are said to be *akyros*, and the sense is clearly 'without binding force' or 'invalid'. The one instance of *akyros* in the *Nicomachean Ethics* is closely related; the arguments or opinions of a person are said to be *akyra* like *psēphismata*: Gauthier and Jolif translate it 'nuls et non avenus' (1959: 650). Again, the instances in the *Constitution of Athens* are similar—in one case the Council is said to be *akyros* in the sense that it does not have jurisdiction; in the two other cases, in the same passage where Aristotle is discussing voting procedures for juries, he refers to one ballot box as *akyros*, and to the ballots which are deposited in this box as *akyroi*. The box which is *kyrios* is distinguished from the one which is *akyros* by its material (wood rather than bronze); this evidently does not affect its function, but serves only to make it identifiable; and nothing at all distinguishes the *kyrios psēphos* from the one which is *akyros*, except the box into which it is deposited.

What all these examples of *akyros* suggest about Aristotle's usage is that the term does indeed mean something like 'without authority'; but that the absence of authority is due, not to any incapacity on the part of that which is *akyros*, but simply to convention.[1] Furthermore, as is particularly evident from the example in which the *boulē* is said to be *akyros*, it is possible for something to be *akyros* at one time or in one respect without being altogether *akyros*.

If this is what Aristotle means to say about the deliberative faculty in women, namely that it lacks authority, but in a conventional and contingent sense, then one can make good sense of Aristotle's claim that the rule of men over women in the household resembles constitutional rule, in which 'the ruler and the ruled interchange in turn (for they tend to be on an equal level in their nature and to have no difference at all). . . ' But, Aristotle adds, 'the male stands in this relationship to the female continuously' (1.12.1259b4-10), that is, although male and female are equal by nature, nonetheless he rules and she is ruled permanently and by convention.

There are passages in the zoological works in which Aristotle's use of *akyros* tells against this interpretation (*G.A.* 772b27; 778a1; *M.A.*

---

1. For an argument that Aristotle, when speaking of the rational faculty of women as *akyros*, did not mean to say that their reason is overcome by their passions, but only to make a factual claim about the relative maturity of husband and wife in Greek upper-class marriages, see Sparshott 1985.

698b7). Both instances in the *Generation of Animals* refer to reproductive incapacity, and the instance in the *Movement of Animals* speaks of an immobile part as 'ineffectual' in the sense of 'unable'. Moreover, there are places in the *Politics* (e.g. 1.5.1254b13-14; 1.12.1259b1-2) where Aristotle speaks of men as naturally superior in command to women. It might be that Aristotle simply means that men are superior in strength; but it seems more likely that these passages are manifestations of Aristotle's view, as expressed in the *Generation of Animals*, that the male is superior in some real if unspecified way. But if that is the case, why does he not claim that the *bouleutikon* of women suffers some real incapacity? The answer to this must surely be that Aristotle understands the relation of husband and wife in the household by analogy with the relation of ruler and ruled in a consti-tutional government. In other words, since Aristotle generally con-siders the male to be *by nature* in command of the female, his language in describing a woman as *akyros* with respect to her husband is an indication of influence from his own political theory, which treats the authority of constitutional government, which is said to be analogous to the marital relation, as conventional.

b. *Authority in the Individual*

In Book 5.7 of the *Nicomachean Ethics* Aristotle asks whether a person can commit an injustice against himself. The answer is, only if one understands a person to have a bipartite soul of which one part is ratio-nal, the other irrational, and understands the injustice itself to be the act whereby the irrational part overrules the rational. This is called *akrasia*.

Aristotle's intention here is to show that injustice must always be analysed in terms of two distinguishable agents. It is of interest here because of what it suggests about justice and authority in the individ-ual, namely, that the rational part ought to rule over the irrational, and that any failure on its part to do so, as in the case of *akrasia*, is a failure of authority within the individual.

Aristotle reports as common belief about the akratic person that he abandons his rational calculation (*logismos*) about what it is best to do in the situation, and that he knows that his actions are base, but does them because of his feelings (*dia pathos*) rather than because of his reason (*dia ton logon*) (7.1.1145b10-14). (This, incidentally, is how Plato, too, characterizes the akratic.)

To solve the puzzle about how it is possible to know that one ought to do something and yet not do it, Aristotle introduces a distinction between two kinds of knowledge (universal and particular) and a distinction between two ways of having knowledge (active and inactive or potential). The former distinction is between recognition of generally formulated desires (for example, 'I like sweet things', or 'I want to avoid sweet things for the sake of health') and acquaintance with particular facts ('all sweet things are pleasant' and 'this is a sweet thing'). The latter distinction is that between knowing something without using or attending to the knowledge, and using or attending to some knowledge (7.3.1146b35–1147a24) which one has. Because of Aristotle's view of the practical syllogism as a way of explaining action, and his view that even apparently irrational actions can be explained, Aristotle does not argue that the akratic person acts without reason, but rather that his reason has been informed by his desires rather than by his *bouleutikon*. The strength of one's desire detaches the particular beliefs, 'all sweet things are pleasant' and 'this is a sweet thing' from the universal belief, which one can still be said to know, though not actively, and since the particular belief, coupled with the desire, gives one reason to act, one does (7.3.1147a31–1147b3).[1]

What can be deduced about authority from this explanation of *akrasia*? First of all, since *aisthēsis* is said to be *kyria* with respect to the particular beliefs, it is *aisthēsis* rather than *logismos* which is the controlling factor in the action of the akratic person; an akratic person is not a person who can offer *no* reason for her/his action, but a person whose reason has been determined by something other than reasoning—by sensation or desire. Secondly, notice that the universal premise is set aside or ignored, but not refuted (this is precisely what distinguishes *akrasia* from intemperance). In effect, the universal belief about one's desires, which has been determined by one's reasoning, is inoperative but not absent. And thirdly, since in order to be akratic one must already have performed a deliberation according to right reason (otherwise one is not akratic but ignorant of some pertinent fact, or simply intemperate) it is clear that *akrasia* involves no incapacity on the part of the deliberative faculty in performing its function of arriving at right decisions; the problem is rather in enforcing decisions.

1. My account of *akrasia* derives from Nussbaum 1978: 201-10 and Wiggins 1980: 247-50.

Furthermore, Aristotle does not view the *engkratic* person as virtuous, but as falling short of virtue precisely because of the struggle in the soul of such a person to enforce the authority of the deliberated decision over the appetites. He also holds that, in general, people who are really virtuous enjoy performing virtuous actions and do not have either to persuade or to force themselves to perform such actions (*E.N.* 1.8.1099a17-18). Therefore, we can see that the failure of authority here is a failure on the part of the deliberative faculty not in terms of carrying out a deliberation but in terms of enforcing the decision that is the conclusion of the deliberation. The authority of the rational part of the soul over the irrational is then natural in the sense that the faculty which deliberates ought to have authority over that which desires because the actions which it prompts one to perform will be in the interest of the person as a whole, while the actions which the appetitive, irrational part of the soul prompts one to do, when not in consultation with the deliberative faculty, will be in the interests of the appetitive part alone. This means that the authority of the rational faculty of the soul resides not only in the function of deliberating, but also in the function of habituating the appetitive and irrational part of the soul to act in accordance with its reason. Thus the exercise of authority is distinguished by Aristotle from the entitlement to authority.

c. *Authority in the Polis*

The reasons that authority can fail to operate in the polis, according to Aristotle, are that the structure of the constitution is innately unjust, or that the ruling part of a government constructed according to a true constitution fails to habituate in the correct manner those who are ruled.

Aristotle refers to both of these as cases of *akrasia*; the first is a case in which the rulers are not entitled to authority, and therefore do not have it, while the second is a case in which the rulers are entitled to authority, but fail to exercise it.

The first sort of failure is described by Aristotle in the passage where he comes closest to an explicit notion of political authority:

> The words 'constitution' and 'government' have the same meaning, and the government, which is the supreme authority in states, must be in the hands of one, or the few, or the many. The true (*orthas*) forms of government, therefore, are those in which the one, or the few, or the many govern with a view to the common interest (*pros to koinon*); but

governments which rule with a view to the private interest, whether of the
one, or of the few, or of the many are perversions (*parekbaseis*) (*Pol.*
3.7.1279a25-31).

What Aristotle proceeds to call kingship, aristocracy and constitutional
government have, then, legitimate authority, while the forms which
deviate from these—tyranny, oligarchy and democracy—have no
authority, although they may, of course, have power. These
constitutions fail as structures to have authority because, by definition,
those who are governing have failed to understand the end or aim of
the state, and hence fail to understand their own function in governing
it. A state which is not governed with a view to the common interest
of the members of the state, but with a view to the interests peculiar to
the rulers, is an unnatural state, a state which is literally deformed,
structured in such a way that it cannot possibly manifest the true
nature or form of a state.

Of the perverted forms of constitution it is oligarchy which
Aristotle refers to as *akratic* in three instances in the *Politics*
(2.12.1273b37; 4.11.1296a2; 5.10.1312b35). The translators render
this as 'pure' or 'exclusive', but given the parallel between state and
individual which, as we have seen, Aristotle develops, one is justified
in understanding it to mean that oligarchies are 'weak-willed' in a way
analogous to people; they deliberate, and make decisions, but their
action can be explained only by reference to the desires of one part
which is not taking into consideration the interests of the whole.

But Aristotle also makes clear that any constitution, even one of the
'true' forms, can be *akratic*. When speaking of the importance of
training the young by habit and education in the ways of the
constitution if one wants to maintain the stability of the state, Aristotle
says, 'there may be a want of self-discipline in states as well as in
individuals' (5.9.1310a18-19). Now this kind of *akrasia* in the state is
not a function of the structure of the constitution but, just as in the
case of the individual soul, indicates a failure on the part of that which
has legitimate authority to exercise that authority by habituating to
obedience that part of city or soul which is to be ruled. This leads in
both cases to an inability to act according to the right reasons.

Conclusion

What I have tried to show, then, is that while Aristotle does have a concept of authority as natural, that concept is rather more complex than it is generally understood to be, and allows for legitimate, conventional authority. This is because, unlike the constituents of the soul, the constituents of domestic and political units cannot always be distinguished naturally as representatives of reason and representatives of desire. When they cannot be so distinguished they must, with a view to the common interest, be so designated.

On Aristotle's account, the parts or powers of the soul are devoted to a single kind of function (reasoning, or desiring, for example) and are quite incapable of performing the functions of the other parts, but this is not true of the members of a household or of a state. That is, the difference between the members is not one of capacity or incapacity (with the exception of natural slaves and the temporary exception of children) but of skill. Some will be better at certain functions than others, but none will be strictly incapable. Hence while authority in the soul belongs naturally to the reasoning part, the authority in a family or a state must be designated. This is partly a consequence of Aristotle's notion of the natural as species-specific, such that he cannot claim that certain people per se naturally have authority over others unless he is willing to divide the human species into sub-species; and, despite his remarks on slaves, he is generally very reluctant to make such a subdivision.

At the same time, just because Aristotle employs so often the analogy between individuals, households and states, he tends to neglect the differences between the parts of the soul (namely, certain capacities or powers) and the parts of the household or state (namely, individual people). Yet these differences are crucial in determining what makes authority natural and therefore legitimate.

BIBLIOGRAPHY

Allen, R.E.
 1980 *Socrates and Legal Obligation* (Minneapolis: University of Minnesota).
Arendt, H.
 1958 'What Was Authority?', in C.J. Friedrich (ed.), *Nomos*. I. *Authority* (Cambridge, MA: Harvard University Press).
Barnes, J. (ed.)
 1984 *The Complete Works of Aristotle: The Revised Oxford Translation*, I, II (Princeton, NJ: Princeton University Press)
Bell, D.R.
 1971 'Authority', in G.N.A. Vesey (ed.), *The Proper Study: Royal Institute of*

Philosophy Lectures IV (1969–1970) (London: Macmillan).

Bradley, A.C.
    1880   'Aristotle's Conception of the State', in E. Abbot (ed.), *Hellenica* (London: Rivingtons).

Gauthier, R.E., and Jolif, J.Y.
    1959   *L'éthique à Nicomaque: introduction, traduction et commentaire* (Louvain: Publications Universitaires de Louvain).

Grene, D., and Lattimore, R. (eds.)
    1954   *The Complete Greek Tragedies*. III. *Sophocles* I (trans. E. Wyckoff; Chicago: University of Chicago Press).

Green, L.
    1988   *The Authority of the State* (Oxford: Oxford University Press).
    1985   'Convention and Authority', *Philosophical Quarterly* 35: 329-46.

Hintikka, K.J.J.
    1967   'Some Conceptual Presuppositions of Greek Political Theory', *Scandinavian Political Studies* 2: 11-25.

Nussbaum, M.C.
    1978   *Aristotle's De Motu Animalium* (Princeton, NJ: Princeton University Press).

Ritter, J.
    1969   'Le droit naturel chez Aristote: Contribution au renouveau du droit naturel', *Archives de Philosophie* 32: 416-57.

Rorty, A.O. (ed.)
    1980   *Essays on Aristotle's Ethics* (Berkeley: University of California Press).

Sparshott, F.
    1985   'Aristotle on Women', *Philosophical Inquiry* 7.34: 177-200.

Wiggins, D.
    1980a   'Deliberation and Practical Reason', in Rorty 1980.
    1980b   'Weakness of Will, Commensurability, and the Objects of Deliberation and Desire', in Rorty 1980.

SOCIAL STATUS AND SOCIAL BEHAVIOUR AS CRITERIA IN JUDICIAL PROCEEDINGS IN THE LATE REPUBLIC

Paul R. Swarney

The narrow aim of this undertaking is to examine the objectives of the defence in three cases argued by M. Tullius Cicero before Roman juries from 80 to 56 BC. The broader purpose is to formulate some observations about the role of evidence in such proceedings which in turn may require us to alter slightly the general clichés often associated with the place of Roman law in the history of Roman society. Any claim that the specific investigation in this analysis is scientific must be coloured by the well-known rhetorical techniques of this model of *latinitas*, and by the fact that we possess only the polished and published versions of Cicero's defences, not a transcript of the words, arguments *and evidence* that may have been presented at the actual judicial event, and on which we might rely as an accurate source for what really occurred.[1]

The analysis which follows will, however, attempt in part to incorporate these liabilities into the material assembled. This will help bolster the conclusion that demonstrating a defendant's place in society —and conversely the prosecutor's social inferiority or deviation—was a primary objective of the defence in each of the cases studied here. That is, while it would be foolish to rely on a published speech to recover exact details about the original and oral presentation, we would be equally foolish to assume that the orator published a text that diverged dramatically from the intention of the original; if the original

---

1. Milo's comment on receiving the polished version of the *Pro Milone* is fair enough warning that Cicero's published speech could be at variance with what was said before the judges. He commented from exile in Marsalla, where he fled after his conviction, that had Cicero in fact delivered the speech which he had sent Milo he would not now have the pleasure of enjoying the famous *bouillabaisse* of Marseilles —to set his words anachronistically in a more modern mode (Dio Cassius 40.54).

relied heavily on concrete evidence to prove a defendant innocent, the published version would hardly ignore this aspect of the defence. Similarly, while the absence of the prosecution's actual or published arguments in their own words will prove a handicap, we must still expect that had cases against clients been based generally on factual evidence any competent orator would certainly have had to account for this in his remarks about the case, perhaps by dismissing such evidence as irrelevant but certainly not by totally ignoring it. Thus, although Cicero's account may be completely misleading about the substance of his or the opposition's arguments, he could not blatantly deviate in his published speech from standard practices employed by speakers for the defence or prosecution.[1]

Some initial observations about the circumstances accompanying the procedures in the three speeches under examination will help indicate the relevance of social structure in shaping arguments for or against individuals on trial. All the cases involve men and women who were socially and economically well situated in land, slaves, friends and those additional criteria and commodities which the ancient world used in measuring wealth and status. No one involved in these cases was in any way a mere individual isolated from their social or economic community. Each had substantial numbers of *clientes* and other dependants directly tied or otherwise connected to them. The setting for each proceeding was significantly public and, if the orator is to be trusted, well attended. Each side presented its arguments at the centre of what is usually called a ring or *corona* with bystanders often participating vocally.[2] A trial was a competition among the well-heeled providing a spectacle for all walks of Roman society. At stake in two of the contests under discussion was that most precious of all Roman commodities, *dignitas*, social standing in the community, the loss of which was almost as horrible as the punishment sought in the earliest of the three cases, death by suffocation, starvation and

---

1.   Cicero is alleged to have admitted that he obscured some important issues in the actual delivery of the defense of Cluentius, and for all we know may have obscured them even more in the published text. Nevertheless the text which has come down to us must represent what was dramatically typical for such a case although the dust which he had managed to fling at the jurors may still survive the centuries (Quintilian 2.17.21).

2.   Catullus, among others, has mentioned this *corona* and the running commentary that might emerge from it (Catullus 52).

exhaustion after having been sewn inside an animal skin and tossed into the Tiber.

This brief survey will review Cicero's published defences of Sex. Roscius of Ameria who was defended in 80 BC, of A. Cluentius Habitus, 66 BC, and of M. Caelius Rufus tried in 56 BC. Each came at a significant stage not only in the life of the defendant but in the career of the orator and the history of the Roman state as well. In the first we have our earliest example from Cicero's career as an orator at a moment when L. Sulla had put the final touches on the vendetta of retribution which had followed his victory in civil war. In the *Pro Cluentio* Cicero as praetor was looking forward to his election as consul and entry into the hallowed circle of the *nobiles*, and back on his own victory over C. Verres while wisely and necessarily courting the favour of Cn. Pompeius, the current star of Roman society. He defended Caelius Rufus after his consular success over L. Catilina and then his humilating exile and return at a moment when the star of Cn. Pompeius was rising beyond imagining at the success of his friend and father-in-law, and at the influence which he, his father-in-law and their good friend M. Crassus exercised over Roman society through their massed *clientelae*.

The three defences are separated by time, circumstances and personalities, yet, as will become evident, each follows a common thread of technique and objective, and each shares common assumptions about the nature of society and the law. Each also betrays a lack of concern for factual evidence in establishing a case for the defence and pays no heed to such evidence if such had been employed by the opposition in arguing its case. The thrust of the cases for and against will be seen as attempting to enhance the social stature of one side, and of all associated with it, and to diminish the other either brutally or gently as circumstances required.

The three cases in question must, further, be clearly understood as personal contests; *nos* and *vos*, 'our side', 'your side', are the terms which we have become accustomed to translate as 'defence' and 'prosecution'. And *nos* and *vos* certainly cannot mean accused and the state. At the most the state, the *res publica Romana*, maintained the venue and, through the magisterial apparatus, supplied the referees. Most importantly the state provided no institutionalized interpretation of law or justice but merely supervised the competition between *nos* and *vos*. For the losers in this contest there was no judicial recourse, only the expectation that his social connections might continue the competition with other players.

A final interesting characteristic shared by the three is the ease with which each case collapses when subjected to a search for the factual evidence that might have substantiated the orator's case or that of the prosecution. The speeches are not models that instruct the novice student at law how to employ factual evidence but rather examples of how to avoid such evidence altogether. They are, however, excellent indicators of the possibility of social mobility and of the means by which social stability was maintained and one's place in the social structure tested.

Sex. Roscius was accused of murdering his father, Sex. Roscius. Of all who were defended by Cicero, the younger Roscius was uniquely liable to actual, and in this case gruesome, execution if found guilty. The speech published by Cicero contains our only source for details about the case, but allows us to set the proceedings in the historical context of the murderous era following Sulla's defeat of his enemies in civil war. The sequence of events leading to the prosecution of Roscius was apparently as follows.

Roscius the father was murdered at Rome while returning home from dinner; his name was placed posthumously among the proscribed and his property auctioned; T. Roscius Magnus and T. Roscius Capito along with L. Cornelius Chrysogonus, a freedman of Sulla the Dictator, entered into control of the estate which was valued at some six million sesterces.

The prosecutor was Eruscius about whom little else is said other than Cicero's deliberate attempt to isolate him from the 'real' prosecutors, the *vos* to whom he continually refers throughout the speech. This device of isolating the prosecutor of record from the perceived enemies of the defendant is yet another characteristic of the speeches under discussion here. While having little in the way of indication of Eruscius's connection to the matters at hand, we should certainly note the abundance of Roscii available in the affair and offer the less than improbable suggestion that they were closely or remotely related.

Viewed superficially from the perspective of modern judicial practice, the obligations of prosecution and defence are simple and straightforward—to establish by direct and concrete evidence that the accused did (or did not) do the deed, or did (or did not) hire, persuade, abet or otherwise assist others to do it on his behalf. In the case of

Roscius both *nos*, the defence, and *vos*, the prosecution, agree that the older Roscius was murdered. Yet in the *Pro Sex. Roscio* there appears not only no factual evidence in support of Roscius's guilt or innocence but not even enough information for us to establish where, when or how Sex. Roscius was in fact murdered. The fatal event occurred 'after dinner' and 'at Rome'. If we are to accept the defence offered by Cicero as one reflecting the actual proceedings, we must assume that neither side was much interested in specific details of the crime or in the mechanical, factual or circumstantial links between crime and accused. According to Cicero's version of the prosecution, the case against Roscius took the form of a character assassination wherein Roscius the son was portrayed at odds with his father. For example, the father's life of the *bon vivant* in Rome and the son's life of the rustic with a fixed residence at Ameria show glaring differences in their temperaments.

Frivolous though such a defence (and prosecution) may seem to us, its seriousness to Cicero can be seen in his construction of both a contrary portrait of Roscius and a devastating picture of those associated with the prosecution. The social standing of Roscius in Cicero's inversion can be seen in his upright behaviour and in the social superiority of those who have come to his defence. Conversely, the weakness of the charge against Roscius can be seen in the deviant behaviour of those associated with the prosecution and the low social standing of members of that group.

Cicero's opening words immediately reveal his rhetorical intentions. On the side of Roscius there sit *summi oratores* ('the cream of influential speakers'), *homines nobilissimi* ('real aristocrats') and men of *aetas* ('age and experience'), *ingenium* ('natural talent') and *auctoritas* ('social influence'). In fact in them reside *summa auctoritas atque amplitudo*.[1] No equivalent to this litany of social excellence exists in a more modern tongue; any attempt to explain fully the implications of each item would divert our attention from the main thrust of this investigation. In brief the men who have encouraged Cicero to speak on behalf of Roscius were themselves the cream of Roman *oratores*, a term which collapses completely if translated as 'lawyer', 'barrister' or the like. To speak in public and more importantly to be called to speak on another's behalf presumes and advertises status in society

---

1. This catalogue of Roman social virtues is found in the opening paragraph of the *Pro Sex. Roscio*.

well beyond the more than ordinary. Such individuals must possess influence—*auctoritas* can be in part so translated—and other qualities which accompany status. This flower of Roman society although endowed with *amplitudo* ('fullness' would be a suitable but awkward rendition), will say nothing in defence of their friend Roscius because of the unfortunate age in which they now live (that is, they fear Sulla and his cronies). Nevertheless they have prevailed upon young Cicero to take up the cause of Roscius, thereby adding their *dignitas* not only to the status of Roscius but also to that of the amateur from Arpinum. From the *dignitas* and *auctoritas* of these men (and, as will be seen, women) the novice *orator* will earn *amicitia* and *beneficia*.[1] Cicero has come forward not to win favour (and certainly not payment) from Roscius but to deposit a store of *gratia*—thanks or obligation—with the cream of Roman society.

While the defendant and his orator glimmer in light reflected from these social stars, the prosecutor is cast into dark shadows of treachery by association with persons who benefitted from the death of Roscius the father among whom is the freedman L. Cornelius Chrysogonus, *adulescens potentissimus*. He has come into the lion's share of the murdered man's estate which he wastes and consumes in *luxuria* day and night. Chrysogonus struggles to enlist the jurors as *adiutores* in his *praeda nefaria*, 'adjutants in his wicked and sacrilegious spoils'. Cicero pleads that the *iudices* resist the crimes of those who are *audax*, 'violently daring'. The *iudices* as men of *dignitas* must stand against those who are *homines sicarii atque gladiatores*, 'cut throats and gladiators'.[2]

Cicero's introduction sets the objective and the tone of the defence. No factual evidence was presented in support either of the claims about Roscius, or, more precisely, about those who have requested Cicero to take up the case, or of the allegations about the dastardly deeds of those associated with the prosecution. The introduction successfully lays the foundation for the contrasting character sketches of defendant and prosecutors which will dominate the rest of the speech but promises and predicts not a shred of evidence to substantiate details in the sketches or of the crime itself. It foretells *oratio* and *argumentio*, not factual evidence.

In his portrait of Roscius in the body of the speech, Cicero claims no

1.   *Pro Sex. Roscio* 4.
2.   The of list anti-social virtues can be found in *Pro Sex. Roscio* 6 and 7.

personal, social superiority on the part of Roscius over his opponents. He does, however, frame his picture with long descriptions of Roscius's association with Caecilia Metella, daughter of Belearicus (cos. 123) and sister of Nepos (cos. 98). At her first appearance in the speech she is a woman in whom all agree can be found an old-fashioned sense of duty—*antiquum officium*. When she is introduced again towards the end she is *spectatissima femina*, her *pater* is *clarissimus*, and her paternal uncles *amplissimi*; her brother *ornatissimus*, and although she is merely a woman, she is perfect in her *virtus* so that she is both affected by the *honos* derived from the *dignitas* of her paternal lineage and male sibling and no less returns to them prestige from her own reputation. M. Massala also supports Roscius.[1]

The need to concentrate on those associated with him in close or remote relationships was probably necessitated by the obvious dullness of Roscius's rustic pursuits particularly when contrasted to the *urbanitas* of his murdered father. Cicero does attempt at one point to invert the slander of rustication levelled at Roscius by his accusers by reciting a favourite Roman formula *in urbe luxuries, ex luxuria avaritia, ex avaritia audacia, inde omnia scelera ac maleficia.*[2] The sequence of city, extravagance, greed, violent daring, crime and dastardly deeds reappears with variations most notably in satire, with Horace and Juvenal as prime examples. In this speech Cicero offered this litany after demanding not that the accusers show evidence that Roscius was involved in the murder of his father, but rather that he could be portrayed as a man of *audacia singularis* ('unique and outrageous daring'), *mores feri* ('savage habits'), *immanes natura* ('grotesque nature') and *vita vitiis flagitiisque omnibus dedita* ('a life completely devoted to vice and deviant behaviour').[3] These qualities which prosecutors tried

1. These essential asides are found in *Pro Sex. Roscio* 27 and again in 147. The social-political achievements of her father and brother—they were both consuls—are not mentioned by Cicero since everyone hearing him would have already known. The descriptive vocabulary applied to her in 147 is completely oriented to her status. She is especially worth looking at—*spectatissima*—not for the good looks with which she might or might not have been blessed, but for the splendid lineage and fraternal connection with which she was born. She is worth a look because she has achieved 'manliness'—*virtus*. M. Massala is probably mentioned in 149 to compensate for the ample references to Caecilia Metella.

2. *Pro Sex. Roscio* 74.

3. *Pro Sex. Roscio* 38. Beastly qualities seem to be part of the general grotesque nature expected of the typical villain and go along with his enormous capacity to

to foist on Roscius are nicely contrasted to the virtues surrounding friends of the defendant and indicate that Cicero expected and dared the prosecution to demonstrate that they suited Roscius before asking the jurors for conviction. 'Unique daring, savage habits, a nature out of control and a life dedicated to every kind of crime and deviant behaviour' is the obligatory portrait of the criminal that must be convincingly drawn before securing conviction.

In fact Roscius's life was so dreadfully dreary that none of these characteristics of criminal behaviour and social deviancy could be made to adhere. He was, nevertheless, notable enough to have inspired the town council at Ameria to send a delegation to Sulla to testify to the character of Roscius the father whose property had been con-fiscated in the name of Sulla's infamous proscriptions.

In direct contrast to this portrait of dull and rustic fidelity to farm and family, Cicero's description of Roscius's enemies is vivid and spectacular. T. Roscius Magnus and T. Roscius Capito, who profited from the death of Roscius's father, were respectively the *vetus et nobilis gladiator*, 'old and established gladiator', and his pupil who in turn outstripped his master in *audacia*.[1] Cicero's vituperations go well beyond mere name-calling, for he inverts the charge by suggesting that Magnus and Capito were responsible for the murder of Roscius in order to acquire his property and now are attempting judicially to remove Roscius the son in order to enjoy secure possession of their ill-gotten gains. The orator offers no factual evidence to enhance his portrait. Instead he enters into a circular argument that their depraved and dissolute natures are such as to have propelled them to murder, which in turn demonstrates the depth of their depravity. They, along with the culprit in chief Chrysogonus, constitute a *grex siciarorum*, 'pack of cut-throats'. Throughout the development of this gruesome description Cicero employs terms like *audio*, 'I hear', to support his reconstruction of events and asks the judges to look at (*cernere*) the picture that he has drawn. He most assuredly was not attempting to base his portrait of these villains on factual evidence nor did he even pretend to do so.[2]

The crowning achievement in this character assassination of the

consume *luxuries*.

1.　The Roscii as gladiators appear in *Pro Sex. Roscio* 17.

2.　The references to hearsay is in 100 and the invitation to the judges to have a look is in 98.

prosecution was Cicero's associating Chrysogonus with Roscius's enemies, Magnus and Capito. While perhaps a daring and dangerous ploy on the part of the young Cicero—for Chrysogonus was the *adulescens potentissimus*, 'all-powerful young man', freedman of Sulla—Cicero was, nevertheless, well connected for the thrust, and Chrysogonus, however *potentissumus* he may have been, was but a *libertus*. In a world where social structure is more important than political institutions, *potestas*, 'power', can have but a temporary victory over *auctoritas*, 'influence'. The social standing, *dignitas*, of the accused, while not self-sustaining, was nurtured and broadcast by his association with the *nobilitas*. The depravity of his enemies was enhanced by their association with a *libertus*. Cicero did not wish to cast aspersion on Sulla who was, after all, Iuppiter Optimus Maximus, but this freedman of his did act as *liberti et improbi*, 'scoundrels', usually act. He led a life of *luxuria* which included *pictae* ('paintings'), *tabulae* ('reliefs'), *signa* ('seals'), *marmor* ('marble statues'), *aedes* ('buildings'), on the Palatine, Corinthian and Delian *vasae*, and even an *authepsa*. Chrysogonus was a veritable proto-Trimalchio anticipating Petronius's wealthy freedman by more than a century. With his *capillo composito et diliburto*, 'well set and oiled curls', he presided over not a *domus* but an *officina nequitiae ac deversorium flagitiorum*, 'factory of vice and den of iniquity'.[1]

Clearly there was no contest. On the one side we have a noted rustic supported by his town and by men and even women of the highest *dignitas* and *auctoritas* sprung from *nobilitas*, *virtus* and *honos* set against gladiators, a gang of cut-throats and a powerful freedman urged on by *cupiditas, avaritia* and *luxuria* ('lust, greed and conspicuous consumption').

This is but a brief résumé of the sustained invective against the prosecution and encomium of the accused fashioned by Cicero. It does, however, allow us to isolate some of the colourful vocabulary which the orator uses. This vocabulary, which is familiar to students of Latin literature in other contexts, will appear with some variation in the other two speeches under investigation here and will be seen to be in fact quite typical in a judicial setting. This quick review of the *Pro Sex. Roscio* has also allowed us to observe how the orator relies

1. The catalogue of museum pieces and exotica, *Pro Sex. Roscio* 132, helps to establish the enormous appetite of the *sumptiosus* Chrysogonus. The *domus* is pilloried in 134.

more on his own dramatic presentation than factual information in constructing the *personae* on whom he would prefer the judges to concentrate as they come to vote in this case. These dramatic characters, or rather characterizations, are good or evil not for specific and documented adherence to or deviation from established law or abstract justice, but for their association with or distance from those who are at the centre of the social structure, and for the type of behaviour acceptable to or frowned upon by those who are chosen to be guardians of this social structure, the present judges.

The methods and rhetorical objectives, and the characteristic vocabulary, which we have observed in the *Pro Sex. Roscio*, are continued and prosper in the defence of Cluentius Habitus 14 years later. The orator is now praetor and on the verge of full entrance into the hallowed ranks of the nobility via his election to the consulship. He is no longer obliged to show a bench full of noble faces to lend *auctoritas* to himself and to his equestrian client; this he is now able to accomplish on his own. Aulus Cluentius Habitus was on trial on a charge of having bribed the judges who condemned a man named Oppianicus. The prosecutor was the condemned man's son who further charged that Cluentius had poisoned his judicial victim. The prosecutor in the former case involving the bribed jurors was this same Cluentius who at that event had accused Oppianicus of attempting to poison himself. Cicero makes no attempt to disguise the personal nature of the dispute which was clearly a matter of retribution, to which Cicero will add familial pressure on the current prosecutor to avenge the shame of father and family on the father's conqueror.

Cicero's portrait of the accused in this case is secondary to the elaborate narrative concerning those whom he wishes to associate with the prosecution, but it does follow the general outline that was established in the *Pro Sex. Roscio*. Cluentius's standing in the community is acknowledged by his townspeople to whom he shows *summa diligentia* ('utmost attention'), *benignitas* ('good will'), *iustitia* ('righteousness') and *fides* ('trust and fidelity'). From 'his ancestors', *a maioribus*, he has inherited *nobilitas* ('aristocratic standing in the community'), *gravitas* ('a serious bearing'), and *constantia* ('reliability'). He also displays *gratia* ('favour and gratitude') and *liberalitas* ('generosity'). Delegations have come from several towns, including, of course, his home town, Larinum. Many equites and some senators are willing to speak on his behalf should they have the opportunity. And he is defended by a most notable senator Cicero, the praetor.

As in the case of Roscius, Cicero focuses on those whom he claims are associated with the prosecution and who are in fact the driving force behind the charge. Their association with the case can only detract from the validity of their case because of their notorious and well-known social deviation. They are, rather spectacularly, the defendant's mother, Sassia, and her heinous husband, the dead Oppianicus himself. The complicated circumstances surrounding the case, the frank but ingenuous admission by Cicero that the panel of judges in the trial of Oppianicus was in fact bribed, and the number of *iudices* involved in the former trial who were themselves convicted or disgraced by censorial decree should have demanded a detailed and factual defence and prose-cution. We might assume that those convicted of having accepted bribes would provide excellent witnesses for the prosecutors by naming those from whom they had received the funds for convicting Oppianicus. Yet Cicero's speech would have us believe that the prosecution merely relied on the argument that the bribery must have come from Cluentius since he won the case against Oppianicus. Cicero offered no factual contradiction against this scenario but simply suggested an amended script for the previous judicial drama involving Oppianicus. In this new—and for Cicero more convincing—version, the obviously guilty Oppianicus initiated the bribery, but so blatant was the case against him that even the most avaricious jurors backed out of the deal. Instead of even a semblance of factual evidence Cicero preferred to delineate a detailed and dramatically fascinating portrait of Oppianicus whose vices drove him to attempt poisoning Cluentius, and of Sassia whose decidely unmaternal hatred of her son had now driven her stepson, the child of the villainous Oppianicus, to prosecute her real son, the virtuous Cluentius.[1]

In the course of the narrative Oppianicus is described as having murdered several of his children, relatives, near relations and assorted others, having procured an abortion to guarantee an inheritance for himself, assassinated fellow townsmen in the chaos following Sulla's victory over his Roman and Italian enemies and, in general, as having

---

1. A sensible explanation for the absence of factual evidence to support Cicero's contention that Oppianicus was responsible for the bribery is, of course, that there was none. Nevertheless, the dramatic portrait presented by Cicero in favour of even a hint of factual evidence supports the contention that neither jurors nor prosecution expected factual evidence as the norm.

demonstrated social behaviour which was, to say the least, beyond the norm. He was *audax, nefarius, immanis ac perniciosa bestia* ('a huge and dangerous monster') and *pestisque* ('a plague upon mankind').[1]

The horrors committed by Oppianicus, while not surpassed in quantity by Cluentius's mother, Sassia, were certainly matched in quality. She began her depraved career by seducing her first son-in-law, 'preferring to conquer her daughter, rather than her lust', *victrix filiae non libidinis.*[2] She was *audax, amentia* ('mindless and unrestrained'), *pecuniosa* ('money mad'), *mater crudelis* ('a mother cruel and without feeling'), moved to *scelus incredibile* ('crime beyond belief') by her *libido effranata et indominata* ('boundless lust'), *furor* ('manic fury'), *audacia singularis* ('unmatched *audacia*') and *cupiditas.*[3] 'She has broken and smashed everything in her greed and fury; her unbounded lust has conquered common decency, her criminal daring fear, her madness common sense and reason.'[4]

Sassia's deviant qualities were in turn shared by all whose association with the bribery in the former case was supposed to implicate Cluentius. Staienus who seems to have been the main conduit for the bribery was *egens sumptuosus* ('consumed by his hunger for luxury'), *audax, callidus* ('crafty') and *perfidiosus* ('treacherous').[5] In stark contrast, those judges who voted 'no case' when they learned about the attempted bribery but could not locate the source were *constans* ('consistent and level headed'), men of *dignitas, virtus, auctoritas, integritas* and *ex vetere disciplina* ('old, established moral behaviour'). L. Quinctius, who while tribune defended Oppianicus and in turn prosecuted Iunius the hapless praetor at Oppianicus's trial, was *insolens* and displayed *superbia* ('blatant arrogance') and *gravis* and *intolerabilis adrogantia* ('serious and unbearable insolence').[6]

This catalogue of adjectives and attributes accompanied by gruesome

---

1. *Pro Cluentio* 41. A better translation for *perniciosa bestia* might be 'dangerous and inhuman monster' indicating that Oppianicus had crossed the furthest boundaries of human behaviour.

2. *Pro Cluentio* 14.

3. *Pro Cluentio, passim*, but particularly in 15 and 18.

4. *Pro Cluentio* 15. Note should be taken of how Cicero continually slips in a more dramatic cameo such as this to give his invective more pictorial impact. The 'facts' which he would wish the *iudices* to fix in their imagination will have been these 30 second spots, not a dry list of factual and documented evidence.

5. *Pro Cluentio* 70.

6. *Pro Cluentio* 107.

details, dramatically recited, of crime, greed and conspicuous consumption constituted the substance of the defence. No substantial factual or documented evidence is brought forward by the orator. The charge of poisoning brought against Cluentius, which rested on evidence extracted from a slave under torture, was dismissed by Cicero in a counter-description of a horrible but unproductive regime of torture inflicted in the presence of Sassia's kinsmen, none of whom was named, and of another session of torture which was in fact investigating another matter.[1] Cicero does not even hint at factual evidence supporting the innocence of Cluentius but asks the jurors to determine whose survival is more important to Roman society, Cluentius a noted equestrian supported by outstanding Italians including that most successful of modern *equites*, the orator himself, or a sexually depraved mother whose many crimes illustrate the extent of her outrageous behaviour, the enormity of which makes her capable of any crime from the seduction of sons-in-law to the prosecution of her own son. And the choice for the judges is not merely between upright son or deviant mother; for on her side we must also place the enormities of her monstrous husband whose social isolation had long preceded his deserved conviction and unmourned death, a man to whom no one offered *aditus* ('access'), *congressio* ('meeting and conversation'), *sermo* ('gossip') or invitations to *convivium* ('parties').[2] Clearly judges interested in the orderly functioning of class and society will understand the social evil intended by the admittedly duped prosecutor and will offer protection not only to the dramatically (but not factually) innocent Cluentius, but also preservation to the Roman social system.

The defence of M. Caelius Rufus ten years later reflects the now familiar emphasis on reputation, *dignitas*, and association with one's socially equivalent fellows, but with some remarkable variations. The questions of social rivalry among and between parties to the cases under review here has received implied attention. Cicero in the *Pro Roscio* as a neophyte to the social structure at Rome was certainly posturing with respect to his support in the case from the Metelli and to his battle against those at the periphery of Sulla's circle. Both

1. *Pro Cluentio* 176-78. Clear proof that information which implicated Cluentius in the death of Oppianicus and which was derived from these torture sessions was irrelevant could readily have been procured by naming the socially prominent relatives and friends who witnessed the torture. (In 176 they are *honesti* and *ornati*.)

2. These marks of social leprosy are in *Pro Cluentio* 41.

groups can only enhance his stature, the one from friendship and *gratia*,
the other from the congratulatory praise (*laus* and *honos*) to be gained
even in defeat for a young man willing to take on the giants of society.
Rather than duelling to the death, the young Roman can gain a place
most rapidly by defeating a known quantity in a legal competition.
Cicero had done as much in his prosecution of Verres, and
Caelius Rufus had accomplished the same with his successful prosecution of C. Antonius, the consul of 63 BC. There are, of course, some
minor complications in the superior social standing won by Rufus after
that trial, for Antonius had been defended by real Roman nobility
including his fellow consul of that year, M. Tullius Cicero. This
victory over the twin *viri consulares* not only greatly improved the
dignitas of Rufus, it probably also paved the way for the disastrous
move against Cicero by Clodius Pulcher which forced Cicero into
exile three years later. Most of these moves and counter-moves have
been examined repeatedly as manifestations of the quixotic Roman
political scene during the last days of the republic, but can be quite
successfully understood within the framework of social rivalry. In a
world dominated by social giants and would be giant killers, a victory
over a social better in the judicial campus could be as effective as a
victory over the enemy on the field of battle. One assumes the standing
of the slain foe, Cicero of Verres and Caelius Rufus of the consular
C. Antonius, every bit as much as Caesar would assume the identity
and status of his defeated son-in-law within the decade. Even the
greatest Roman of his day, Cn. Pompeius Magnus, could meet his
match and suffer the indignity not only of death on the Egyptian shore
but of immediate and effective historical revision.

It is in the context of these social fireworks that the delightful
ironies of the defence of Rufus are set. The newly restored Cicero
speaking on behalf of Caelius Rufus who had previously defeated his
fellow consul, and against Clodius Pulcher and his monstrous sister,
who had forced Cicero into exile! The case is, nevertheless, comfort-
ably and superficially mired in a banal world of familial vendetta.
Rufus was prosecuted by a young man whose father was being prosecuted by Rufus. Cicero would have been severely hampered had this
been the only possible opponent (and, arguably, there probably would
not have been a prosecution against Rufus had the young Atratinus
been acting *solus*). Cicero compliments the young man on his pietistic
zeal and turns his righteous indignation against the siblings for whom

he had probably rehearsed the ensuing invective during his exile.

The version of the case which we have from Cicero again does not advertise the presence of abundant factual or documented evidence brought against Rufus by the prosecution. From Cicero's mock-embarrassed explanation of the matter some care was taken to show a Rufus closely bound to the evil of evils, Catiline, at a time when he should have been more carefully connected to Cicero himself.

The main thrust of the defence is, however, against Clodius Pulcher and his sister, Clodia. They are worthy opponents, for their clan had a history of office, *auctoritas* and *dignitas* which had stamped the name of their ancestor, Appius Claudius, on such essential services in the life of Rome as the *aqua Appia,* one of the main water supplies, and the *via Appia*. Their standing in history and society was matched by wealth which included prime real estate in Rome and around the Bay of Naples. Cicero smoothly makes this familial duet his prime target after dismissing Attratinus in a cloud of filial compliments. The high quality, *dignitas* and *auctoritas* that he had genetically associated with the *nobilitas* in the *pro Roscio* are similarly swept aside in a narrative of social and sexual deviation that is contrary to accepted norms of behaviour, and a betrayal of the ancestors of these two who provide all Romans with standards of proper social etiquette. The dramatic *tour de force* of the speech will be the condemnation of the accusers by the persona of their own ancestor.

From the opening moments of the defence Caelius Rufus is, for us predictably, portrayed as *adulescens inlustris* ('a brilliant young man shining in') *ingenio* ('native talent'), *industria* ('hard work and drive') and *gratia* ('favour given and expected'), that is, social connections.[1] This, of course, is far different from the portrait drawn by the prosecutors who would have us see a Caelius driven by *luxuria, libido,* and *vitia iuventutis* ('vices of youth').[2] It is, however, obvious to Cicero that the only lust in this case is the *libido* of the whore who has inspired the charge against Caelius, that *amica omnium, haec Palatina Medea,* 'everyman's female companion, this Palatine Medea'.[3] She

---

1. *Pro Caelio* 1.
2. *Pro Caelio* 25.
3. *Pro Caelio* 18. Quintilian (8.6.53) noted that Caelius had called her 'a two bit Clytemnestra' in his own speech to the judges. The occasion must have been one of the most dramatic, in the most literal sense of the word, in Cicero's career.

'along with her husband—I mean her brother!'[1] are the real enemies facing young Caelius.

Clodia's deviant activities began after the 'suspicious' death of her husband, the consular Metellus Celer, whose *virtus, dignitas* and *gloria* were not enough to prevent his wanton widow from associating with men who were not *cognati, adfines*, or even *viri familiares*, 'relatives, kin or friends of her husband'.[2] She and her household were devoted to lust and to destroying young Caelius. Indeed the list of adjectives describing her behaviour permeates the speech, and her wicked house is contrasted with those houses who provide testimony about Caelius's outstanding social qualities. Her house, *domus*, is *infamis* ('notorious'), *crudelis, facinerosa* ('crime-ridden'), and *libidinosa*. The lady herself is *temeraria* ('rash and imprudent'), *procax* ('aggressively bold and forward') and *irata* ('insanely mad').[3]

The portrait of Clodia reaches its supreme completion in the dramatic appearance of her great ancestor, Appius Claudius Caecus, the blind censor whose name remains on the via Appia 'along which her lovers parade to her' and the *aqua Appia*, the water supply she employs in her lustful lustrations. The role of Appius is played brilliantly by Cicero who in the *gravis persona*, 'the dramatic mask', of the blind censor accuses Clodia of not following the clear and famous examples of virtuous living handed down by her female progenitors. Cicero lays aside the serious mask of old Appius to put on the more modern character of that man about town, her brother Clodius Pulcher, who as tribune initiated the law which drove Cicero into exile. In the persona of Clodius he castigates Clodia not for betraying the mores of her ancestors but for ignoring the rules of her class by associating with someone who was a social and economic inferior. There certainly were equally handsome young men available to satisfy her desires who would have caused no trouble, or at least less trouble than Caelius. The dramatic presentation by Cicero was completed by his introducing the familiar stern and moderate fathers from comedy and the recitation of lines from some plays themselves.[4]

1. *Pro Caelio* 32.
2. *Pro Caelio* 34. The words are placed in the mouth of the *persona* of her great ancestor, Appius Claudius Caecus.
3. *Pro Caelio* 53-55 contains most of the attributes connected to Clodia throughout the speech.
4. *Pro Caelio* 37-39.

The comic interlude is significant in forcing us to focus on the essential techniques of the defence. Entertaining and diverting though it is, Cicero's performance accomplishes the essential task of degrading the characters of his noble opponents without reference to testimony or evidence. And in so doing he cleverly enhances the position of high standing attributed to his friend Caelius without having to introduce a shred of evidence to demonstrate his point. The behaviour of the Palatine Medea and her husband/brother at scandalous parties and musical events at Baiae near Naples, in her gardens in Rome, in her household with freedmen and slaves is a betrayal of class and family and overshadows the weak allegations about moral turpitude aimed at Caelius. The success or failure of the ploy depended entirely on the orator's abilities as actor and rhetor to convince his audience that the characteristics which he attributed to the accused and prosecutors were more believable than those the opposition had attempted. He certainly does not reveal a network of investigators whose diligent sleuthing had uncovered incontrovertible evidence that Caelius was innocent of the many charges laid against him.

Having established his version of the true picture of the accused and the true picture of the true prosecutor, Cicero asks the *iudices* to choose either to preserve (*conservate*) a noted equestrian of accomplishment and hope for his family and for the state, or to trust in the jealous rantings of a noted whore. The judges were asked, then, to judge the truth of competing portraits, not the validity of evidence, the dramatic impact of the orator as playwright and actor, not the tedious tangle of real or manufactured evidence.

Those who are even vaguely familiar with other examples from Latin literature will be able to recognize aspects of Cicero's artistry. What was obviously required in these three judicial events was not so much character assassination but characterization. The orator had at the ready, and the audience seemed to expect, a stock supply of appropriate phrases and scenarios. Those associated with 'us' must be said (but not proved) to be *constans* (or *fidelis*), *nobilis, inlustris*, (men and women) of *honos, virtus, dignitas, auctoritas* and *gratia*. Those associated with the other side, *vos*, must repeatedly, but with suitably clever variation, be labelled *audax* (or *procax*) *sumptiosus*, and *egens*, who are motivated by *cupiditas, libido, avaritia* and *potestas*. And they can be no better than the *liberti*, 'former slaves', that they are or with whom they associate.

The orator's skills in this matter are not investigatory or inquisitorial but dramatic. He must carefully suit the personal portrait of his subject to well-established types. The *pestis* that Cicero had discovered in Oppianicus was the same 'plague' that the poet Catullus was later to discover under the armpits of his rival.[1] The lustful and socially deviant Clodia is painted with the same brush as Catullus's Lesbia, including details about her fondness for her brother.[2] The characteristics marshalled for and against are shared most obviously by the satirical tradition. Even Cicero's brief description of the evils of town life can be seen gently repeated in Horace and more violently in Juvenal.[3] Near-contemporary historians also participate in this tradition of typecasting. Sallust in his remarkably vivid portrait of Catiline offers even less factual foundation than did Cicero in his Catilinarians for the evil man presented to his reader, and certainly no more documented evidence than Cicero in these speeches.[4]

The objective of defence and of prosecution at this stage of the judicial process was to establish the high or at least respectable position of its side and their friends in the social structure and to demean correspondingly the place of its opponents and their friends in the same structure. Both aspects of this objective were accomplished by associating with the one side adjectives, social qualities and intimate acquaintances all illustrating acceptable social behaviour. This duty of orator was, of course, inverted with respect to his opponents with whom he associated adjectives, anti-social qualities and intimate acquaintances of the worst sort all illustrating unacceptable and repulsive social behaviour. The desired result would be to move the one side as close as possible to the accepted centres of the social order and the other to the furthest edges. The challenge for the speaker-actor would have been to rescue his side from the social obscurity or social notoriety to which it rightly belonged by surrounding his cause with as many named social giants as possible. The first part of this challenge was well met in the *Pro Sex. Roscio*, and the second in the *Pro*

1. Rufus (but probably not Caelius Rufus) in Catullus 69.
2. Catullus 79.
3. Horace, *Sermones* 2.6; Juvenal 3.
4. Sallust, *Bellum Catilinae*, 5. George Paul demonstrated in a paper presented to the Canadian Historical Association in Hamilton in June 1987 how Sallust's portraits bear remarkable resemblance to typological prototypes found in Hellenistic historians.

Caelio. The corollary to this challenge was the equally serious duty of reducing the reputation of one's opponents by associating them with the worst sort of individuals and activities or by manufacturing censure from their social peers if their standing in society was immune to ordinary invective. The first of these strategies may be seen in all three of the speeches reviewed here and the second beautifully employed in the *Pro Caelio*.

The trial in all three cases examined here was not of evidence and documented reports about the crimes, or legally definable versions of the truth, but of reputations and of place within the community.[1] Therefore, when witnesses come forward, they testify not so much to the facts of the alleged crime but to the reputation of the accused criminal or of those bringing the charge. The townspeople who were at hand to testify in all three trials were not witnesses to the criminal event but to the most important evidence arguing for the acquittal of the defendant, his standing in his community. As we read through these speeches we are tempted from our modern judicial perspectives to trip lightly over these passages as asides or diversions from the real matter of the speech and process. They may, if this analysis should survive further investigations along these lines, be the very essence of the defence and the heart of the charges brought forward by the prosecution. What we witness in these events is less a judicial and more a social occasion.

---

1. J.M. Kelly (*Studies in the Civil Judicature of the Roman Republic* [Oxford: Clarendon Press], pp. 93-111), has come closest to noting the involvement of reputation in judicial proceedings. His concern is, however, more specifically directed at reputation as a deterrent to litigation. J.A. Crook (*Law and Life of Rome* (Ithaca, NY: Cornell University Press, 1967]) has aptly described the proceedings as an upper class game. An excellent discussion of the socially oriented vocabulary can be found in A. Wallace-Hadrill (ed.), *Patronage in Ancient Society* (London: Routledge, 1989).

INSTRUMENTA IMPERII:
LAW AND IMPERIALISM IN REPUBLICAN ROME[*]

Jonathan Edmondson

One of the liveliest current academic battlegrounds in Roman Republican history is the debate about the nature of Roman imperialism. The theory of defensive imperialism (that is, that the Romans did not actively seek imperial expansion, but were drawn into conflicts to protect their friends and allies) held the fort for many years, but is now under siege from those who prefer to see the Roman elite as consciously expansionist, fully aware of the economic gains to be made from conquest and empire. Moreover, continuous warfare gave the Roman elite the opportunity to win personal prestige and glory. This in turn helped to keep them (and their families) at the forefront of Roman politics and society (Brunt 1978; Harris 1979; Harris 1984). This debate about the motives for Roman conquest should not obscure the fact that there were structural elements in Roman society that encouraged, or even demanded, continuous warfare: the military role of the leading magistracies, the importance of the triumph for members of the Roman elite and the fact that the Roman military levy served as a crucial means for the Roman elite to maintain social control over citizen legionaries and allied auxiliaries alike (Richardson 1975; Momigliano 1975: 41-46; Hopkins 1978: 1-98; Nicolet 1980: 89-148; North 1981).

Much of the recent debate about Roman imperialism has focused on the conquerors; but for a balanced picture it is necessary—in addition—to consider the impact of Rome on the subject and allied peoples that made up Rome's Republican Empire. The study of other ancient empires has recently been stimulated by the use of new frameworks for analysis derived from sociological discussions of state development.

* I am most grateful to all members of the Seminar for their comments, but also to Michael Crawford, Virginia Hunter, Christopher Jones, Robert Kallet-Marx, John Richardson and Armin Stylow for their kindness in reading and commenting on a subsequent written version. All dates are BC unless otherwise stated.

Of these, the centre-periphery model is arguably the most useful (Wallerstein 1974; Ekholm and Friedman 1979; Rowlands, Larsen and Kristiansen 1987; Campion 1989). This has encouraged some historians of the Roman Empire to concentrate more on the impact of Rome on her subject peoples, rather than just focusing on the political centre, Rome (e.g. Price 1984; Cunliffe 1988). The changing relationship between Rome and her subjects (first in peninsular Italy and subsequently in the wider Mediterranean world) is very revealing of Rome's attitude towards Empire. This paper seeks to explore one new avenue of approach, as a contribution towards understanding the general nature of Roman imperialism.

Rome's Empire during the Republic was marked by a high degree of diversity. Regions were conquered in much the same way, but received very different forms of treatment thereafter. Some areas were directly controlled from an early date: for example, Sicily, Sardinia, or the two Spanish *provinciae*.[1] A Roman ex-praetor or ex-consul was sent on an annual basis with military support to ensure Roman control, and taxation, of each of these territories. Other regions (for example, Italy or the Greek East) were left relatively self-governing. Here Rome relied on a series of alliances with individual city-states or peoples and looked to the local elites to ensure that Rome's interests were served (that is, to ensure that taxation and demands for military manpower were met).[2] Elsewhere Rome spurned any formal modes of control, but established informal links with allied (or 'client') kings (Braund 1984). In theory, the Roman senate supervised all Rome's dealings with Italian and overseas territories; but in practice much depended on, and much was entrusted to, the 'man on the spot'; namely the Roman pro-magistrate who commanded Roman troops in the provinces (Richardson 1986: 172-80).[3] Control over the Empire was thus initially much diffused or centrifugal. Even so, there is no doubt that Rome still made a considerable impact on the local societies that made up her Empire. For example, the non-Roman communities of Italy, bound to Rome only by treaties (*foedera*), gradually adopted

1. For the problematic definition of *provincia* see Richardson 1986: 1-10.
2. There is no good recent monograph on Roman provincial administration under the Republic, to replace the somewhat outdated account in Stevenson 1939: 53-93; but see Badian 1972 (on taxation); Richardson 1986 (on Spain); Salmon 1982 (on Italy); Gruen 1984 (on the Greek East).
3. Cf. Polybius 29.1, for senators back in Rome discussing and affecting generals' conduct of campaigns overseas.

Latin as their official language and also modelled their political systems and their urban centres very much on those of Rome.[1]

Greater central control can be seen to develop from the end of the second century BC, as revealed, for example, in the law regulating praetorian provinces of 100 BC (Hassall, Crawford and Reynolds 1974 = *RGE* 55). But it was only under the early emperors that a more centralized and unified system of provincial administration and taxation was worked out, control for the first time being centrifocal (Millar 1981: 52-80). Rome maintained control over her conquered territories with a minimum of administrative manpower on the spot or in Rome (Hopkins 1983: 186).

The whole question of Rome's impact on conquered territory is obviously a vast subject. In this paper I would like to suggest one new avenue of approach: that is, by examining the impact that Roman legal and administrative regulations made upon Rome's emerging Empire. It will be suggested that such regulations were important in three overlapping and interlocking ways. First, at an immediate level, the regulations themselves made an impact on a functional/administrative level: they helped to articulate and ensure Roman control of subject territory. Secondly, a more long-term, cultural effect: they provided the subject communities with models of Roman administrative, judicial and even legal practices to imitate. Thirdly, the regulations also had a symbolic function as 'instruments of Empire' (to borrow Suetonius's phrase: *Life of Vespasian* 8.5). The physical impact of the plaques on which such regulations were inscribed and the context in

---

1.   Inscriptions reveal that the predominant language of central and southern Italy, Oscan, first adopted the Latin alphabet and the Latin practice of left-to-right arrangement, before it eventually gave way to Latin: see Vetter 1953: nos. 1-221 (nos. 8-72 from Pompeii); note no. 14: an Oscan building inscription: 'V(ibius) Popidius, son of V(ibius), *meddix tuticus* (Oscan chief magistrate) gave money for the building of this portico and also approved the work'; cf. Latin inscription (*CIL* X 794): 'V. Popidius, son of Epidius, q(uaestor), oversaw the construction of porticoes'. However, when Italy revolted from Roman rule in 90 BC, coins were minted by the Italian confederacy with legends defiantly in Oscan: Vetter 1953: 139; Sambon, 1903, 125-36. For Oscan institutions based on Roman ones see Vetter 1953: nos. 11, 12, 17, 18, 19 (Pompeii); 180, 181; Adamesteanu and Lejeune 1971- 72: 66 (Rossano di Vaglio, Lucania—in Greek script): all attesting a 'kvaistur', clearly derived from the Roman magistrate's title 'quaestor'. The last cited also uses the Oscan term 'senateis tanginod' (= Latin *senatus consulto*). For an Oscan municipal charter: Galsterer 1971. For Latin inscriptions *ILLRP* passim; in general Zanker 1976; Crawford 1981.

which such plaques were set up is also revealing of the relationship between ruler and ruled in the emergent Roman Empire.[1]

The discussion that follows will be able to consider only a tiny fraction of the surviving documents. A detailed study of all relevant material would be needed to see if there was a change over time both in Roman and in provincial attitudes to the setting up of such regulations, in their content and in their style or tone. Such a study lies beyond the scope of this paper. Instead, some lines of approach will be suggested, and some hypotheses articulated. These hypotheses will need to be tested against the whole range of data. The discussion will concentrate on the second and early first centuries BC, since this was the crucial formative period during which the structures of the Roman Empire were emerging and evolving. It will focus on three main geographical areas: Italy, the Greek East and the Iberian peninsula, so that the impact of Rome on areas at different stages of cultural development may be discussed.

1. *Modes of Communication*

In the Roman Republican Empire regulations between centre and periphery were articulated in a variety of ways:

a. through treaties or alliances, the terms of which were ritually made public in both Rome and the allied community;

b. through settlements imposed by Rome on a foreign community after defeat in war or after the quelling of a revolt; these were imposed first by the commander on the spot, but then had to be confirmed by votes of both the senate and people in Rome;

c. through Roman adjudication of disputes between subject or allied communities, usually by commissioners (*legati*) appointed by the Roman senate; their decisions also had to be confirmed by the senate;

d. through letters (*epistulae*) sent by Roman magistrates from Rome or by pro-magistrates in the provinces to the subject or allied community;

e. through 'decrees' of the senate (*senatus consulta*), literally advice given by the senate to individual magistrates who had consulted it; these decisions did not strictly speaking have the force of law, but in practice became the main means of

---

1. For the symbolic importance of Roman texts see Williamson 1987; Corbier 1987; Beard 1985.

administrative regulation of subject territory. Such decrees were often cited in a magistrate's letter to a community; and

f.   to a lesser degree, through the promulgation of Roman laws or statutes.

It is only occasionally that Roman law in the strict sense will be relevant to the discussion. Roman laws (that is, *leges*, passed by the Roman people in the *comitia tributa*, or *plebiscita*, passed by the Roman *plebs* in the *concilium plebis*, which had the force of laws from 287 BC) were normally passed by definition only for the *populus Romanus*. Even by the early second century AD Rome did not seek to impose her private law outside Roman colonies (cf. Galsterer 1986): for example, local legal systems were clearly still in place in Bithynia and Pontus (cf. Pliny, *Letters* 10.108 and 109). *A fortiori* it is implausible that Rome under the Republic sought to impose any legal uniformity on her emerging Empire. But, as we shall see, laws which were primarily intended for Roman citizens occasionally had a wider application. But in the main this paper will largely be concerned with 'Roman law' in the sense of 'Roman administrative law or regulations'.

Several ancient authors claim to quote such laws or regulations or magistrates' letters (e.g. Polybius 3.22; Josephus, *Jewish Antiquities* 14.190-216; Philo, *Embassy to Gaius* 314-315). It is very difficult to ascertain how closely these literary versions follow the original texts of the regulations; they shall, therefore, not be discussed in this paper. Much more valuable are the copies of such regulations inscribed on bronze plaques or marble stelae that have survived from Rome, but especially from Rome's subject communities. The surviving documents obviously represent only a fraction of all regulations set up in public, and they are in no way evenly spread in either chronological or geographical terms. Furthermore, they were themselves to a certain extent 'versions' of the original decrees. They do not necessarily present a complete verbatim record of the original decree, but are rather just edited copies (Millar 1983: 82, 98-110). They could be inscribed to suit whoever was arranging for their erection. But if sufficient attention is paid to the circumstances that led to their publication, they can provide a useful index of the changing relationship between Rome and her Italian and provincial subjects.

Laws, administrative regulations and treaties had been communicated both orally and in writing since the early Republic. The procedures for the publication of the Twelve Tables provide a good illustration from the mid-fifth century:

These decemvirs drafted a body of laws... and exposed them on ten plaques to the scrutiny of any who wished... And for a long time they also had many public meetings with the best men concerning these laws and examined them with the greatest care. When they were satisfied with their formulation, they first assembled the senate and, since there were no further objections made to the laws, they secured its ratification of them. Then they summoned the people in the centuriate assembly; and after the pontiffs, the augurs and other priests present had conducted the performance of the customary rites, they took the votes of the centuries. When the people too had confirmed these laws, they caused them to be engraved on bronze plaques and arranged in sequence in the most conspicuous place in the Forum (Dionysius of Halicarnassus, *Roman Antiquities* 10.57.5-7).

Dionysius was writing under Augustus and so the historicity of his account might be questioned. But for my argument that is not important, since even if not historical, his account must rely on his own knowledge—or that of his source(s)—of later procedures for publication of laws and is thus still revealing of general Roman practice. Laws such as the Twelve Tables were published in a clearly ritual setting. This gave the laws divine legitimation and helped to ensure their enforceability. To reinforce their original promulgation, schoolboys were required to learn their contents and recite them orally, a practice that continued until the early first century B C (Cicero, *de Legibus* 2.23.59).

As for treaties, they were also engraved on bronze plaques and set up in a public place: for example, the treaty between Rome and the Latins of 493 BC (the so-called *foedus Cassianum*) was engraved and written up on a bronze pillar which stood behind the rostra in the forum at Rome almost until Cicero's day (Cicero, *pro Balbo* 23.53; cf. Livy 2.33.9; Dionysius of Halicarnassus 6.95.2 for the terms).

As for *senatus consulta*, the senate communicated its decisions to the communities concerned by sending a magistrate or specially appointed delegate (*legatus*) to announce its decision orally. But this official also carried with him a written copy of the decision (e.g. Polybius 28.3.3; 29.27.2; 30.19.7; Livy 45.12.4) The recipients kept copies of these *senatus consulta* and could refer to them when necessary. Thus, for example, Polybius when addressing the Achaean League in 170-169 'called to his assistance the *senatus consultum* which ordered that no one should take notice of requests made by (Roman) commanders, unless they were acting on the strength of a *senatus consultum*' (Polybius 28.13.11). He was presumably able to quote verbatim from a copy of the relevant *senatus consultum*.

But how were these copies generated? To what extent were all *senatus consulta* recorded in writing at the time of their being passed by the senate? A law of Caesar passed in 59 BC laid down that all *senatus consulta* should be officially recorded in writing and published in Rome as part of the proceedings of the senate (*acta senatus*) (Suetonius, *divus Iulius* 20.1). This presupposes that it had not been the regular practice hitherto; and it did not remain regular practice for very long, since it was abolished by Augustus (Suetonius, *divus Augustus* 36). Before 59 BC some *senatus consulta* were written up and witnessed by a small committee of senators (presumably those who had advocated the particular measure), as the preambles to many surviving copies of *senatus consulta* reveal (e.g. *RDGE* 2 = *RGE* 21: ll. 3-5; *RDGE* 5 = *RGE* 28: ll. 19-23; *RDGE* 9 = *RGE* 38: ll. 10-14). The chairman of this committee then deposited one written version in the Treasury of Saturn, the official records office at Rome, and another in the sanctuary of Ceres, traditionally the archives of the plebeians (Mommsen 1907: 290-313; Tibiletti 1956; Frederiksen 1965: 184-87; Sherk 1969: 7-9; Schwind 1973: 14-69, 195-206; Culham 1984; 1989; Lewis 1986; Crawford 1988).

Mommsen argued (1907: 296) that all *senatus consulta* had to be written up and lodged in the archives even before Caesar's law. This is by no means certain and is unlikely on *a priori* grounds, since on many occasions *senatus consulta* would consist merely of small pieces of advice for a magistrate on how he should proceed. However, if the *senatus consultum* concerned Rome's relations with her subject communities, then it would have been useful to keep a record of it for future consultation. If the regulation was disobeyed, a copy of the relevant part of the *senatus consultum* could be despatched to reinforce Rome's requirements and to ensure their enforcement.

None of these official records of laws, treaties and *senatus consulta* survive, since they were written on papyrus rolls or wax tablets bound together into *codices*, each volume containing the records from one year (e.g. Josephus, *Jewish Antiquities* 14.219: 'file two, page 1'; Reynolds 1982: document 8, ll. 1-3: 'file [?one, pages four], five, six, seven eight, nine').[1] However, edited copies of these regulations survive in the form of inscriptions—either on bronze plaques or on marble stelae. Therefore, it is important to differentiate between two types of document: (a) the copy of the regulation (on wax tablets or

---

1. We also hear of members of the Roman elite having copies made of these records: e.g. Plut. *Cato Minor* 18. For archives in communities other than Rome (under the Empire) see Sherk 1970: 83-84. The same filing system by year was used in the record office of the *curatores* of the public revenues: cf. Engelmann and Knibbe 1989: ll. 4 and 7.

papyrus) for deposition in the archives and (b) the copy (on bronze plaques or stone stelae) for public display. This same differentiation between the archival copy and the copy for public display was made in the Hellenistic world, even when Rome was not involved. Thus, for example, after the settlement of a frontier dispute in Epiros in c. 167 BC copies of the agreement are to be deposited in the sanctuary of Zeus Olympios at Elis and of Apollo Kerdoios at Larissa 'on bronze stelae' (*SEG* XXXV 665 and 1845, ll. 36-38; cf. Cabanes and Andreou 1985; Charneux and Tréheux 1988), while further copies (?on wax tablets or papyrus) are to be deposited in the archives of Ambracia and Charadros, the contestant cities (*SEG* XXXV 665 and 1845, ll. 38-40).

But the surviving copies of such regulations raise several important questions: what were the mechanisms and motivation which lay behind and led to their publication? Did Rome require the publication of such documents in allied or subject communities, or did these communities decide to publish such texts of their own accord? If the former is right, this would provide evidence for considerable Roman interventionism in the administration of her subject peoples; if the latter, this would suggest a much more passive form of Roman administration. Rather, I hope to show that both mechanisms were at work; there was imposition from the centre, but also impulse from the periphery.

2. *Imposition from the Centre*

An occasion on which Rome often imposed a decree was after the formal surrender of a people to Rome after military defeat. The conduct of L. Aemilius Paullus in 167 BC in announcing the Roman administrative settlement of Greece after his defeat of Perseus in the Third Macedonian War is illustrative of some of the techniques employed by Rome after conquest.[1]

> Paullus had ordered ten leading citizens from each state to meet him at Amphipolis and to gather up all the king's (i.e. Perseus's) money and documents, which had been deposited everywhere. The day for the meeting arrived. Paullus entered with the ten commissioners (*legati*); a whole crowd of Macedonians poured all around, while he took his seat on his official platform (*tribunal*). The Macedonians were familiar with royal power; but this new sovereign power was displayed to them in such a way as to inspire terror: the consul's seat of judgement, his entrance after a path had been cleared, the herald and the attendant: their eyes and ears were all unaccustomed to such things. And these things might have

---

1.   Gruen 1984: 423-29, as part of his general argument that Rome was not yet interventionist in the Greek world, plays down the impact of this settlement.

frightened even allies, let alone conquered enemies. Silence was imposed by the herald; Paullus proclaimed in Latin the decisions of the senate [Livy here uses a periphrasis for *senatus consultum*], as well as those decisions of his own, made on the advice of his council. These pronouncements were translated into Greek by the praetor, Gnaeus Octavius, who was also present.

[Livy then gives the terms of the settlement].

After Paullus had made public these administrative arrangements for Macedonia, he gave notice that he would also lay down laws (*leges*) (Livy 45.29-31, with omissions).

Various points stand out, but I should like to emphasize two. First, the carefully staged ritual that accompanied, and emphasized, the pronouncement of the new administrative settlement of Greek affairs; it was meant to strike fear into a conquered people. This was not the only ritual following the Roman victory—earlier Paullus had forced Perseus to surrender at the Roman camp, a stunning sight, as Livy remarks (45.7). Later Paullus staged Panhellenic games 'on such a scale as to excite admiration not only for the splendour of the display, but also for the well-organized showmanship in a field where the Romans were at the time mere beginners' (Livy 45.32.10); not just games, but also an exhibition of all the booty captured from the Macedonians (Livy 45.33), just to rub salt in the wounds. Thus Roman superiority was not only celebrated, but publicized in the most visible way. Secondly, Paullus addressed the crowd in Latin—a gesture again calculated to emphasize Roman sovereignty over Greece: it was not that Paullus was not bilingual (Livy 45.8.6; Polybius 29.20.1, where he addresses Perseus in Greek). Although neither Polybius nor Livy mentions any physical publication of the terms of 167 in the Greek cities, it would be quite consistent with Paullus's conduct. He wanted to make it quite clear to the Greeks that there had been a shift in political control from Macedonia to Rome. The publication of these terms in writing—on a bronze plaque or a marble stele—would reinforce the impact made by their oral pronouncement and the ritual which surrounded this oral pronouncement. It would help to emphasize symbolically the Greek world's subjection to Rome.[1]

Although no physical confirmation survives from the settlement of 167, evidence is to hand from the same phase of Roman relations with Greece: a copy of the *senatus consultum* settling affairs after a revolt in

---

1. For the similar importance of inscriptions and reliefs as imperial propaganda in the provinces of the neo-Assyrian Empire see Machinist 1983 with further bibliography.

the Boeotian town of Thisbai of 170 BC (SIG^3 646 = *FIRA* I 31 = *RDGE* 2; translated at *RGE*, 21). In this decree the pro-Roman leaders are cemented in their position of power; the territory of Thisbai, which had been confiscated on the surrender of the city and turned into Roman public land, is to be returned to the city; and the magistrates for the next ten years are to be selected only from the pro-Roman group, who are given permission to fortify themselves on the acropolis for their own protection. Rome's presence is now clearly felt. But this is not strictly speaking a document imposed by Rome, since Thisbaian envoys of the pro-Roman party had requested Roman intervention. But Rome, once invited, had no qualms in intruding visibly into the political and social conflicts of this Greek community.

More direct intervention can be seen in two documents from Spain. A bronze plaque records that the Roman general, L. Aemilius Paullus, decreed on 19 January, 189 (or just possibly 188) that the 'slaves' of the people of Hasta dwelling in the Turris Lascutana should be free and confirmed them in possession of an urban centre and territory (*CIL* I^2 614 = II 5041 = *ILS* 15 = *ILLRP* 514, translated at *ROL* iv, p. 255). It appears that he was creating a new community for people previously dependants of the citizens of Hasta (Richardson 1986: 118). The Roman general was thus openly intervening in a local social conflict. Furthermore, a plaque was erected to commemorate his actions. The plaque served no doubt as a record of the settlement, as proof and legitimation of the newly-won liberty, and territory, of these former 'slaves' in case their former masters, the people of Hasta, tried later to reassert themselves. But the plaque also advertised the power of Rome to intervene in local affairs, and thus the Roman general was seen as a source of equity and justice.

Secondly, a surrender pact, arranged by the Roman commander on the spot, L. Caesius, in 104 BC for a defeated people (the *populus Seanoc*...), has recently been discovered at Villavieja, near Alcántara (Cáceres) (*AE* 1984, 495; López Melero, Sanchez Abal and García Jiménez 1984; Richardson 1986: 199-201). It confirms the format for such surrenders outlined by Polybius (36.4.1-3). The people had as their political centre a hill-fort in a highly Celticized region, and one not yet marked by much state development (Edmondson 1990). The document reveals the startling potential power that a Roman army commander could wield when on campaign, even though his measures did require confirmation by the 'people and senate of Rome' (ll.10-11). The Roman commander, if he had wished, could have imposed a system of laws on the defeated community, an act which would have deprived that community of a vital symbol of its own cultural and political autonomy—its laws (Reynolds, Beard and Roueché 1986: 127).[1] The bronze plaque on which the terms of the settlement were recorded may have been the first public document to appear in the community; as such, it is hard to imagine that it was set up on the initiative of the inhabitants of the hill-fort, as Beard has tentatively suggested (Reynolds, Beard and Roueché 1986: 127, n. 21). It is more likely to have been set up on the orders of the Roman commander, advertising as it does that he was responsible for returning to the community their possessions and laws; he is in effect claiming the status of patron of the community. The bronze plaque with its adventitious Latin inscription was designed to be set up in a public place; its very presence symbolized to the Alcantarans that they were now part of the expanding Roman Empire. The political geography of their region was now very much changed.

However, it is not just settlements after conquest that required regulations to be imposed by the centre on the periphery. Other Roman documents contain very precise instructions as to how and where they should be published in the allied or subject communities. Two examples will suffice. First, the *senatus consultum* of 186 BC which outlawed the establishment or operation of any Bacchic shrine (Bacchanal) in peninsular Italy (*CIL* I² 581 = *ILS* 18 = *ILLRP* 511; translated in *ROL* iv, pp. 255-9 and LR I 472-3; cf. Livy 39.8-19; North 1979). The decision was promulgated by a letter of the consuls sent to Rome's allies (*quei foederatei esent*: ll. 2-3). Thus it does not follow, as some have claimed, that the regulation was solely aimed at Roman citizens throughout Italy, even if the copy of the regulation to have survived was found in the Ager Teuranus, part of Roman, and hence not allied, territory (cf. Galsterer 1976: 132). Provision was made both for oral and written publication:

> You shall proclaim (*exdeicatis*) these orders at a public meeting (*in conventionid*) for a period covering not less than three market-days (ll. 22-23).

> And the senate resolved that it was right and proper that you engrave this proclamation onto a bronze plaque and that you order it to be fastened up where it can most easily be read (*ubi facilumed gnoscier potisit*) (ll. 25-27).[2]

---

1. Cf. Meiggs 1972: 220-33 for law and cultural autonomy under the fifth century BC Athenian Empire.

2. Williamson 1987: 172 and n. 49 has argued that *gnoscier* should not be translated as 'to read', but merely as 'to know' as part of her argument to stress the visibility and the illegibility of these documents on bronze. But *nosco* and its cognates all include the idea of mental understanding, not just visual recognition: cf. *Thesaurus*

The text explicitly states that the instructions, written on an official document (*tabelai*: i.e.,? on wax-tablets), were actually 'given' to the communities throughout Italy:

> See to it that those Bacchanals are broken up within ten days from the time when the document (*tabelai*) shall have been given to you (ll. 29-30).

This implies that the consuls had to ensure that a physical copy of the regulation was sent to each allied community. The tone of the instructions is very precise and uncompromising. Rome was adamant about visible publication of the *senatus consultum* and the eradication of Bacchic cult groups, on the grounds that they formed a major focus for disloyalty and a threat to security. The precision may also be explained by the possibility that this was one of the first times such Roman interventionism had been necessary.

Secondly, the Law on the Praetorian Provinces of 100 BC (often misleadingly called the 'Piracy Law'), known from copies at Delphi and now also from Cnidos in Asia Minor (Hassall, Crawford and Reynolds 1974 = *RGE* 55).[1] This is not a *senatus consultum* or a letter from a magistrate, but a law passed by the Roman people (or, strictly speaking, a plebiscite of the Roman *plebs*). First, it contains very precise penalties for magistrates or pro-magistrates who fail to carry out its terms (Delphi Copy C, ll. 7-30). This precision again suggests that Rome was anxious to deal with a threat to public security: for the law includes measures to be taken against pirates in the Aegean (hence its usual title). But it also contains very precise details concerning its communication:

> The senior consul (i.e., the one elected first) is to send letters to the peoples and states as he thinks fit, announcing that the Roman people [has taken steps to ensure that] the citizens of Rome and the Latin allies and those of the nations outside (Italy) who are in the friendship of the Roman people may be able to sail the seas in safety... And likewise he is to write to the king ?holding power in Cyprus and to the king ruling in Alexandria and Egypt and to the king ruling in Cyrene and to the king[s... [text breaks off, but picked up by Delphi Copy B]... (Cnidos, column III, ll. 28-35, trans. Hassall *et al.* 1974)

> In Cyrene and to the kings ruling in Syria [who all] have friendship and alliance [with the Roman people and] is to [make clear] that it is also right that they should also take action to prevent any pirate from [using as a

---

Linguae Latinae, sv. *nosco*. Also see Crawford 1988 for arguments as to the legibility and widely diffused knowledge of the texts and style of statutes on bronze.

1. *RGE* 55 incorporates some new—unpublished—readings by Joyce Reynolds and provides further recent bibliography on the inscription.

base of operations] their kingdom, land or territories [and that no officials
or garrison commanders] appointed by them should harbour the pirates
and to take action, as far as is in their power, to ensure that the Roman
people [shall have in them zealous contributors to the safety of all] (Delphi
Copy B, ll. 9-12, trans. Hassall *et al.* 1974).

The law further prescribes that the pro-magistrate responsible for
Asia,

is to send a copy of this law to the cities and states to whom [he is
required] to send in accordance with this law. [According to the custom of
each of those] to whom the letters are sent in accordance with this law the
letters [are to be] engraved on a bronze plaque [or else on a marble slab
or] on a whitened board, in order that they may be clearly exposed in the
cities [in a temple] or market-place, (in a position) in which [anyone who
wishes] may stand and read [at eye-level]. He is to write in this way [and
no other] in order that [the kings and the peoples] over whom they rule
may carry out these instructions (Delphi Copy B, ll. 22-27, trans.
Hassall, Crawford and Reynolds *et al.* 1974).

Especially striking is the fact that strong-termed letters, no doubt
including copies of relevant sections of the law, are to be sent not just
to subjects of Rome, but also to allied (or 'client') kings, who were
nominally independent and not strictly part of the Roman Empire at
all.[1] All this clearly reveals the growing confidence of Rome in the
Greek world and a willingness to impose her will when required.

The publication of such laws and decrees should not be viewed in
isolation, but as part of a much larger process: that is, the visible
entry of Rome into the public consciousness and political space of the
Greek cities.[2] During the second century Romans appeared increasingly
in person in Greek cities: thus, for example, a Roman commander
intervened in a purely local dispute between Euromos and Mylasa in
Asia Minor (*SEG* XXXIII 861). But Roman generals also set up
victory monuments in the major centres of the Greek world. A
particularly dramatic example concerns L. Aemilius Paullus. After
defeating king Perseus of Macedon in 168, Paullus simply appropriated
for his own use a monumental pillar that was being erected for
Perseus at Delphi, a major international sanctuary. Moreover, the
pillar stood outside the temple of Apollo, the most prominent place at
the sanctuary (Polybius 30.10.2; Livy 45.27.7); it displayed a sculpted
frieze representing the defeat of the Macedonians by the Romans and
it was topped by an equestrian statue of Paullus himself. At an

1.   The geographical and conceptual definition of the *imperium Romanum* at this
period is by no means clear: for discussion see Lintott 1981; Richardson 1979.
2.   On political space see Kuper 1972.

estimated 9.58 metres tall, it dwarfed the two pillars that stood near to it, both of which honoured mere Hellenistic kings, Eumenes II of Pergamum and Prusias of Bithynia (Kähler 1965; Pollitt 1986: 155-58 and figs. 162-64; Ferrary 1988: 556-60). An inscription in Latin at the bottom commemorated Paullus and his achievement: 'L. Aemilius Paullus "imperator" [dedicated this from the spoils which he] took from King Perseus and the Macedonians' (*CIL* I² 622 = *ILLRP* 323).[1] Just as Paullus used Latin to announce the terms of the settlement of Macedonian affairs after the cessation of war, so again he used Latin to emphasize his supremacy over the Greeks. In short, the monument constituted a very clear symbol of the intrusion of Rome into the Greek world. It may be significant that the Delphians chose to inscribe the copy of the Roman law on praetorian provinces on this pillar, a monument redolent with the ideology of Roman conquest and foreign domination.[2]

3. *Rome and Italy: A Changing Relationship*

Rome seems, therefore, to have had no compunction in intervening visibly in the communities of her Empire in the latter part of the second century. But did she make a similar impact in Italy? The senate was responsible for dealing with any crimes committed in Italy 'which require a public investigation'—that is, treason, poisoning and assassination (Polybius 6.13.4; cf. McDonald 1944: 13-17; Harris 1972). We have already seen the senate intervening throughout the peninsula to deal with the threat posed by Bacchic cult activity. Was this typical of Rome's attitude towards her Italian allies or exceptional? In other words, should the imposition of Roman regulations on nominally independent communities be seen as a regular and burdensome practice? If so, this would then form part of the reason that led some Italians to take up arms against Rome in 90 BC.

All known plaques (whole or fragmentary) containing Roman regulations or statutes from Roman Italy datable to the period before 90 BC are listed in Table 1. Very few texts have been found dated to the early or mid-second century, the period when Rome, with Italian military aid, was conquering the Mediterranean world. Relations in

---

1.   I prefer the translation of Pollitt 1986: 156-7 to *RGE* 24.

2.   However, a variety of other decrees and deeds of manumission were also inscribed on this pillar (Colin 1930: 29-116, texts nos. 36-73). The pillar, therefore, served as something of an inscribed 'archive', on which see further Sherwin-White 1985: 74-75; Reynolds 1982: 65-66.

this period were relatively cordial. Rome granted Italians a share of the booty of these foreign wars (e.g. *ILLRP* 573 from Cora) and many Italians emigrated overseas to take advantage as businessmen of the economic openings created in the newly conquered territories (Wilson 1966). Rome was also relatively generous in bestowing Roman citizenship on those Italians of Latin status who had held a magistracy in a Latin community (Piper 1988) and on those who simply migrated to Rome (Sherwin-White 1973: 96-133). Rome also allowed Italians to participate in the foundation of colonies in peninsular Italy or Cisalpine Gaul (Livy 33.24.8-9; *CIL* I^2 3201). But from the mid-second century Rome became more exclusive with her citizenship and stopped founding further colonies. Incidents between Italians and Roman magistrates become more frequent (Livy 42.1.6-12; Aulus Gellius, *Attic Nights* 10.3.3). Military service became much more unpopular, especially if it involved Spain, where campaigns were long, drawn out and not very rewarding in terms of booty. Exemption from military service thus became a real privilege for the Italians.[1] It is against this background that the spread of Roman legal documents in Italy has to be discussed. Although, as stated earlier, the epigraphic record is only a very partial one, it is surely significant that so many fragments of Roman laws can be dated to the last two decades of the second century (see Table 1).

It is not just the date of most of these fragments that is important, but also the sheer geographical range of their findspots. They have come to light from Etruria, Umbria and even Cisalpine Gaul in the north; from Lucania, Apulia and Bruttium in the south. This distribution strongly suggests that Roman laws and regulations circulated widely in Italy at the end of the second century. The establishment of clearly defined judicial procedures for redress against Roman magistrates and their assistants on charges of extortion provided some kind of protection for Rome's allies (Richardson 1987); and the extortion law of C. Gracchus allowed any non-citizen who successfully brought a prosecution against a corrupt Roman magistrate to be enrolled as a Roman citizen, or, if he so preferred, to be granted the right of appeal against Roman magistrates and

---

1.   Cf. e.g. *ILLRP* 528 from Aletrium for a local magistrate's son exempted from military service, after his father had funded an immense public building programme; and when C. Gracchus tightened up procedures for trying cases of extortion in 123, he offered as a reward to an Italian who successfully brought such a case exemption from military service (*CIL* I2 583 = *FIRA* I 7, ll. 78-79, translated at LR I 247-51 or *ROL* iv, pp. 317-71; Sherwin-White 1982).

1. *Roman Regulations on Bronze from Italy up to 90 BC*

	location	type of regulation	date	ref.
1.	Tiriolo, Bruttium	*SC de Bacchanalibus*	186	581
2.	Tibur, Latium	letter of praetor + SC (? re. levy)	159	586
3.	?Forum Sempronii, Umbria	extortion law of C. Gracchus (Tabula Bembina)	122	583*
4.	Tarentum, Apulia	judiciary law	after 122	2924
5.	Florence, Fragment A	judiciary law	after 122	595**
6.	Florence, Fragment B	judiciary law	after 122	596**
7.	Clusium, Etruria	judiciary law (on reverse of Etruscan text: *CIE* 3230)	after 122	597
8.	Guardia Vomana, Umbria	judiciary law	after 122	598
9.	Nicotera, Bruttium	judiciary law	after 122	2925a+
10.	Nicotera, Bruttium	judiciary law	after 122	2925a+
11.	Velia (Fragment 3)	?judiciary law	after 122	599
12.	Isoverde, near Genoa	*Sententia Minuciorum*	117	584
13.	?Forum Sempronii, Umbria	agrarian law (Tabula Bembina)	111	585*
14.	Bantia, Lucania	judiciary law (Tabula Bantina)	after 122	582++
15.	Bantia, Luciana	Oscan municipal charter (Tabula Bantina)	after no.14	*Chiron* 1 (1971) 191-214++
16.	Falerio, Fragment 1a	?	?	2677
17.	Falerio, Fragment 1b	?	?	2677
18.	?? (Bauer, Fragment A)	?	?	2925+++
19.	?? (Bauer, Fragment B)	?	?	2925+++

Notes

a. all refs. to CIL I^2 (except where stated)

b. *, **, +, ++, +++: on obverse/reverse of same plaque

c. nos. 3, 13: for the possible origin of the Tabula Bembina at Forum Sempronii (modern Fossombrone) see Campana 1947–49: 13

d. for the relative dates of nos. 14 and 15 see below

exemption from military service (*CIL* I^2 583, ll. 76-79). The texts of these judicial laws (especially that on the Tabula Bembina) constantly seek to enforce the open, public scrutiny of the judicial procedure. It would be quite consistent with this for the laws to include a clause requiring their publication in all Italian communities. Although no such demand can be found in the preserved portions of the texts, Tibiletti (1953: 47-48) argued that the text of the fragment from Tarentum (*CIL* I^2 2924, ll. 12-14) should be restored to include just such a clause (cf. Lintott 1982: 134-5). This intervention in the towns of Italy would be consistent with the regulation in the extortion law on the Tabula Bembina that,

> the praetor (in charge of the standing court) shall give orders for evidence to be collected within Italy in the towns (*oppida*), market-towns (*fora*), *conciliabula* where prefects are customarily sent to give jurisdiction (*CIL* I^2 583, ll. 30-31).

An examination of the physical plaques on which these laws were inscribed is also instructive. For some Roman regulations clearly replaced earlier local texts published in languages other than Latin. This shows Rome again intervening physically, or symbolically, in the communities of her Empire. One example is clear-cut—the fragment from Clusium in Etruria was engraved on the back of an Etruscan text (*CIL* I^2 597; *CIE* 3230). Similarly at Heraclea, originally a Greek colony, various Roman laws and regulations of the 40s BC (*CIL* I^2 593 = *FIRA* I 13, translated at LR I 408-412, 416-20) were engraved on the back of a bronze plaque which had first been used for a Greek sacred law (*IG* XIV 645). Finally the plaque from Bantia in Lucania, which has on one side part of a Latin judiciary law (*CIL* I^2 582 = *FIRA* I 6, translated at *ROL* iv, pp. 295-303), but on the other a local muncipal charter in Oscan (Galsterer 1971, translated at LR I 412-14). It used to be thought that the Latin text was the later. On this view we would have a Latin law replacing a local charter, another symptom of the eclipse of local languages and practices and a visible symbol of Roman intervention. But a relatively new fragment of the plaque incontrovertibly proves that the Latin law was earlier than the Oscan. For the Oscan text had to circumnavigate an already existing nail-hole, which was driven through the plaque well below the Latin text (Adamesteanu and Torelli 1969). Thus at Bantia a Latin law was taken down and replaced by a municipal charter in Oscan. The publication of a Latin law at a time when the community was still clearly Oscan represents in some ways an even greater intrusion by Rome. Its replacement at a later date by an Oscan document, possibly in the decade leading up to the Social War, suggests that such forced publication of Roman laws was seen by a nominally independent community of Italy as an imposition, as a visible loss of its own civic and cultural autonomy.[1]

As further evidence for this increased intrusion of Roman administrative regulations at the end of the second century, we may adduce three examples of Roman adjudication of local territorial disputes in Cisalpine Gaul. In 117 Q. and M. Minicius Rufus arbitrated between the Genuates and the Veiturii (*CIL* I² 584 = *ILLRP* 517, translated at *ROL* iv, pp. 263-71 and LR I 334-36). What is important here is the strong language of their adjudication. After hearing each side of the case, the Roman commissioners pronounced an edict on how the territory was to be split and then,

> they ordered them (that is, the Genuates and the Veiturii) to fix those
> limits and to have boundary stones erected; they ordered them to come to
> Rome in person when these commands were carried out (ll. 3-4).

The adjudication of a land dispute is one thing to require the contestants to come all the way to Rome to confirm that the senate's will has been carried out is quite another. Similarly, physical boundary stones survive from the adjudication of two other land disputes in the same period (*ILLRP* 476, 477).[2] Again they explicitly state that the proconsul of Cisalpine Gaul has 'ordered' them to be set up 'as a result of a senatorial decree'. Rome, it seems, was in the later second century much more self-confident than before and no longer needed to cloak her potential power in diplomatic language. Thus I would argue that the increasing imposition of Roman regulations and law was an important factor in the souring of relations between Rome and the

1. Cf. Torelli 1983, where he has reverted to believing in the priority of the Oscan text by what seems to me a forced argument based on a new inscription. Michael Crawford points out to me that the plaque with the Latin law may have been acquired from the nearby Latin colony of Venusia; Bantia was therefore just reusing a bronze plaque no longer needed at Venusia. Even if this is so, we would still have evidence (a) for the publication of a Roman law in a Latin colony, where it was strictly not applicable; and (b) for an Oscan community being influenced by the practices of a neighbouring, but more Romanized centre, in the public erection of a municipal document on a bronze plaque in its own urban centre. There is, however, no firm evidence for the plaque having come from Venusia. Brunt (1988: 139-43) assumes that the Latin law was posted in Bantia, but stresses that there must have been special reasons for this exceptional act of publication.

2. *ILLRP* 476 concerns a dispute between the Patavians and Atestini: three boundary stones were set up either in 142 or 117, depending on which L. Caecilius is being referred to as proconsul in l. 1. *ILLRP* 477 is dated to 135 BC and concerns the resolution of a dispute between the Atestini and the Veicetini.

communities of Italy in the later part of the second century BC, a souring that eventually led to war in 90 BC.

In addition to this political effect, the increasing publication of such Roman regulations also had a cultural impact on the peoples of Italy, because locally generated documents to a certain extent came to adopt not only the precise legal language of these Roman regulations. For example, a law of the *vicus* of Furfo concerning temple lands survives from the first century BC (Laffi 1978, improving the text of *ILLRP* 507). Its repetitious formulae are clearly derived from Roman legal texts and must owe something to the increased diffusion of Roman legal documents throughout Italy.[1] But in addition locally inscribed documents come increasingly to imitate Roman documents in terms of their style of presentation of written text. The Oscan charter from Bantia is one example—the Oscan community borrows from Roman documents how best to present a municipal charter on a bronze plaque (Galsterer 1971). But even more striking are the Iguvine Tables, a series of seven plaques containing sacral regulations from Iguvium (modern Gubbio) in Umbria (Poultney, 1959 with photographs; Prosdocimi, 1984). The regulations are written in Umbrian and most are inscribed in Umbrian script, arranged right to left across the plaque (Tables I–Vb). But on Table Vb the script (but not the language) changes from Umbrian to Latin. Even more strikingly, on Table VIIa the script is much smaller and much more neatly arranged than before. In short, it closely resembles the style of writing common in Roman legal documents. Poultney (1959: 23-4) dates the tables in Umbrian script to the third and second century, those in Latin script to the early first century BC. Thus, the change to Latin script and a Roman style of arrangement of text occurs at a time when Roman laws on bronze were more widely diffused throughout Italy than ever. It further suggests that the visible impact of these Roman texts was not just symbolic, but also cultural. The communities of Italy used them as a model of how to formulate and style their own public documents on bronze.

Roman documents on bronze also had a similar influence in the western provinces. The imposition by Rome of such plaques as those from Hasta (*CIL* I^2 614) or Alcántara (*AE* 1984, 495) had an important acculturating effect on such less developed regions of Spain. Such plaques introduced the cultural practice of displaying documents in the civic centre of the community to regions outside the cultural orbit of

---

1. For further comments on the linguistic influence of Roman laws see Crawford 1988.

the Greek and Phoenico-Punic colonies. This in turn helped the community to articulate a clearly defined political space. It helped to give the community a civic focus. The small number of surviving Republican documents (Roman and non-Roman) from Spain makes it difficult to come to any firm conclusions. But one example may be illustrative. The community of Contrebia (modern Botorrita) near the Ebro valley at some date in the second century BC decided to erect a bronze plaque containing a sacral law in Celtiberian (Beltrán 1980; Beltrán and Tovar 1982). But even though it is not in Latin, in the physical organization of its text it owes a clear debt to Latin sacral laws (de Hoz 1979: 242, comparing it especially to *ILLRP* 505 from Spoleto, Italy). Its erection also represented an important stage in the urban development of Contrebia. Some time later the same community put up a bronze plaque containing a document in Latin: it had clearly adopted the Greco-Roman cultural habit of posting major documents in its political centre. At least in this region of Spain the use of public documents on bronze and even the organization of the texts of these documents owed much to Roman practice.

4. *Peripheral Initiatives: Communication and Loyalty*

By no means all Roman regulations posted in foreign communities however, were imposed from the centre. Many documents—especially from the Greek East—were generated out of initiatives from the periphery. Millar (1977) has argued that under the Principate the Roman Empire was administered essentially by a process of requests made of the emperor by provincials and the emperor's response to such requests. He sees the Roman emperor as a passive, rather than active, administrator. The origin of this administrative process goes right back into the second century BC. For if provincial subjects and (*a fortiori*) 'allies and friends of the Roman people' suffered at the hands of other provincials, they would despatch an embassy to the Roman army commander (or later the provincial governor) on the spot and/or to the senate in Rome. Such embassies were heard by the senate for the most part in February, presumably since the consuls would still be present before assuming their military duties. But occasionally ambassadors—especially those who had patronage links with individual Roman senators or those who had been granted the right as a special privilege—were able to jump the queue and be heard out of order (*extra ordinem*) (e.g. Reynolds 1982: document 8, ll. 78-83, with comments *ad loc.*). Once they had stated the problems (in Latin and hence often through interpreters), the envoys were dismissed; the senate deliberated; the presiding magistrate took a vote and no doubt usually, but not necessarily, took the majority advice of the senate. The *senatus consultum* was written down by the officially appointed committee and deposited in the state archives. The envoys then received a letter on wax tablets from the presiding magistrate, containing the *senatus consultum*, or at least the relevant portions of it, to convey back to their community. If the senate had decided in their favour, they would want to have the decision inscribed on a marble stele or engraved on a bronze plaque and set up in a prominent public space, as a confirmation or legitimation of their rights, say, to a piece of territory or to ensure symbolic protection against future encroachments by hostile neighbours. The bronze plaque or marble stele was often erected within a sacral space; it thus elicited not only Roman, but also divine support. Enhanced by its physical context, it conveyed a very emphatic public message.

This construct is no doubt grossly over-simplified, but is borne out by many documents. It would be instructive to look at the whole range of inscriptions and try to ascertain what proportion of them were imposed by Rome, what proportion were generated out of this dialogue between periphery and centre, a dialogue that was usually initiated from the periphery. It will be possible to look at only a few selected documents here, to consider how this dialogue was conducted.

First, a series of three interrelated documents from Delphi dated to 190-188 are generally revealing:

1. In 190 a Roman army under M. Acilius Glabrio liberated Delphi from the Aetolians, who had seized and occupied some of its territory, and restored this land to the Delphians. A letter of Glabrio, laying down the regulations about this land, was inscribed on the base of an equestrian statue set up in his honour at Delphi (*SIG*[3] 609 and 610 = *RDGE* 37A & B, translated at *RGE* 12). The letter contains explicit instructions that 'all these regulations be engraved on a stone stele and displayed in the [?sanctuary]' (*RDGE* 37A, l. 2). The disputed estates are listed on the bottom of the inscription (*RDGE* 37 B, ll. 1-80), no doubt to act as proof of the Delphians' right to them, if ever the Aetolians should return to claim them. The Delphians seem to have appealed to the Roman pro-magistrate while in the field; there is no question of referral of the matter directly to the senate in Rome at this initial stage. The Roman commander is seen as the first and obvious source of equity, as he also was in the dispute over access to a water channel between various Spanish peoples in 87 BC (*CIL* I[2] 2951a).

2. To validate the pro-magistrate's action, the Delphians sent ambassadors in 189 to the senate. As a result, the senate declared the

sanctuary of Apollo at Delphi inviolable and granted the city and territory of Delphi 'autonomy and freedom' and 'immunity from taxation'. The praetor, Sp. Postumius, sent two identical copies of letters, appending the *senatus consultum* confirming this grant, with the Delphic envoys: one was for the 'magistrates and city' of Delphi, the other for the Amphictyonic League, based at Delphi (*SIG*³ 612 = *RDGE* 1, translated at *RGE* 15).

3. These envoys, however, were murdered by some Aetolians as they were returning to Delphi and the replies that they were carrying from Rome were destroyed. The Delphians decided to send more envoys to Rome with letters explaining what had happened. In response, the Roman consul of either 189 or 188 sent a letter to M. Fulvius Nobilior, the Roman general fighting in Greece at the time, instructing him to sort the matter out, 'when the events at Same have turned out favourably' (*SIG*³ 611 = *RDGE* 38, translated at *RGE* 16, ll. 10-12). The consul then gave the new envoys copies of the original letters to take back to Delphi and the Amphictyonic League. A copy of this last document was inscribed on a block that also formed part of the honorific equestrian monument of Acilius Glabrio. The monument with its letters and senatorial decrees protecting Delphi against intrusion by Aetolians visibly advertised that Delphi owed this protection to Rome, and more specifically to the armed power of Rome. At the same time, the inscription also records Rome's respect for the traditional gods of Delphi. For in his letter the Roman consul asserts that the Romans

> will always try to be the authors of some good for the Delphians because of the god (Apollo) and because of you and because of our ancestral custom to revere the gods and to honour them as the cause of all good things (ll. 22-25, trans. Sherk).

Thus, a letter or a *senatus consultum*, even if elicited from the periphery, provided an excellent opportunity for the Romans to impose their will on their Greek subjects, but also to create an image of themselves as political masters, powerful, but pious and fair.

The Greek cities clearly saw this dialogue with Rome as important. For they paid many visible honours to those members of their elite who acted as the go-betweens in this process of dialogue with Rome: that is, their envoys, especially if they had successfully negotiated important privileges for their community. For example, in 112-111 Epidauros honours one of its leading citizens with a bronze statue to be erected 'in the most conspicuous place of the sanctuary of Asklepios' (*IG* IV² I.63, translated at *RGE* 51, ll. 11-13). He and his descendants are granted immunity and exemption from local taxation, as well as front-row seats at the theatre in city festivals (*IG* IV [2] 1.63, translated at *RGE* 51, ll. 15-17). He is granted all these honours because he had acted as envoy of the Epidaurians to Rome, negotiated a treaty of alliance and friendship and delivered copies of this alliance to the public archives at Epidauros (ll. 8-9).[1] The importance of those who communicated with the Romans, and by extension the channel of communication itself, is clearly demonstrated. The inscription does not mention the erection of a copy of the alliance in Epidauros, but this doubtless occurred, as attested, for example, at Maronea in Thrace: 'this treaty should be engraved on a bronze plaque and set up in Rome on the Capitol and in Maroneia in the Dionysion (that is, sanctuary of Dionysus)' (Touchais 1978: 725-26, ll. 42-43; Stern 1987).[2]

For the sort of ceremonial that accompanied the successful negotiation of a treaty with Rome, a document probably from Elaia in Asia Minor, dated c. 129 BC, is revealing (*SIG*[3] 694 = *IGRR* IV 1692, translated at *RGE* 44).[3] After the conclusion of a treaty of friendship and alliance, a bronze plaque containing the senatorial decree authorizing the treaty and the terms of the treaty itself was erected on the Capitol in Rome (ll. 23-27), while two were also to be set up in Elaia: one in the sanctuary of Demeter, the other in the council chamber beside a statue of Democracy (ll. 27-31). Elaia was modelling itself in this regard on Rome; Rome did not in any way impose publication of the treaty. But the erection of plaques in the equivalent sacral spaces at Rome and at Elaia (the Capitol and sanctuary of Demeter respectively) symbolically strengthened the bond between the two states. The further publication of the treaty in the key political space of Elaia (the council chamber) also did much to advertise its new political relationship with the now dominant power in the area, Rome. Elaborate ceremonials accompanied the erection of the plaques; the priests, priestesses and magistrates were to open the temples, offer frankincense and utter prayers for the good luck and safety of Elaia and Rome, and for the alliance with Rome to be everlasting. Children

---

1. There is also reference to procedures in Rome: the senatorial decree authorizing the grant of this alliance was deposited in the Roman treasury and the alliance was put up on a bronze plaque on the Capitolium (ll. 6-8).

2. For other examples see Williamson 1987: 171, n. 44, to which one might add the alliance between Rome and Heraclea Pontica (Memnon in Jacoby 1957: 3B, 434F 18); see also in general Gruen 1984: 54-95.

3. For the debate about its provenance see Robert 1984 *contra* Sherk, *RGE* 44, who argues for Pergamum.

were to be let off their studies and slaves their work. Sacrifices were to be offered to the goddess Roma, to Demeter and Kore (the patron deities of the community) and to all the other gods and goddesses, followed by parades of boys and young men.

Such sacrifices to the goddess Roma (Greek Rhome, appropriately the Greek word for 'strength') were especially important in the ritual ratification of a recently acquired treaty with Rome. The cult was also an important focus for celebrations connected with the renewal of a treaty with Rome.[1] The development of the cult of Roma throughout the Greek East vividly demonstrates the way in which the Greek elite sought quickly to identify with their new powerful masters (Mellor 1975; Price 1984: 40-43; Errington 1987). In between renewals, treaties were read aloud each year in the local assembly (as at Astypalaia: *RDGE* 16, ll. 14-15), an event also marked by a religious ritual.

However, it is not just the cult of Roma itself that is significant here, but the fact that written copies of treaties were often set up in the physical context (that is, in the sacral space) of the cult of Roma. Thus, for example, a plaque recording Rome's treaty with Kibyra was set up beneath the gold statue of Roma (*OGIS* 762, translated at *RGE* 25, l. 15).[2] Williamson has argued (1987: 180) that Rome instructed such Greek communities exactly where to erect these documents. This seems unlikely, since the Greek envoys could have been asked in the Roman senate about the most appropriate place for the placement of such plaques. How precise a topographical knowledge, one might ask, did Roman senators have of the tiny Greek island of Astypalaia? Rather, the choice of precisely where to erect the treaty with Rome was another initiative left to the local elite. At Chios a member of the local aristocracy went even further. At the time of the establishment of the cult of Roma there (in the later third or early second century), he set up an inscription describing, or possibly a sculpted relief depicting, the birth of Romulus and Remus and their descent from Ares/Mars (Derow and Forrest 1982: 79-92, ll. 25-27). He also had

1. Cf. Polybius 28.2 for a Rhodian attempt in 169 to renew their treaty; the Astypalaea document (*RDGE* 16) seems to be a renewal, rather than the initial grant, of a treaty.

2. For discussion of its date see Gruen 1984: 731-33. Williamson (1987: 180) also claims that the treaty with Astypalaia of 105 BC (*IG* XII 3.173 = *RDGE* 16, translated by Sherk, *RGE* 53) contained a similar regulation (at ll. 48-50), to the effect that it should be published in the Temple of Athena and Asklepios and near the altar of Roma. These lines, however, concern not the publication of the treaty, but the setting up of votive offerings (*anathemata*).

myths glorifying the Romans depicted on arms given out as prizes in the gymnastic competitions at the inaugural festival (Derow and Forrest 1982: 79-92, ll. 30-31; cf. Ferrary 1988: 223-29). Such very visible acts, loaded with symbolic meaning, allowed the local elites to demonstrate further their loyalty towards Rome.

Romans were also lauded as the 'common benefactors' of the Greeks (Gruen 1984: 196-97; Ferrary 1988: 124-32). At Troezen a local historian in 157 gave recitations praising the Romans as 'common benefactors of the Greeks' (*SIG*[3] 702). Iulia Gordios in Lydia went one step further in the 130s and praised the Romans as the 'common benefactors of all' (*SEG* XXXIV 1198). In much the same spirit, certain Greek communities (no doubt again on the suggestion of members of their elite) also erected honorific statues to individual Roman generals, or even exceptionally paid them cultic honours (Gruen 1984: 169-70; Price 1984: 42-47). Rhodes could even erect a colossal statue representing the 'Roman people' in the temple of Athene (Polybius 31.4.4). Such ceremonials and rituals became regular events and helped to bind these allied/subject communities ever more closely to the imperial centre, Rome.

The many surviving documents from various parts of the Mediterranean world help us to uncover some essential features of the evolving relationship between Rome and her emerging Empire in the Republican period. But to get the most out of these documents, we need to look beyond their mere texts and reconstruct the entire political context out of which, and the entire ritual context in which, they were formulated. These written copies of regulations and honours represent just one small part of a continuous and ongoing dialogue between ruler and ruled. The process of dialogue consisted of an inextricable mixture of the oral and the written—embassies and adjudications, oral pronouncements and written agreements. Roman decisions were often communicated in ritual settings, which increased their authority and efficacy. The precise relationship between allied or subject community and Rome was often reaffirmed in ritual contexts. Such regular acts of communication allowed both Rome and her provincial subjects and allies gradually to formulate, debate and sometimes to modify the precise nature of their relationship. At various times and stages of this discourse Rome imposed her regulations and emphasized their importance by publishing them in very visible contexts, often laden with symbolic meaning. But at other times Rome allowed the initiatives to come from the periphery, and especially from the local elite. It was this group of provincial society who stood to gain most from the Roman presence. Since Rome did not set up a large bureaucracy to run her

Empire, she relied to an enormous degree on the work of these local aristocrats. In return for this work, Rome buttressed those leaders who supported Rome's interests in their position of local power, a process that was still fundamental to Roman rule in the Greek world, for example, in later periods (Bowersock 1965: 1-41).

Furthermore, this whole process of discourse between centre and periphery had an important unifying effect throughout Rome's emerging Empire. On the one hand, at Rome the regular act of writing up regulations encouraged the development of a formulaic language of administration. Thus, we can, for example, compare the formula in the edict of L. Aemilius Paullus from Alcalá de los Gazules, southern Spain, dated to 189:

> the territory and the town which they had possessed at that time, he ordered that they should possess and hold as heretofore, as long as the people and the senate of Rome were willing (*CIL* I² 614 = *CIL* II 5041 = *ILS* 15 = *ILLRP* 514).

with that in the surrender document of 104 from Alcántara in western Spain:

> he returned to them such territory, buildings, laws and other things that they had possessed on the day before they surrendered, as long as the people and senate of Rome were willing (*AE* 1984, 495; López Melero, Sanchez Abal and García Jiménez 1984).

with that in the *senatus consultum* of 170 BC on the affairs of Thisbai, Greece:

> whereas the Thisbaians spoke about their territory and harbours and revenues and about mountain lands, whatever of those had been theirs, it was decreed that they be permitted to possess them (*SIG*³ 646 = *RDGE* 2 = *RGE* 21, ll. 15-20).

The development of such formulaic language led in turn to increasingly formulaic administrative practice (cf. Goody 1986). Such linguistic and administrative formulae gradually led to a more standard and uniform style of Roman rule in various parts of her Empire.

On the other hand, the cities of the Greek East also developed ever more standardized forms for articulating their relationship with Rome. The terms of alliances struck with Rome became more and more standardized, similar honorific language was used to praise the Romans ('common benefactors', for example), and the growth of cults of Roma and then even of Roman magistrates led to the frequent re-enactment of the same sort of ritual language. Local differences were gradually being eroded. Such documents and the ceremonials associated with them were not only 'instruments of Empire', but were also instrumental in creating a greater homogeneity in Rome's relations with her provincial subjects.

5. *Roman Regulations and Local Legal Practice*

In 242 BC a division of jurisdiction between the two praetors took place at Rome. The urban praetor henceforth was responsible for jurisdiction when both parties were Roman citizens and the peregrine praetor when one party was Roman and the other a 'peregrine' or non-citizen, or when both parties were non-citizens (Crook 1967: 68; Daube 1951). The very appearance of a peregrine praetor illustrates Rome's clear perception of her own imperial expansion. Rome realised that as her Empire grew there would be an increasing need to provide arbitration between Romans and non-Romans and even between conflicting non-citizens. This is not to say that Roman law was necessarily envisaged for the settlement of such disputes, but at least Roman legal procedures had now been established for cases involving non-citizens. Once these non-citizens became familiar with Roman legal procedures, they may then have decided to introduce aspects of them into their own local judicial procedures.

Where Rome imposed her own regulations on subject communities or settled disputes between rival provincial communities, this gradually led to changes in local legal practice. In part the process was stimulated by the increasing Roman and Italian presence overseas—Roman soldiers who settled in their area of service, Roman and Italian businessmen who took advantage of new economic openings overseas and Roman *publicani* who leased the right to collect Rome's taxes or to supply Rome's armies while on campaigns (Wilson 1966; Badian 1972). This will have led to disputes arising between such Romans and the locals, which would occasionally have required legal adjudication. If the dispute involved a Roman, he is likely to have sought Roman officials to act as adjudicators, or at least to set the terms of the adjudication. Such adjudication need not necessarily have been conducted under Roman law, but Roman officials are likely to have operated legal practices familiar to them.

The *senatus consultum* regulating the affairs of Thisbai after its revolt in 170 provides an example (*SIG*[3] 646 = *RDGE* 2, translated at *RGE* 21). Certain Thisbaians had a partnership agreement with Cn. Pandosinus, an Italian businessman (*negotiator*), involving grain and olive oil (Mommsen 1913: 287, 295-96). The Roman commander,

C. Lucretius, is instructed to 'assign them judges, if they wish to be assigned judges' (ll. 53-56). Presumably they had lodged some complaint that the terms of their agreement were not being fulfilled by Pandosinus. They appealed to the Roman commander in the field as the most effective source of justice and equity in the region. He then took on the role, as it were, of the peregrine praetor at Rome; he heard the details of the case and assigned judges, even if the legal proceedings were not conducted according to Roman legal practice (Nicholas 1962: 19-25). Such disputes between provincials and Romans or Italians would have gradually made an impact on the way in which provincials conducted legal actions among themselves, even when no Romans or Italians were involved. In the Greek East the structures of legal practice were long established and so this impact of Roman practice may not have been very strong. But in the western provinces of the Empire, where state structures were not well developed before Roman conquest, Roman legal practice would have provided a convenient model for the locals to adopt. One final example from Spain is strikingly revealing of this.

In 1977 a Latin inscription on a bronze plaque was discovered near the Ebro valley at Contrebia (modern Botorrita) (*CIL* I^2 2951a [with bibliography]; Fatas 1980; Richardson 1983; Birks, Rodger and Richardson 1984). The inscription records the adjudication in 87 BC of a dispute between two native peoples, the Salluienses and the Allavonenses, over whether the former were entitled to route a canal to a water source over territory belonging to a third people, the Sosinestani. Interestingly, the plaintiffs, the Salluienses, are known to have provided cavalry to fight with Cn. Pompeius Strabo in Italy during the Social War three years earlier, for which they were rewarded with Roman citizenship (*CIL* I^2 709 = *ILLRP* 515, partially translated at *ROL* iv, pp. 273-75). Possibly these new Roman citizens had returned to their native community and been elected to their local council. Their experience fighting in a Roman army had taught them the efficacy of dealing directly with a Roman general. The details of the dispute (which are problematic) do not concern us here. What is important is the nature of the legal procedure. The plaintiffs, the Salluienses, had brought the defendants, the Allavonenses, before the Roman proconsul, C. Valerius Flaccus. Flaccus had been urban praetor, possibly in 96 (Broughton 1952: 9), and was thus experienced in Roman procedures of jurisdiction. In true Roman fashion, he set the framework for the case and appointed the 'senate' of another local community, Contrebia, as judges.

The Tabula Contrebiensis is highly significant in this context in three ways. First, it suggests that Roman legal procedure made a considerable impact on the subject communities of the Roman Empire. Although this particular case was not judged according to Roman law, very sophisticated Roman legal procedures (including legal formulas and legal fictions) were used to settle a local dispute (Birks, Rodger and Richardson 1984: 50-73). Such procedures may well have provided the model for future legal proceedings in the area. In short, the adoption of Roman legal forms contributed to the general Romanization of the Celtic west. Secondly, the case emphasizes how clearly the potency of Rome was perceived in subject areas. Such purely local disputes which required Roman intervention advertised and enhanced the reputation of Rome (in the person of the Roman pro-magistrate) as an effective, if not the only effective, source of administrative and/or judicial action in the region. In short, such an appeal to Rome or to a Roman pro-magistrate helped to legitimate Rome's authority over her subject territory (Birks, Rodger and Richardson 1984: 50).

Finally, the fact that the resolution of this dispute by Contrebia was recorded on a bronze plaque throws further light on the nature of discourse between ruler and ruled at this crucial phase of Roman imperial expansion. The plaque was found near a two-storeyed building fronted with a colonnade in the urban centre of Contrebia (modern Botorrita), whose senate had been appointed to judge the case (Beltrán and Tovar 1982: 22-23; Richardson 1983: 40). It has six nail holes around the edge and so was clearly intended for erection— possibly on this colonnaded building. The plaque was not found at Zaragoza, the urban centre of the successful plaintiffs, the Salluienses (although there is nothing to prevent another copy from having been posted there too). It did not serve, therefore, to confirm the legal decision made in their favour. Rather, the Contrebians sought to commemorate a highly prestigious moment for their local senate, a moment that had no doubt boosted their prestige in the eyes of the neighbouring, and presumably rival, communities (Richardson 1983: 40). Thus the impetus for publication of such a document came not from the centre, but from the periphery, a process already familiar from some of the documents from the Greek East discussed above in Section 4. But the quality of the highly technical, legal Latin suggests either an extremely high degree of Romanization in at least one Contrebian or (more plausibly) that the services of a Roman, rather than Celtiberian, engraver were involved. Contrebia may, therefore, have appealed to Flaccus for just such a man. Flaccus, I would argue, would not have been slow to respond, since with his administrative experience he would have recognized the important symbolic value of such a plaque. For, even if it could not be read by the majority of Contrebians, its very presence in their urban centre visibly advertised Roman power. Therefore, the motivation for publication was twofold; it enhanced the reputation of the elite of Contrebia, while at the same time also advertised the effectiveness of Rome as an administrative and judicial force. It was beneficial to both ruler and ruled alike.

6. *Conclusion*

Thus, a study of the nature and diffusion of Roman legal and administrative documents allows us to reconstruct several important aspects of the complex and shifting relationship between Rome and her subjects or allies during the crucial formative phase of Rome's imperial expansion. But to get the most out of these documents, they must be viewed on two levels: first, for the details of Roman administrative practice that they contain; and secondly, for the physical significance of their context and place of publication. They should be read as both functional and symbolic texts. Such documents helped to formulate and regularize the relationship between centre and periphery. Not only the texts themselves, but also the context in which they were generated allowed an essential discourse to be conducted between ruler and ruled. This discourse helped to articulate and emphasize the new configurations of power throughout the Mediterranean world, as Rome came to dominate more and more of this area. Furthermore, the nature of the texts themselves and the context of their publication tellingly reflect the shifting attitudes that Rome adopted both at different stages of her imperial expansion and in different regions of her Empire. At some periods, in some places Rome was keen to impose her statutes on her subject communities; this allowed a powerful statement about Roman dominance. Elsewhere and at other times, Rome was happy to allow the initiative to come more from the periphery. Both processes were essential to the articulation of the norms of administrative practice in the emerging Roman Empire. Finally Rome's attitude towards law and Empire was marked by an initial imposition of regulations, but then by a subsequent unwillingness to develop a universal legal system throughout her Empire (Galsterer 1986). Rome's attitude towards law thus reflects very closely her general conduct towards Empire—after the initial savagery of conquest, Roman administration of conquered territories was, in stark contrast, relatively unobtrusive. In the same way, the initial publication of a Roman decree was a powerful symbol of the major political change that had occurred in the locality, but Rome refused to go further and unify the Empire by imposing Roman law on citizens and non-citizens alike; it was simply not worth the effort in terms of manpower or time.

BIBLIOGRAPHY

Adamesteanu, D., and M. Torelli
    1969   'Il nuovo frammento della Tabula Bantina', *Archeologia Classica* 21: 1-17.

Adamesteanu, D., and M. Lejeune
    1971-72   Il santuario lucano di Macchia di Rossano di Vaglio, *Memorie: Atti della Accademia Nazionale dei Lincei, serie ottava. Classe di Scienze morali, storiche e filologiche* 16: 39-83.

Badian, E.
    1972   *Publicans and Sinners: Private Enterprise in the Service of the Roman Republic* (Oxford: Basil Blackwell).

Beard, W.M.
    1985   'Writing and Ritual: A Study of Diversity and Expansion in the Arval Acta', *Papers of British School at Rome* 53: 114-49.

Beltrán, A.
    1980   'El bronce ibérico de Botórrita y su contexto arqueológico', *Caesaraugusta* 51-52: 103-109.

Beltrán A., and A. Tovar
    1982   *Contrebia Belaisca (Botórrita, Zaragoza). I. El bronce con alfabeto iberico de Botórrita* (Monografías arqueológicas, 22; Zaragoza: Universidad de Zaragoza, Departamento de Prehistoria y Arqueología).

Birks, P., A. Rodger, and J.S. Richardson
    1984   'Further Aspects of the *Tabula Contrebiensis*', *JRS* 74: 45-73.

Bowersock, G.W.
    1965   *Augustus and the Greek World* (Oxford: Clarendon Press).

Braund, D.C.
    1984   *Rome and the Friendly King: The Character of Client Kingship* (London: Croom Helm).

Broughton, T.R.S.
    1952   *The Magistrates of the Roman Republic*, II (American Philological Association Monograph, 15.2; New York: American Philological Association).

Brunt, P.A.
    1978   'Laus Imperii', in P. Garnsey and C.R. Whittaker (eds.), *Imperialism in the Ancient World* (Cambridge: Cambridge University Press): 159-91.

    1988   *The Fall of the Roman Republic and Related Essays* (Oxford Press: Clarendon).

Cabanes, P., and J. Andréou
    1985   'Le règlement frontalier entre les cités d'Ambracie et de Charadros', *Bulletin de Correspondance Hellénique* 109: 499-544, 753-57.

Campana, A.
1947-49   'Storia dei frammenti della Lex Acilia repetundarum e della legge
           agraria', *Rendiconti della Pontificia Accademia Romana di
           Archeologia* 23-24: 13.
Campion, T.C. (ed.)
1989   *Centre and Periphery: Comparative Studies in Archaeology* (London:
           Unwin Hyman).
Charneux, P., and J. Tréheux
1988   'Sur le règlement frontalier entre Ambracie et Charadros', *Bulletin de
           Correspondance Hellénique* 112: 359-73.
Colin, G.
1930   *Fouilles de Delphes. III. Epigraphie. Fasc. iv, Inscriptions de la
           terrasse du temple et de la region nord du sanctuaire* (Paris: de
           Boccard).
Corbier, M.
1987   'L'écriture dans l'espaçe romain', in *L'Urbs: Espaçe urbain et
           histoire* (Collection de l'Ecole française de Rome, 98; Rome: Ecole
           française de Rome): 27-60.
Crawford, M.H.
1981   'Italy and Rome', *JRS* 71: 153-60.
1988   'The Laws of the Romans: Knowledge and Diffusion', in J. González
           and J. Arce (eds.), *Estudios sobre la Tabula Siarensis* (Anejos de
           Archivo Español de Arqueología, IX; Madrid: Consejo Superior de
           Investigaciones Científicas): 127-40.
Crook, J.A.
1967   *Law and Life of Rome, 90 BC–AD 212* (Aspects of Greek and Roman
           Life; Ithaca, NY: Cornell University Press).
Culham, P.
1984   'Tablets and Temples: Documents in Republican Rome', *Provenance*
           (Journal of Society of Georgia Archivists) 11.2: 15-31.
1989   'Archives and Alternatives in Republican Rome', *Classical Philology*
           84: 100-115.
Cunliffe, B.
1988   *Greeks, Romans and Barbarians: Spheres of Interaction* (New York:
           Methuen).
Daube, D.
1951   'The Peregrine Praetor', *JRS* 41: 66-70.
Derow, P.S., and W.G. Forrest
1982   'An Inscription from Chios', *Annual of the British School at Athens*
           77: 79-92.
Edmondson, J.C.
1990   'Romanization and Urban Development in Lusitania', in T.F.C. Blagg
           and M. Millett (eds.), *The Early Roman Empire in the West* (Oxford:
           Oxbow): 151-78.
Ekholm, K., and J. Friedman
1979   ' "Capital" Imperialism and Exploitation in Ancient World Systems',
           in M.T. Larsen (ed.), *Power and Propaganda: A Symposium on
           Ancient Empires*, (Mesopotamia, 7; Copenhagen: Akademisk Forlag):
           41-58.
Engelmann, H., and D. Knibbe
1989   'Das Zollgesetz der Provinz Asia: eine neue Inschrift aus Ephesos',
           Epigraphica Anatolica 14: 1-206.

Errington, R.M.
    1987   '*Thea Rhome* und römischer Einfluss südlich des Maanders im 2. Jh. v.
                Chr.', *Chiron* 17: 97-118.
Fatás, G.
    1980   *Contrebia Belaisca*. II. *Tabula Contrebiensis* (Monografías arqueológ-
                icas, 23; Zaragoza: Universidad de Zaragoza, Departamento de
                Prehistoria y Arqueología).
Ferrary, J.-L.
    1977   'Recherches sur la législation de Saturninus et de Glaucia', *Mélanges
                de l'Ecole française de Rome: Antiquité* 89: 619-660.
    1988   *Philhellénisme et impérialisme: aspects idéologiques de la conquête
                romaine du monde hellénistique* (Bibliothèque des écoles françaises
                d'Athènes et de Rome, 271; Rome: Ecole française de Rome).
Frederiksen, M.W.
    1965   'The Republican Municipal Laws: Errors and Drafts', *JRS* 55: 183-98.
Galsterer, H.
    1971   'Die Lex Osca Tabulae Bantinae: eine Bestandsaufnahme', *Chiron* 1:
                191-214.
    1976   *Herrschaft und Verwaltung im Republikanischen Italien* (Munich:
                Beck).
Galsterer, H.
    1986   'Roman Law in the Provinces: Some Problems of Transmission', in
                M.H. Crawford (ed.), *L'impero romano e le strutture economiche e
                sociali delle province* (Biblioteca di Athenaeum, 4; Como: Edizioni
                New): 13-27.
Goody, J.
    1986   *The Logic of Writing and the Organization of Society* (Cambridge:
                Cambridge University Press).
Gruen E.S.
    1984   *The Hellenistic World and the Coming of Rome* (2 vols.; Berkeley:
                University of California Press).
Harris, W.V.
    1972   'Was Roman Law Imposed on the Italian Allies?', *Historia* 21: 639-
                45.
    1979   *War and Imperialism in Republican Rome* (Oxford: Clarendon Press).
    1984   (ed.) *The Imperialism of Mid-Republican Rome* (Papers and
                Monographs of the American Academy in Rome, 29; Rome:
                American Academy in Rome).
Hassall, M.W.C., M.H. Crawford and J.M. Reynolds
    1974   'Rome and the Eastern Provinces at the End of the Second Century
                BC: The So-called "Piracy Law" and a New Inscription from Cnidos',
                JRS 64: 195-220.
Hopkins, K.
    1978   *Conquerors and Slaves* (Sociological Studies in Roman History, 1;
                Cambridge: Cambridge University Press).
Hopkins, K. (with G. Burton)
    1983   *Death and Renewal* (Sociological Studies in Roman History, 2;
                Cambridge: Cambridge University Press).
de Hoz, J.
    1979   'Escritura e influencia clásica en los pueblos prerromanos de la
                peninsula', *Archivo Español de Arqueología* 52: 227-250.

Jacoby, F.
1957   *Die Fragmente der griechischen Historiker: Neudruck verm. um Addenda zum Text, Nachtrage zum Kommentar, Corrigenda und Konkordanz* (Leiden: Brill).

Kähler, H.
1965   *Der Fries von Reiterdenkmal des Aemilius Paullus in Delphi* (Monumenta artis Romanae, 5; Berlin: Mann).

Kuper, H.
1972   'The Language of Sites in the Politics of Space', *American Anthropologist 74*: 411-425.

Laffi, U.
1978   '*La Lex Aedis Furfensis*', in *La cultura italica: atti del convegno della società italiana di glottologia, Pisa, 19 e 20 dicembre 1977* (Pisa: Giardini): 121-44.

Lewis, N.
1986   'The Process of Promulgation in Rome's Eastern Provinces', in R.S. Bagnall and W.V. Harris (eds.), *Studies in Roman Law in Memory of A. Arthur Schiller* (Leiden: Brill): 127-39.

Lintott, A.W.
1978   'The *quaestiones de sicariis et veneficiis* and the Latin Lex Bantina', *Hermes* 106: 125-38.
1981   'What Was the "Imperium Romanum"?', *Greece and Rome* 28: 53-72.
1982   'The Roman Judiciary Law from Tarentum', *ZPE* 45: 127-38.

López Melero, R., J.L.Sanchez Abal and S. García Jiménez
1984   'El bronce de Alcántara. Una *deditio* del 104 a.C.', *Gerión* 2: 265-323.

McDonald, A.H.
1944   'Rome and the Italian Confederation (200-186)', *JRS* 34: 11-33.

Machinist, P.
1983   'Assyria and its Image in the First Isaiah', *JAOS* 103: 719-737.

Meiggs, R.
1972   *The Athenian Empire* (Oxford: Clarendon Press).

Mellor, R.
1975   *Thea Rhome: The Worship of the Goddess Roma in the Greek World* (Hypomnemata, 42; Göttingen: Vandenhoeck & Ruprecht).

Millar, F.G.B.
1977   *The Emperor in the Roman World* (London: Duckworth).
1981   *The Roman Empire and its Neighbours* (London: Duckworth, 2nd edn [London: Weidenfeld & Nicolson, 1967]).
1983   'Epigraphy' in M.H. Crawford (ed.), *Sources for Ancient History* (Cambridge: Cambridge University Press): 80-136.

Momigliano, A.
1975   *Alien Wisdom: The Limits of Hellenization* (Cambridge: Cambridge University Press).

Mommsen, T.
1907   'Sui modi usati da' Romani nel conservare e pubblicare le leggi ed i senatusconsulti', *Annali dell'Instituto di corrispondenza archeologica* 30: 181-212, in B. Kubler (ed.) *Gesammelte Schriften—Juristische Schriften*, III (Berlin: Weidmann): 290-313.

1913   'Observationes Epigraphicae 'XV' SC de Thisbaeis', in H. Dessau
               (ed.) *Gesammelte Schriften: Epigraphische und Numismatische
               Schriften*, VIII (Berlin: Weidmann): 274-96.

Nicholas, B.
1962   *An Introduction to Roman Law* (Clarendon Law Series; Oxford:
               Clarendon Press).

Nicolet, C.
1980   *The World of the Citizen in Republican Rome* (trans. P.S. Falla,
               Berkeley : University of California Press).

North, J.A.
1979   'Religious Toleration in Republican Rome', *Proceedings of the
               Cambridge Philological Society* 25: 85-103.

1981   'The Development of Roman Imperialism', *JRS* 71: 1-12.

Piper, D.J.
1988   'The *ius adipiscendae civitatis Romanae per magistratum* and its
               Effects on Roman-Latin Relations', *Latomus* 47: 59-68.

Pollitt, J.J.
1986   *Art in the Hellenistic World* (Cambridge: Cambridge University Press).

Poultney, J.W.
1959   *The Bronze Tablets of Iguvium* (American Philological Association
               Monograph, 18; Baltimore: American Philological Association).

Price, S.R.F.
1984   *Rituals and Power: The Roman Imperial Cult in Asia Minor*
               (Cambridge: Cambridge University Press).

Prosdocimi, A.
1984   *Le Tavole Iguvine I* (Lingue e iscrizioni dell'Italia antica, 4; Florence:
               L.S. Olschki).

Reynolds, J.M.
1982   *Aphrodisias and Rome: documents from the excavation of the theatre
               at Aphrodisias conducted by Professor Kenan T. Erim, together with
               some related texts* (*JRS*, Monograph 1; London: Society for the
               Promotion of Roman Studies).

Reynolds, J.M., W.M. Beard and C. Roueché
1986   'Roman Inscriptions 1981-5', *JRS* 76: 124-146.

Richardson, J.S.
1975   'The Triumph, the Praetors and the Senate', *JRS* 65: 50-63.

Richardson, J.S.
1979   'Polybius' View of the Roman Empire', *Papers of the British School
               at Rome* 34: 1-11.

1983   'The *Tabula Contrebiensis*: Roman Law in Spain in the Early First
               Century BC', *JRS* 73: 33-41.

1986   *Hispaniae: Spain and the Development of Roman Imperialism 218–82
               BC* (Cambridge: Cambridge University Press).

1987   'The Purpose of the *Lex Calpurnia de repetundis*', *JRS* 77: 1-12.

Robert, L.
1984   'Documents d'Asie Mineure. XXXII.2. Un décret d'Elaia', *Bulletin
               de Correspondance Hellénique* 108: 489-96.

Rowlands, M., M. Larsen and K. Kristiansen
1987   *Centre and Periphery in the Ancient World* (New Directions in
               Archaeology; Cambridge: Cambridge University Press).

Salmon, E.T.
1982   *The Making of Roman Italy* (Aspects of Greek and Roman Life;
        London: Thames & Hudson).
Sambon, A.
1903   *Les Monnaies antiques de l'Italie: Etrurie, Ombrie, Picenum,
        Campania (Cumes et Naples)* (Paris; repr. Bologna: Forni, 1967).
Schwind, F.
1973   *Zur Frage der Publikation im römischen Recht* (Münchener Beitrage
        zur Papyrusforschung und Antikenrechtgeschichte, 31; Munich: Beck,
        2nd edn).
Sherk, R.K.
1969   *Roman Documents from the Greek East: Senatus Consulta and
        Epistulae to the Age of Augustus* (Baltimore: Johns Hopkins University
        [= *RDGE*]).
1970   *The Municipal Decrees of the Roman West* (Arethusa Monograph, 2;
        Buffalo, New York: State University of New York at Buffalo).
1984   *Rome and the Greek East to the Death of Augustus* (Translated
        Documents of Greece and Rome, 4; Cambridge: Cambridge University
        Press [= *RGE*]).
Sherwin-White, A.N.
1973   *The Roman Citizenship* (Oxford: Clarendon Press, 2nd edn [1939]).
1982   'The *Lex Repetundarum* and the Political Ideas of Gaius Gracchus',
        JRS 72: 18-31.
Sherwin-White, S.M.
1985   'Ancient Archives: The Edict of Alexander to Priene, a Reappraisal',
        JHS 105: 69-89.
Stern, J.
1987   'Le traité d'alliance entre Rome et Maronée', *Bulletin de
        Correspondance Hellénique* 111: 501-509.
Stevenson, G.H.
1939   *Roman Provincial Administration till the Age of the Antonines*
        (Oxford: Clarendon Press).
Tibiletti, G.
1953   'Le leggi de *iudiciis repetundarum* fino alla guerra sociale',
        Athenaeum 31: 1-100.
1956   'Pubblicazione delle leggi', in E. de Ruggiero (ed.) *Dizionario
        Epigrafico di Antichita Romane* IV, 23 (Rome: Pasqualucci): 707-10.
Torelli, M.
1983   'Una nuova epigrafe di Bantia e la cronologia dello statuto municipale
        bantino', *Athenaeum* 61: 251-57.
Touchais, G.
1978   'Chronique des fouilles et découvertes archéologiques en Grèce en
        1977', *Bulletin de Correspondance Hellénique* 102: 641-770.
Vetter, E.
1953   *Handbuch der italischen Dialekte* (Heidelberg: Winter).
Wallerstein, I.M.
1974   *The Modern World System: Capitalist Agriculture and the Origins of
        the European World* (New York: Academic Press).
Williamson, C.
1987   'Monuments of Bronze: Roman Legal Documents on Bronze Tablets',
        Classical Antiquity 6.1: 160-83.

Wilson, A.J.N.
　　1966　　*Emigration from Italy in the Republican Age of Rome* (Manchester: Manchester University Press).

Zanker, P. (ed.)
　　1976　　*Hellenismus in Mittelitalien: Kolloquium in Göttingen vom 5. bis 9. Juni 1974* (Abhandlungen der Akademie der Wissenschaften in Göttingen, Philologisch-historische Klasse, 3rd series, 97; 2 vols.; Göttingen: Vandenhoeck & Ruprecht).

THE IMPACT OF LAW ON VILLAGE LIFE IN ROMAN EGYPT

Deborah W. Hobson

What was the impact of the imperial legal system on the everyday life of the inhabitants of rural communities in Roman Egypt? This seems like a simple and straightforward question, but in fact it points to an area of scholarly investigation which has been remarkably ignored until quite recently, namely, the life of the ordinary peasant in antiquity.

Students of Greek and Roman history have long been accustomed to drawing their information primarily from the major literary and historical sources of Greece and Rome, which record the past in terms of major events, usually from the perspective of the ruling class and conquerors. The Greek papyri from Egypt, which generally cover the period from the death of Alexander the Great in 323 BC to the Arab conquest in AD 640, provide an incomparable collection of evidence of a different sort. These are the documents of ordinary life, as it was lived by ordinary people, most of them indigenous peasants, in a country which was during the first part of this timespan a Hellenistic monarchy ruled by the Macedonian descendants of Alexander's general Ptolemy, and in the second part a Roman province governed by a prefect who was a Roman equestrian acting as the personal representative of the emperor.

Even the study of Greco-Roman Egypt has been dogged by the tendency to study history primarily from the perspective of the rulers—that is, from the top down. This is because we are confined by our linguistic limitations (Hobson 1988: 353-54), which means that the only evidence which is easily accessible to classical scholars is the documentation which was written in Greek, the official language of communication in Egypt throughout the whole Greco-Roman period. Those Egyptians who wanted to communicate with the government had to do so in Greek; thus we can only examine the lives of those peasants who were able to use the system, and the life of the Egyptian community as a whole is most easily accessible in relation to the ruling bureaucracy through whose institutions it is recorded. One sees the limitations of this view of Roman Egypt most clearly in the realm of law. There is a strong tradition of excellent scholarship in the field of juristic papyrology, and yet, though much important work has been done in this area, it is virtually all from the theoretical perspective of legal structures which seem rather remote from the mundane concerns of the humble peasant.

I propose here to examine the system from the bottom up, to see how and when a villager had recourse to 'the law', and what he or she knew about the law. In order to define a useful body of information for this study I have limited the investigation to papyri from only three locations. First, Soknopaiou Nesos, a village on the far western edge of the Arsinoite nome, well removed from the 'civilized' world, and therefore a good test of how far-reaching the arm of the law might have been, since if it reached Soknopaiou Nesos, it must have been widely disseminated. Secondly, I have used papyri from Tebtunis, another small but more centrally located village of the Arsinoite nome, sharing some features of Soknopaiou Nesos (for example, both villages were relatively small and had strong native priesthoods), but otherwise more likely to be affected by the legal system, one might think, because of its more central location in the nome. Finally, I have collected evidence from Oxyrhynchus, partly because there is so much of it and it is so easily accessible, primarily in the many published volumes of the Egypt Exploration Society, and also because as a metropolis it might be expected to provide a contrast with the two small villages in terms of its legal sophistication. Previous experience with examining particular problems documented by papyri from Egyptian villages has taught me that there is a great deal of local variation (Hobson–Samuel 1981: *passim*), and that it is thus dangerous to generalize about life in Roman Egypt on the basis of evidence drawn at random from a variety of sites.

This investigation is also limited chronologically to the first three centuries AD, a period for which the documentary evidence is relatively plentiful and administratively coherent. The reign of Diocletian (AD 284–305) brought substantial changes to the administrative structures of Roman Egypt, so the end of the third century seems a logical terminus for this inquiry.[1]

---

1.   In an unpublished Duke University doctoral dissertation, Peter D.M. Witt

Before turning to the documents from these particular sites, it is important to identify the general legal context to which they belong. What exactly constitutes 'the law' in Roman Egypt? This in itself is a fairly thorny question, since the relationship between Roman imperial law and Greek law as well as indigenous local custom is complicated, and is itself the subject of a vast bibliography.[1]

Broadly speaking the imperial law in Egypt was embodied in a conglomeration of prefectorial edicts, codes, and imperial constitutions and rescripts. At the same time, however, there were the so-called 'laws of the land', which were the survivals of Ptolemaic and Egyptian law, and there were also a series of special legal arrangements affecting particular groups, for example, the Jews in Alexandria, the Antinopolites and the Roman citizens.[2] For the present purposes these complexities need not concern us, since we are focusing on the general question of how law (whatever the source of the law was) impacted the lives of the native people of Egypt, who themselves would have been largely oblivious to such juridical distinctions.

Roman law as such was promulgated to the people of Egypt primarily through the edicts of the prefect, who was the provincial governor and also the supreme judicial authority of the country during his term of office. As one measure of the impact of law on Egyptian natives, one might ask whether these prefectorial edicts actually reached the small villages of the country. A recent publication of all the extant prefectorial edicts (Katzoff 1980; cf. Katzoff 1978: 45-56) lists 59 entries from 4 BC to the fourth century. The papyri on which these are preserved appear to come from all over Egypt, though Oxyrhynchus is the most frequent provenience (20 out of 59). There is certainly evidence in the Soknopaiou Nesos papyri of knowledge of edicts of the prefects in both the early first century and in the beginning of the third century,[3] so the edicts must have been widely circulated. They

(1977) has collected all of the references to the strategos in the papyri, and he reports (pp. 118-19) that the latest document in which this official is attested as being involved in civil matters is *P. Lond.* V 1651 (AD 363).

1. For a useful synthesis of the current (as of 1970) state of the question, see Modrzejewski 1970: 317-77.

2. A good general discussion of this is given by Bowman 1986: 73-74.

3. *SB* I 5235 (AD 12) refers to a prefectorial edict exhorting people to refrain from ὕβρις or πληγαί, interesting in view of the subject of the present investigation. *P. Gen.* I 16 and *SB* I 4284 (both AD 207) refer to an edict of the prefect Subatianus Aquila asking people to return to their ἴδια (place of origin). These references are not

were officially promulgated at the prefect's office in Alexandria, from where copies were sent to the strategoi of the nomes, who instructed local officials to post them.[1] In this way, the prefect's edicts were made available to every community in Egypt.[2] Of course they were written and promulgated in Greek (which is interesting in that the prefects themselves were native speakers of Latin, and the audience for the edicts included Romans and Egyptians as well as Greeks), so even though they may have been posted everywhere, only those villagers who were literate and could read Greek actually had direct access to them.[3]

The subject matter of the edicts is wide-ranging, from the very particular to the very general, but all together the extant edicts, fragmentary though most of the texts are, offer pronouncements in such areas as fiscal administration, religious practices, criminal and civil law and government abuses. They appear to have had widespread currency, since we find them cited in judicial cases long after the term of a particular prefect.[4]

If one uses as the criterion of impact the extent to which the law, as manifested in the prefectorial edict, was disseminated throughout the country, one would have to conclude that the impact of law was very extensive. On the other hand, the prefect as the provincial representative of the emperor was not only the supreme judicial authority, but he was at the same time the supreme fiscal, administrative and military

included in Katzoff's article.

1. Katzoff (1982a) articulates an important distinction between prefectorial edicts (διαστάγματα), addressed to the population at large, which never contain references to their own publication, and letters (ἐπιστολαί), addressed by the prefect to subordinate officials, which often contain instructions for their promulgation.

2. An interesting example of the wide geographical range of the prefect's pronouncements is to be found in *P. Oxy*. XVII 2131, a petition to the prefect from an Oxyrhynchus woman requesting exemption from a local liturgy. It was number 1009 in a roll of conjoined petitions and was displayed in the temple of Antinous at Antina, fifty miles from Oxyrhynchus.

3. A good general discussion of the judicial system as it affected individuals is found in Lewis 1983: ch. 9, '*Insciam Legum* or The Administration of Justice'.

4. See, e.g. *P.Oxy*. VI 899, a petition to the strategus of AD 200 in which a woman claiming on the basis of her gender that she should be released from responsibility for the cultivation of crown land cites legal precedent going back as far as the prefecture of Ti. Julius Alexander in AD 69.

authority.[1] How could an Egyptian villager distinguish between these various realms of authority?[2] From his perspective there was a series of authorities which governed his everyday life. In the first place, the agricultural activity which was the centre of his life was stringently regulated by the government. Land was measured, crops were weighed, property was registered, taxes were paid, all according to a set of amazingly detailed procedures which extended to the most remote corner of the countryside. No one could have been unaware of the existence of the machinery of government, if not the mechanics of the law. The taxation system alone would have had an enormous impact on local activity, since taxes had to be paid, both in money and in grain, for virtually every kind of activity. In this sense, then, the initial question posed in this paper can be answered quite simply, since it is clear from even a cursory reading of the papyri that imperial law, in its manifestation as bureaucracy rather than legal codes, was ubiquitous and inescapable, whether or not the individual villager perceived this as law.[3]

Prefectorial edicts are not the only type of papyrus document which contains evidence relevant to the general topic of law; there are records of legal cases and judicial proceedings (Coles 1966), orders for arrest, and predominantly there are hundreds of petitions from villagers to officials in which they ask for assistance.[4] It is these petitions which give us the most direct information about how and when the village inhabitants appealed to legal bodies to assist them in settling

1. See the chart showing the structure of the bureaucracy of Roman Egypt in Bowman 1986: 67 fig. 3.

2. This point is also observed by Bowman 1986: 73, n. 8: 'there is, in practice and probably even in principle, very little distinction between administration and jurisdiction'. See also Bowman 1976: 163: 'The supposed distinction between administrative competence and juridical competence is one which has bedevilled the study of Roman Egypt (and other areas) for many years. I suspect that it is a distinction which serves no useful purpose and which no Roman administrator would have understood.'

3. Of course the papyri are by their very nature instruments of the bureaucracy, so those residents of Egypt whom we know from these documents have had at least this direct experience of 'the law' in its bureaucratic guise. One wonders how many Egyptians were able to go through life without any contact with officialdom.

4. Petitions from Oxyrhynchus in the early Roman period form the basis of a study by Morris (1981).

Law, Politics and Society

disputes,[1] and these documents therefore give us the most realistic insight into how individuals actually experienced the judicial system in their everyday lives. From the three sites which provide the focus of this paper, we have a total of 182 petitions, 95 of which are from Oxyrhynchus, 52 from Soknopaiou Nesos, and 35 from Tebtunis. It is hard to extrapolate from these numbers a statistical idea of how often people may have sought outside intervention to protect their rights, because we have in each case differing quantities of papyrological evidence overall,[2] such that it is difficult to estimate what proportion of the total these figures might constitute. However, one possible index of the litigiousness of an Egyptian population is provided by the evidence of an interesting archive of papyri from the record office of Tebtunis in the reign of Claudius.[3] A sequence of two Michigan papyri (*P. Mich.* II 123 and *P. Mich.* V 238) in this archive provides a record day by day of every transaction drawn up in the record office of Tebtunis for a period of sixteen consecutive months in the years AD 45 and 46. Here among a total of 1048 separate entries we find a total of 70 recorded as ὑπομνήμα, ὑπομνήματα or ἀναφόριον, all Greek terms which might be used to refer to petitions. From this we might conclude that 6.7 per cent of the transactions in the yearly activity of a typical village were petitions.

Whereas the prefectorial edict gives us the official voice of the government in relation to its subjects, the petition shows us the more personal side of that relationship, where the inhabitants turn to the governmental representative for help in solving local problems.[4] In

1.   On dispute settlement in village communities, an interesting historical study for the purposes of comparison with our materials is Davies 1985. For an anthropological perspective, see Nader and Todd 1978, dealing with ten contemporary societies and containing an excellent bibliography.

2.   For example, we have about 1000 published papyri from Soknopaiou Nesos, whereas we have over 4000 from Oxyrhynchus, which was in any case a much more populated place.

3.   This archive was the subject of an unpublished Duke doctoral dissertation by Lori Reed Toepel (1973).

4.   Morris (1981: 63) asserts as his reason for choosing petitions from Oxyrhynchus as a subject for study, 'Petitions have been selected for this investigation because such documents represent occasions on which individuals formally requested the government to intervene in their lives, and in such a request there is the obvious expectation that some benefit will result. Furthermore, such documents reflect individual perceptions of rights and the role of government in their protection.'

this respect the petition shows us the way in which the law has potential for functioning as a means of regulating relations between people in a community rather than between the community and the central government. However, it is unclear whether the average Egyptian could have had any concept of the law when he filed a petition. Indeed, the lack of distinction between law and other jurisdictions as mentioned above becomes apparent when one considers how the process of invoking the law might begin. Any communication of an individual with officialdom, no matter what the jurisdiction, could have begun with a trip to the local record office, where trained scribes could record the person's concern in appropriate language and direct it to the proper official.[1] Thus a petition, which is a recourse to the judicial authority of the state, might emanate in the first instance from the same physical location as a contract for the sale of a house, which belongs to the category of fiscal authority.

The petition to an official for help in settling a local dispute is actually the end of the disputing process rather than the beginning. Legal anthropologists identify seven stages in the disputing process, with adjudication, which involves invoking the law, as the final stage. Other and less formal stages are (in declining order of formality) arbitration, mediation, negotiation, coercion, avoidance and 'lumping it' (Nader and Todd 1978: 9-12). 'Lumping it' describes the situation where one of the aggrieved parties in a dispute decides to ignore the problem, so the dispute ceases without actually having been settled. Avoidance, on the other hand, occurs when one of the parties withdraws from the dispute (by moving away, for example). Coercion involves using force or the threat of force to resolve the conflict. These three aspects of the disputing process involve unilateral action by one party or the other. Negotiation is the term used to describe dispute settlement where the two parties come to an agreement on the subject at issue without the intervention of a third party. Mediation, by contrast, describes a situation where the two disputing parties agree to have a third party help them settle the disagreement. Arbitration also involves the agreed-upon use of a third party, but here the two disputants agree in advance to abide by the decision of the adjudicator,

1. Presumably one could prepare a document without going to the record office, but given the need to do so in Greek legalistic language, it is hard to imagine that in an unhellenized community like Soknopaiou Nesos there could have been many people outside of the record office with the necessary language skills.

and they do not themselves come to a settlement. And finally, where all else fails, adjudication involves the presence of a third party who has the authority to settle the dispute in whatever way he wants, whether or not the two disputants agree to this intervention.

Any one dispute may involve more than one of these methods of settlement, but there is a clear progression from the informal to the formal, with recourse to the law at the pinnacle of the process. Now, when we apply this anthropological construct to the kind of evidence we have from Roman Egypt, it becomes immediately apparent that the petitions which we have do not constitute the disputing process itself, but rather represent the final stages of that process, where all other possible remedies have been exhausted. In the case of the papyri the earlier stages of the disputing process are not for the most part documented, since they are by their very nature informal and not official, whereas papyri, because they are written documents, tend to deal with official matters. This disparity between documentary evidence and social reality would be particularly acute for small villages like Soknopaiou Nesos and Tebtunis, where strong ties of kinship must surely have functioned to maintain social order in ways which would never have been recorded. Among those written records many documents suggest that the strategos or centurion may have interceded to ward off a court case, which fits the categories of arbitration and mediation,[1] but the vast majority of our material relates to the adjudication process. Thus the cases we are looking at are almost all ones with long histories of which we are ignorant. It is probably safe to assume that a person does not file a petition the first time an otherwise friendly neighbour beats him up in a fight. A petition is the last chapter in a story of which we rarely have access to the previous episodes. We must always bear this in mind when considering what petitions tell us about life in Roman Egypt.

Individuals who had a grievance for which they needed outside intervention could petition to several levels of officialdom. Petitions were nearly always formulated in more or less the same way.[2] The

1.   There is a remarkable absence of scholarly writing on the subject of non-legal dispute settlement in Roman Egypt. Modrzejewski (1952) claims to describe the situation for Greco-Roman Egypt, but virtually all of the evidence he cites is Ptolemaic or Byzantine. For the later period we have Schiller 1970 and *idem* 1971, but I know of no comparable work for the Roman period.

2.   For a discussion of the format of a petition, see Thomas 1982: ch. 2. See also

petition begins with the name and title of the official in the dative, followed by παρά and the name of the sender in the genitive, usually identified with the name of his father and his village (for example, Petesouchus son of Apunchis from Soknopaiou Nesos). There follows an account of the grievance, usually a description of someone who has behaved unacceptably. Two words figure very prominently in complaints: βία (violence) and ὕβρις (insolence); most petitions complain of one or the other of these modes of behaviour. After the complaint comes the specification of the action requested from the official to whom the petition is directed, then a farewell (for example διευτύχει) and the signature of the petitioner followed by the date. The same format is followed, with only slight variations, no matter what the official, though there is a tendency to be more obsequious the further up the official is in the hierarchy. The strategos is usually addressed simply as κύριε (sir), but the prefect is 'you, my preserver'.[1]

Various officials are addressed in these petitions, but the bulk are addressed to the strategos,[2] the epistrategos[3] or the prefect.[4] Many Soknopaiou Nesos petitions are addressed to the centurion, a Roman military official who had some policing powers in local communities.

Not infrequently a petitioner wrote substantially the same petition to two different officials at the same time,[5] presumably in a desperate

White 1972.

1.   See, for example, *P. Oxy.* I 38, and (my personal favorite) on one occasion a grammarian who is the public grammaticus of Oxyrhynchus addresses the emperor in the following way: 'Your heavenly magnanimity, which has irradiated your domain, the whole civilized world, and your fellowship with the Muses (for Education sits beside you on the throne) have given me confidence to offer you a just and lawful petition' (*P. Coll. Youtie* II 66, AD 253–260; the translation is the editor's).

2.   On the strategos the most comprehensive work is still that of Hohlwein (1924–25). For prosopographical details see Bastianini 1972; for the Oxyrhynchite nome see Whitehorne 1978; cf. Whitehorne 1981. Witt's unpublished doctoral dissertation (1977) deals only with the judicial function of the strategos, and is a fairly limited study, but useful for the references contained therein.

3.   On the epistrategos the definitive work is that of Thomas (1982).

4.   On the prefect see Humbert 1984 and Foti Talamanca 1974. Prosopographical material has been collected by Reinmuth (1935 and 1967). See also Bastianini 1975 and 1980 and Brunt 1975.

5.   See *SB* I 5238 to the centurion versus *SB* I 5235 to another official, AD 12; *P. Lond.* II 276 to the centurion versus *SB* I 5239 probably to the strategos in AD 15; *BGU* I 165 to the basilikos grammateus and strategos in AD 159-160; *P. Gen.* I

attempt to bring their plight to the attention of *anyone* who might resolve it. The proportional difference between the officials addressed in the three localities under consideration here is probably significant; although all have a strong tendency to direct complaints to the strategos (42 per cent of Soknopaiou Nesos complaints are addressed to the strategos, against 33 per cent for Tebtunis and 36 per cent for Oxyrhynchus), Soknopaiou Nesos on the one hand has many (19 per cent) directed to a decurion or centurion, both military officials with some apparent authority to deal with local disputes,[1] who presumably traveled around more than the prefect and therefore would have been more accessible to people in the outreaches. The Oxyrhynchus group contained only two petitions directed to a centurion, whereas on the other hand 25 per cent of the Oxyrhynchus petitions in this study were addressed to the prefect, while only two Soknopaiou Nesos petitions, both from the same archive, were addressed to the latter official. This suggests that those in the more central locations were more accessible to the machinery of judicial power than those on the periphery. On the fringes, disputes were more likely to be settled by show of strength than by court of law. Additionally, it may be that the mediative powers of the strategos were more effective in settling disputes between neighbours in local communities before matters got to court, whereas the relatively greater impersonality of life in a metropolis made it difficult to bring disputing parties together to reach a settlement.

It is probably significant that almost all of the petitions which make specific reference to laws are those from Oxyrhynchus,[2] and almost all of these are addressed to the prefect; for example, there are several petitions from women asking for appointment of a guardian who invoke the Julian and Titian Law.[3] There are also several references

16 to the centurion versus *SB* I 4284 to the strategos in AD 207; *BGU* I 322 to centurion versus *BGU* I 321 to strategos in AD 216.

1. On the judicial authority of the centurion see Meyer 1920: 281-82; Mitteis 1912: 28-30; Lesquier 1918: 235-57; Davies 1973: 199-200.

2. There is one notable exception to this, and that is a reference in *P. Mil. Vogl.* IV 229, a Tebtunis papyrus of c. AD 140, to a father (with a Greek name) having power over his daughter, a clear allusion to *patria potestas*. I am referring here only to references to specific laws; more general references to legal precedent occur earlier (see, e.g., *P. Oxy.* VI 899, c. AD 200, cited above). On the question of citation of precedents in petitions see Katzoff 1981 and *idem* 1982b.

3. *P. Oxy.* XII 1466 (AD 245); *P. Oxy.* IV 720 (AD 247); *P. Oxy.* XXXIV 2710 (AD 261).

to women acting without a guardian according to the *ius liberorum trium*[1]. In one document (*P. Oxy.* XII 1468, c. AD 258) there is a reference to 'decreed penalties of laws' for misdeeds, and in another (*P. Oxy.* IX 1202, AD 258) a petitioner who applies for succession to an inheritance from his father who has died intestate states that it is 'in accordance with that portion of the edict which grants succession to lawful heirs'. A more general reference to the laws is found in a petition to the strategos (*P. Oxy.* II 284) where the plaintiff complains that he has been nominated to a liturgy 'contrary to all the laws' (cf. *P. Oxy.* VIII 1121, AD 295, addressed to the *beneficiarius*).

This kind of reference[2] is not found in petitions from Tebtunis or Soknopaiou Nesos, though occasionally a villain is described as ἄνομος, 'lawless'. There are several possible explanations for this discrepancy between Oxyrhynchus and the villages. First, it should be noted that the Oxyrhynchus papyri which invoke the law are all later in date than the bulk of evidence from the two villages; indeed, the earliest reference to the law is in an Oxyrhynchus papyrus of AD 245 (*P. Oxy.* XII 1466, cited above), which was almost certainly after Soknopaiou Nesos had ceased to exist. This apparent familiarity with the law may have arisen with the development of jurisprudence itself, which occurred in the third century. Secondly, the petitions would not have been actually formulated by the petitioner himself, but by the scribe in the record office, who knew the proper way to word such documents. In Oxyrhynchus, a metropolis, the scribes would very likely have had a higher level of training than those in the small villages.

Petitions cover a variety of situations where the individual turns to the authority of the state for assistance; some are just simple requests, as for the appointment of a guardian for minor children, or for exemption from a liturgy,[3] but most petitions are seeking assistance in settling a dispute where one party is complaining about the actions of another, and it is this kind of petition which is particularly relevant here. Among our group of 182 petitions, 143 involve disputes.[4] Some

1. *P. Oxy.* XII 1467 (AD 263); *P. Oxy.* XLVI 3302 (AD 300).
2. With the one exception cited above (p. 205 n. 2).
3. *P. Mich.* XIV 675 (Oxyrhynchus AD 241); *P. Oxy.* XVII 2131 (AD 207); *P. Oxy.* XLVI 3286 (AD 222/223); *P. Oxy.* VIII 1119 (AD 254); *P. Oxy.* IX 1204 (AD 299); *SB* VIII 10196 (Tebtunis c. AD 180); *P. Tebt.* II 328 (AD 191/192), *P. Lond.* III 846 (p. 131, Soknopaiou Nesos, AD 140).
4. Even those documents referred to above in which the petitioner seeks

of these are relatively straightforward cases involving debts or property ownership where adjudication is required by a third party, but no transgression of a law is implied. However, the great bulk of petitions are occasioned by unacceptable or abusive behaviour on the part of someone, usually someone known personally to the petitioner.

Two important studies of crime in Egypt, both based on the evidence of these petitions (Baldwin 1963 and Davies 1973), fail to take account of the social context which is presupposed by the petition, and therefore in my view misinterpret the nature of the actions which form the basis for the complaints. One in particular (Baldwin 1963) uses as his point of departure a remark of Seneca (*Epistles* 51.13) about Egyptian criminals (to the effect that it is proverbial to speak of Egyptians as being criminals) and concludes by agreeing with this view of Seneca's, talking about the 'seamy side of life' in Egypt (Baldwin 1963: 262). This approach seems to ignore the fact that the vast majority of petitions are directed against persons whom the complainant *knows by name*. This is not a situation of rampant street muggings by strangers. In any case, of the 182 petitions which form the evidence for this paper, only 74 (41 per cent) are occasioned by what one might call a criminal act (for example, assault, fraud, extortion, misappropriation of property). Of these only 12 involve a 'criminal' act where the perpetrator is unknown and unnamed. A recent article about theft containing a table of all attested complaints of theft in Roman and Byzantine Egypt (Lukaszwicz 1983: 112-19) identifies a total of 96 cases of theft documented in the papyri, of which only 34, about a third, were committed by unknown perpetrators. In the vast majority of cases, the deed has been committed by a personal acquaintance of the complainant, not infrequently a relative. These are not cases involving hardened criminals, as Baldwin's approach implies. These are cases where the normal expectations of civilized behaviour have not been met, and the complainant is unable to resolve the problem by himself without outside intervention. One does not rush to law when a so-called criminal deed has been perpetrated; one complains only where help is needed to restore the lost object or to protect the community from a perceived threat to its security. Furthermore, there is no evidence from the petitions that the complainant was even aware that a law had been violated.

exemption from a liturgy are often formulated as a dispute with the official who has wrongfully assigned the liturgy, e.g., *P. Oxy.* XVII 2131 and *P. Oxy.* IX 1204.

The petitioning process exists on the perimeter of what is essentially a system of self-help rather than a penal system as we know it.[1] This is evidenced in several ways. First of all, note that the complaint is filed by the victim rather than by a police officer.[2] The complaint is not filed on the legal principle of the matter, but because some act of restitution is required—either the return of the stolen property or the restraint of a violent person who cannot otherwise be brought under control. For example, in *P. Oxy.* L 3555 (first/second cent.) Thermouthion petitions to the strategos because her slave had been knocked down by another slave and had her hand mutilated. At the time this happened Thermouthion had not petitioned, but now it seems that her slave's condition has worsened so that she is in danger of her life; the basis of the petition is that Thermouthion is 'a woman helpless and alone', and is dependent on this slave. Thus if this slave dies as the result of the injury, presumably Thermouthion wants to have stated a claim to a replacement at the expense of the accused (or in this case, since the accused is himself a slave, his owner). In other words, Thermouthion is not filing a petition because of the intrinsic injustice of the attack, but out of economic self-interest.

Not infrequently the petition indicates that the victim had attempted to rectify the situation himself before calling for outside help; often it says that he remonstrated with them (λογοποιούμενος πρὸς αὐτούς),[3] but the accused then got violent, thus providing the grounds for the petition. For example, in *P. Oxy. Hels.* 23 (AD 212) the petitioner accuses a camel driver of stealing some equipment. The man threatens him, and thus 'to prevent him carrying out his threats and to protect myself I present this petition'.

Where there has been a robbery in the home of the petitioner

1.   Taubenschlag (1959) discusses the technicalities of when self-help was or was not admissible in Greco-Roman Egypt. He states at the outset (p. 135), 'Selfhelp in the technical sense of the term exists when somebody unilaterally secures or satisfies his real or pretended claim... Selfhelp in this sense is forbidden in Greco-Roman Egypt'. Yet he does not set these technical distinctions into the broader context of social institutions. The petitions clearly reflect a system of self-help in the sense that this term is generally applied to pre-institutionalized societies.

2.   It is this feature of the self-help system which probably explains the paucity of cases of murder attested in the papyri; the victim of this particular crime was hardly in a position to file a petition! On this point see Baldwin 1963: 259.

3.   E.g. *P. Tebt.* II 331 (c. AD 12); *P. Oxy.* XIX 2234 (AD 31); *P. Mich.* V 229 (Tebtunis AD 48); *P. Oxy.* XXXIII 2672 (AD 218); *SB* VI 9458 (late second cent.).

during his or her absence (as is the case in a number of documents), the victim attempts to track down the perpetrator before making an accusation; that is, he is his own detective, though he usually seems to take a local official with him to make a house search. For example, in *P. Mich.* V 230 (Tebtunis, AD 48) Papontos claims that someone came to his house and stole ten wooden beams and a mortar. Investigating the matter with the village police officer, he found five of the beams at the home of a certain Patunis. He remonstrated (λογοποιούμενος) and Patunis committed an act of ὕβρις such that the boy[1] who was on his shoulder (!) fell to the ground and was in danger of his life.[2] The plaintiff then asks that the accused be summoned to the district court. Similarly, in *P. Oxy.* X 1272 (AD 144) a woman has had jewelry stolen while she was away; she suspects a neighbour, so she asks the official to whom she addresses her petition to come for a personal inspection so that the suspect can be brought for inquiry so that she can get her stolen goods back. Note that she asks for nothing more than the simple recovery of her stolen goods.[3]

In other words, it is up to the victim to try to find out who has committed the crime and get an official to summon the accused to court for questioning. It is then up to the victim to provide the evidence which will convict the accused. Although the administrative machinery exists to support the process, the ultimate disposition depends on the ability of the complainant to provide enough evidence to win the case.

It is interesting to note that in a number of documents where the perpetrator's identity is unknown, the petitioner says that he wants to find out who is responsible so that he (the perpetrator) can be held accountable to him (the plaintiff): πρὸς το μένειν μοι τὸν λόγον. It is not so that the perpetrator can be punished by the arm of the law, but so that the victim of the crime can settle his own accounts. This formula is used where an irreparable act of vandalism has occurred, even when the perpetrator is identified, as for example *BGU* I 2

---

1. The ambiguity of the Greek word παῖς is such that we don't know whether this is a slave or his own child.
2. In this case we have also *P. Mich.* V 229, a different petitioner but the same offender also commits an act of ὕβρις such that the victim is in danger of his life.
3. Cf. also *P. Oxy.* XLIX 3467 (AD 98) where someone dug through the wall of a building from the street and stole the petitioner's sheep. He searches and finds them in a temple, and shows this to a village official before filing his petition.

(Soknopaiou Nesos AD 209), where some bullies have dug up the land after the petitioner had seeded it.

The examples given thus far have been those where the theft or injury has been personal, but a number of petitions are collective ones which express a threat to the community as a whole. In *P. Oxy.* XXIV 2410 (AD 120) some villagers complain about a certain Horion who has usurped some of their crown land and prevents them from accessing the village irrigator; they ask for assistance so they can remain in their own place: ἵν ἰσχύσωμεν ἐν τῇ ἰδίᾳ συμμένειν. In *SPP* XXII 49 (AD 201) the state farmers of Soknopaiou Nesos complain that a man from the nearby village of Heraklia has usurped their shore land (which in Soknopaiou Nesos was the majority of the arable public land); similarly *P. Gen.* I 16 and *SB* I 4284 (both AD 207) involve the complaint of the collectivity of public farmers of Soknopaiou Nesos that they have just returned to their land as the result of the edict of Subatianus Aquila, to find Orseus and his brothers cultivating it. Here the appeal is to the self-interest of the government to restore order—because the land is most productive when the peasants remain on their ἴδια[1] and work their allotments. If they are oppressed, they flee, thus deserting the land and also avoiding payment of taxes, a double loss to the government. The concentration of these collective petitions at the beginning of the third century, and all but one from Soknopaiou Nesos, probably reflects the growth of the large estates which gradually absorbed the small peasant communities in the third century.[2]

So far I have focused on those petitions which deal with complaints about abusive behaviour from members of the village community or outsiders to the village community. In these cases the point of law (if we call it such) is a criminal one by our definition: primarily assault causing bodily harm and theft, though, as I have emphasized above, the petitioners never invoke the law, per se, as a frame of reference for their complaint, even if occasionally the behaviour of the assailant is described as lawless.

1.   That is, the place where they were registered for the purpose of the Roman census.

2.   On this phenomenon, see Crawford 1974. In addition to the documents cited in the text, papyri which contain similar collective complaints are *P. Lond.* III 924 (AD 187/188), *BGU* I 2 = *MChr* 113 (AD 209), *BGU* I 23 (second/third cent.). Morris (1981) cites this kind of petition as evidence of a breakdown in relations between the individual and the government after the first century of Roman rule.

However, many petitions arise not from accusations of ὕβρις or βία, but from property disputes among members of the same family, usually arising as the result of an inheritance. Thirty-three petitions from the sample I have looked at involve family disputes.[1] For example, a woman from Soknopaiou Nesos complains that her husband has died and his brother, who is the legal guardian of her children, has sold her husband's property which should have gone to the three children (*BGU* I 98, AD 211); a priest from Soknopaiou Nesos petitions about losing his share of a property of his maternal grandfather inherited by him and his two cousins, one of whom has prevented the complainant from claiming his share (*P. Mich.* III 175, AD 193); a woman from Oxyrhynchus complains that whereas she nursed her mother when she was sick, when the mother died intestate, leaving the petitioner heir 'according to the law', two neighbours in the house of the mother (it was undoubtedly a commonly owned house) carried off all the moveables (*P. Oxy.* VIII 1121, AD 295). Another Oxyrhynchus person complains of having been defrauded by his mother, who was his guardian (*P. Oxy.* VI 898, AD 123). A Soknopaiou Nesos man (*P. Gen.* I 6, AD 146) complains about trying to collect a loan made by his late father to two fellow villagers twelve years previously; one of the debtors has died and the other looks down on him, so he says, either because of his youth or because he is only a camel driver. Marital discord surfaces in this category of domestic disputes. One Tebtunis petitioner (*P. Mich.* V 227, before AD 47) complains on behalf of the daughter of his sister, who has apparently

1.   Documents which involve family disputes: from Oxyrhynchus, *P. Oxy.* II 281 (AD 20–50); *P. Oxy.* II 282 (AD 30–35); *P. Oxy.* II 315 (AD 37); *P. Oxy.* XLIX 3466 (AD 81–96); *P. Oxy.* XXXVIII 2852 (AD 104–105); *P. Oxy.* XLVI 3274 (c. AD 99–117); *P. Oxy.* VI 898 (AD 123); *P. Oxy.* XXXIV 2708 (AD 169); *P. Oxy.* XII 1468 (c. AD 258); *P. Oxy.* IX 1201 (AD 258); *P. Oxy.* VIII 1121 (AD 295); *P. Oxy.* XXXIV 2713 (AD 297); *P. Oxy.* XLVI 3302 (AD 300–301); *P. Oxy.* XLIX 3468 (1); *P. Oxy.* XVII 2133 (late third cent.); from Soknopaiou Nesos, *BGU* I 226 = *MChr* 50 (AD 99); *P. Lond.* II 358 (p. 171) = *MChr* 52 (c. AD 150); *P. Münch.* III 174 (AD 158); *BGU* II 467 (c. AD 177); *SB* VI 8979 (c. AD 180); *P. Amh.* II 78 = *MChr* 123 (AD 184); *P. Lond.* II 342 (p. 173, AD 185); *P. Mich.* III 175 (AD 193); *BGU* I 98 (AD 211); from Tebtunis, *P. Mich.* V 232 (AD 36); *P. Mich.* V 227 (before AD 47); *P. Mil. Vogl.* VI 264 (AD 127); *P. Mil. Vogl.* VI 265 (AD 135); *SB* VI 9314 = *P. Mil. Vogl.* III 129 (AD 135); *P. Mil. Vogl.* TV 229 (c. AD 140); *P. Tebt.* II 334 (AD 200/201); *P. Mil. Vogl.* II 73 (second cent.); *P. Tebt.* II 335 (mid third cent.).

suffered abuse at the hands of her husband. A Tebtunis woman (*P. Tebt.* II 334, AD 200–201) complains that her husband, who received a large dowry of 5000 drachmas from her parents while they were alive, has, now that they have died, made off with everything they had left her. An Oxyrhynchus man (*P. Oxy.* II 282, AD 30–35) complains that his wife has run off taking all his property.

A most complicated domestic tragedy is that of Diogenes of Tebtunis (*P. Mil. Vogl.* IV 229, c. AD 140), married to his sister Herakleia, with a married daughter named Ptolema. Diogenes had a quarrel with his wife, and apparently transferred some of his property to the ownership of his daughter. Ptolema then applied for a divorce from her husband, allegedly so that she would have control over this property. Her father appealed to the strategos to restore his *patria potestas* over his daughter, and she made a counterappeal to the archidikastes. Diogenes appeals to the archidikastes to instruct the strategos to settle the differences between him and his women before the daughter's divorce goes through.

It may be appropriate at this point to summarize the characteristics of these petitions which are instructive for our purposes. First and foremost, petitions appear to be a cry for help from someone who is unable to assert his or her own rights. In this sense the frame of reference is not 'the law', though a violation of some law may be involved, but rather the belief that the rights of the individual, the petitioner, have been violated in some way which needs to be rectified. Implicit here is the notion that one did not go to law on the principle of the matter, but only because it was necessary to do so in order to assert one's rights or claim one's rightful property or even to re-establish one's dignity; in other words, if you could do this for yourself, you didn't make a petition. So, for example, many of the thefts occur when no one is home, and thus the victim does not know how to recover the stolen property. However, where the thief gets caught in the act, the victim seems generally to begin by trying to assert his own rights (λογοποιούμενος), and only files the petition when this attempt at negotiation has failed and resulted in violence to himself rather than in the restitution of the stolen goods.

It is interesting to note in this context how many petitions are filed by women (a total of 39 out of 134 where we can identify the gender of the petitioner, which is 29 per cent overall, of which only 9.8 per cent come from Soknopaiou Nesos, 33 per cent from Tebtunis and 39 per cent from Oxyrhynchus). They were on the one hand significant owners of property through dowry and inheritance (Hobson 1983), and thus would have been a logical target for usurpation and theft, but on the other hand they were more physically defenseless than men.[1] Women seem to have particular difficulties in asserting their rights to commonly inherited property as against the male heirs (see, for example, *P. Oxy.* XXXIV 2713, AD 297).

In general, the object of the petition is nothing more than the restitution of the property or the settlement of the dispute; only occasionally is any more general notion of punishment involved.[2] 'I make this petition to *obtain my right*', τῶν δικαίων τυχεῖν, is the way it is expressed (for example, *P. Oxy.* I 37, AD 49–50).

The substance of the disputes recorded in the extant petitions is very much the same for the three communities under examination, with the exception of the collective petitions, which come almost entirely from Soknopaiou Nesos, the smallest and most vulnerable of the three sites. The trivial nature of many of the complaints suggests the extent to which the natives must have looked to the government to help them regulate their daily lives, and perhaps reflects a faith in authority which does not appear to be justified by the results evidenced in our documents.

When one begins to examine what happened to a petition after it was filed, one is struck forcefully by the improbability of an individual ever actually receiving a satisfactory resolution of his difficulty. The treatment accorded a petition varied according to the level of official to which it was addressed. Those addressed to the strategos fall into three categories of action: (1) either the strategos is asked directly to summon the accused and (implicitly) make a judgement ('summon NN [the accused] and hear me against him/them' is the formula).[3] This is the remedy that is sought when the culprit is

1. Women often assert their helplessness in formulating their petitions, e.g., *P. Oxy.* VIII 1120 (first/second cent.), 'I am a feeble widow'; *P. Oxy.* L 3555, 'I am a woman helpless and alone'; *SB* XIV 11904, 'a woman helpless and widowed'; *BGU* II 522, 'a woman widowed and helpless'.

2. Though of course we would expect to find the details of punishment in the record of a court case, not in the original petition which prompts the case. Nevertheless, the focus of dispute settlement is on restitution rather than punishment.

3. See, e.g., *P. Gen.* I 28; *P. Gen.* I 6; *SB* I 4284; *P. Oxy.* II 282; *P. Oxy.* IX 1204; *P. Oxy.* IX 1202; *P. Oxy.* II 284; *P. Oxy.* L 3561; *P. Oxy. Hels.* 23; *P. Oxy.* XXXVI 2758; *P. Lond.* III 924 (p. 134); *P. Tebt.* II 331; *P. Oxy.* XIX

identifiable, presumably a member of the same community and ready to hand for a court proceeding. The remedy that is sought in these cases is generally restitution of the stolen goods. Where the damage is irreparable, either because the culprit is unknown or because the injury has been physical assault, then (2) the request is made that the petition be filed in the register, ἐν καταχωρισμῷ, so that the villain (if he appears, or repeats his action) will be held accountable to the petitioner, πρὸς το μένειν μοι τὸν λόγον πρὸς τοὺς ἐνκαλουμένους.[1] A third form that petitions to the strategos take is referral for action either upward, to the prefect for the circuit court,[2] or through some local official to get the accused for court proceedings.[3] It should be noted here that the strategos did not have judicial power in his own right, but only as the delegate of the prefect, so his function in the petitions which direct him to summon an accused person for a court proceeding is probably to conduct a preliminary hearing prior to sending the case to the prefect for judgment. Presumably in many cases he was able to effect a resolution at this stage so the case never got any further. In this sense then the strategos acted as an arbitrator rather than a judge.

Petitions to the centurion, of which we have only a handful, follow the same general format as those to the strategos, except that the object tends to be to have the accused summoned for questioning, to explain his actions (for example, *P. Gen.* I 3, *P. Gen.* I 16).[4] Illustrative in this regard is the difference between two Soknopaiou Nesos documents, *BGU* I 321 and 322, two versions of the same petition, one addressed to the strategos (321) and the other to the centurion.

2234; *P. Oxy.* XXXIII 2672.

1.   *BGU* I 321 (theft of grain where culprit has promised to repay but hasn't yet done so), *P. Oxy.* L 3561 (unknown thief), *BGU* I 35 (ox slaughtered by unknown person), *BGU* I 45 (SN man's son has been beaten up by named assailant from neighbouring Herakleia), *BGU* I 12 (named SN men have dug up ground where petitioner has seeded), *P. Tebt.* II 330 (theft in house while occupant was away).

2.   *BGU* I 226; *P. Oxy.* II 283; *P. Mich.* V 226; *P. Oxy.* III 484.

3.   *P. Mich.* V 228 (get elders of Oxyrhynchus to send accused for the coming assizes); *P. Mich.* V 229 (get village police chief of Talei to send accused for coming assizes). Cf. directives from strategos to local officials to do something: *P. Oxy.* XXVII 2473 (instruct keepers of property registers to make appropriate entries), *P. Oxy.* XXXIV 2709 (ask the city clerk to assign a guardian for minor children).

4.   On the competence of the centurion as a police official to receive appeals and bring about a settlement, see Mitteis 1912: 28-30, 33-36 and Meyer 1920: 281-82.

The one addressed to the strategos asks that the petition be filed in the registry so that the accused can be held accountable to the plaintiff (a bureaucratic solution); the version addressed to the centurion ends with the statement 'I flee to you for refuge' and asks that the accused be brought in (presumably for questioning) so that 'with your authority I can get back [the stolen 7 artabs of wheat]' (a practical solution).[1]

As one climbs up the administrative ladder one begins to see how complicated it could be to get action on a complaint. *P. Amh.* II 77 (AD 139) is pretty straightforward; a Soknopaiou Nesos man complains of fraudulent activities on the part of the customs house person and asks the epistrategos to summon the man for an inquiry; similarly in *P. Oxy.* XXXIV 2708 (AD 169) a man is being thrust out of a commonly owned property by his nephew and niece, and asks the epistrategos to assign a judge. However, more commonly the petition up to the epistrategos necessitates a chain of command down to the local level to accomplish the petitioner's objective. For example, a man (*P. Oxy.* IV 487 AD 156) who has been appointed by the grammateus of Oxyrhynchus to act as guardian for some minor children *requests* the epistrategos to *instruct* the strategos to *compel* the grammateus to pick another guardian.[2] In other words, petitions to the epistrategos are not aimed at getting direct action from him, but on having him use his authority to put pressure further down the line to accomplish the objective.[3]

1. Cf. *P. Gen.* I 16 (AD 207) a version to the centurion of the same petition as *SB* I 4284 to the strategos; the version to the strategos asks him to summon the accused and 'hear us against them'; the version to the centurion asks him to summon the accused to him and ask them to give an account to him concerning the charges. This sounds almost like a preliminary hearing, perhaps an attempt to settle the matter out of court using the threat of violence implicit in having a Roman military officer interrogate the accused. The same phraseology about giving an explanation to the centurion is found in *P. Gen.* I 3; *BGU* I 98; *P. Amh.* II 78.

2. Cf. *P. Oxy.* III 488, where the scribe of the komogrammateus has registered the petitioner as having more land than she claims to have, which makes her liable for more taxes than she should pay; she asks the epistrategos to have the strategos see to it that this is corrected. See also *P. Tebt.* II 327 and *P. Oxy.* IV 718.

3. Most petitions to the epistrategos deal with matters relating to the duties of an office. In addition to the documents cited above in the text, cf. also *P. Oxy.* III 718, also concerning unjust assessment for payment of *demosia* on public land (in all of these cases involving erroneous property registrations the accused in the legal format is the local official who made the mistake); *P. Oxy.* III 487, where a man protests being appointed guardian of two children because he is too busy and too much in

Petitions to the prefect fall into a couple of categories. One is in the form of a simple request—to be assigned a guardian for minor children,[1] or permission to leave the country[2] or to return home from Alexandria.[3] These are requests which could have been handled administratively. Disputed issues which must be adjudicated are either referred back to the epistrategos (for example, *P. Oxy.* XLVII 3364) or to the nome strategos for local action (for example, *P. Tebt.* II 326, *P. Oxy.* XLVI 3302).

Very few of the petitions to the prefect ask him to take action directly in the first instance. Most often, however, petitions to the prefect indicate a long process where the petitioner has been shunted from one level of adjudication to another without obtaining the object of his request. *P. Oxy.* XVII 2133 (late third cent.) describes a woman who is having a dispute with her paternal uncle with regard to her share of an inheritance from her father who has died intestate. She says 'I have several times taken legal proceedings against him but he just insults me'. In other words, she appeals to the prefect because the decisions of lower bodies have not had sufficient weight to be enforceable.[4] This shows the difficulty of enforcing legal decisions in a self-help society where there were no workable sanctions applied for non-compliance. Similarly in *P. Oxy.* XLIX 3468 an Oxyrhynchus man petitions against the co-owner of a commonly shared property; he says that he has already petitioned the strategos but the accused has disregarded the official order (that is, to stop claiming possession of the plaintiff's half of the house in dispute) because he (the accused) is βίαιος. The plaintiff asks the prefect to ask the strategos to send for the accused (that is, for trial) 'so that I may obtain my rights from you and be relieved'.

A question that naturally arises when one looks at these petitions is,

---

debt; *SB* VIII 10196, where a petitioner has been chosen by lot for the job of tax collector, but does not have the wherewithal (*poros*) to perform this liturgy; *SPP* XXII 39, a complaint about a sitologos, though we also find complaints of this sort directed to the strategos on occasion: see *P. Oxy.* II 284 and *P. Oxy.* I 285, both complaints against tax collectors, and *P. Oxy.* IX 1204, a petition to the strategos by someone complaining that he has been nominated illegally to a liturgy.

1. *P. Oxy.* IV 720; *P. Oxy.* XXXIV 2710; *P. Oxy.* XII 1466; *P. Oxy.* XXXIV 2711; *P. Oxy.* XII 1467

2. *P. Oxy.* X 1271; *P. Oxy.* XVII 2132.

3. *P. Oxy.* XXXV 2740.

4. Cf. *P. Oxy.* XXXIV 2713, almost the same situation.

was this process an effective way for an individual to gain justice? One is struck in reading through the petitions by how many refer to more than one attempt at securing a successful outcome. Again and again the petitioner describes a process where he or she is referred back and forth between one level and another of the system. This would have been one of the major difficulties in a self-help system; the aggrieved party had to pinpoint the culprit, request a judge, file this request in person at the appropriate office (which might mean traveling for miles to the capital city of the district or even, in the case of petitions to the prefect, to Alexandria), provide the evidence, and at the end of this lengthy process it seems that enforcement depended on the moral authority of the judgment for its efficacy. One Oxyrhynchus woman (*P. Oxy.* VIII 1120, early third cent.) complains that she has filed a petition regarding an act of ὕβρις suffered by her son-in-law at the hands of a named person; but, she says, 'the influence of the perpetrator secured the failure of the petition'. I assume that it is the unlikelihood of success which causes petitioners to tell their story simultaneously to two different levels of the system, for example, the centurion and the strategos.

Of the group of documents I have examined here, at least twenty-one refer to previous levels of adjudication of the case. It is probably significant that only two of these come from Tebtunis and four from Soknopaiou Nesos. The vast majority come from Oxyrhynchus, and the names of the petitioners are mostly (but not all) Greek rather than Egyptian. Does this mean that metropolites are given the run-around more frequently than villagers? On the contrary, I think it indicates that villagers had more difficulty accessing the system, and therefore gave up along the way, their grievances unsatisfied. A Yale papyrus of AD 209 (*P. Yale* I 61) tells us that when the prefect was sitting at the *conventus* in Arsinoe[1] (where he went once a year to review the management of the nome and hear cases that were brought before him), he received 1804 petitions in just over two days. Most of these he would have taken back to Alexandria and responded to over the next few months. The little man who seeks justice because his fellow-villager is ploughing up his seeded earth is not likely to achieve satisfaction before the next planting season, if ever.

The process by which even the simplest justice was obtained was very

---

1. On the prefect's *conventus* in Arsinoe, see Foti Talamanca 1974: I, 31-78, 165-201; Lewis 1981.

cumbersome. An example is an Oxyrhynchus brother and sister petition to the epistrategos (*P. Oxy.* VII 1032, AD 162); they enclose a copy of a prefect's decision rendered in AD 147–48 regarding a small piece of land which they had converted to a vineyard by obtaining a special permit and making a payment to the government. Some necessary formality had been omitted at that time, so nine years afterwards (AD 156–57) the prefect at that time ordered this payment to be made, and the order was communicated to a third sibling, a brother now dead. In AD 161 the government was still after its payment (now 14 years later) so the prefect referred the matter to the dioicetes who sent it to the epistrategos to deal with.

This paper began by posing the question of how imperial law impacted the lives of villagers in rural Egypt. This question has provided a framework for examining the petitions by which individuals could appeal to the governmental judicial system for assistance in solving their problems. The problems brought to light in this way illuminate the values and standards of behaviour of rural society. We see the importance attached to 'civilized' behaviour: violence (βία) and insolence (ὕβρις) are an affront to the safety and dignity of the individual, and as such must be dealt with forcefully to maintain the harmony of the community. Indeed, Demosthenes himself said, in reference to a law against ὕβρις in Athens, that 'nothing is more intolerable in the world than ὕβρις' (21.46).[1] We see the difficulties caused by property ownership, and particularly commonly owned property which devolved to relatives through inheritance. We see the concept of the collective in operation whenever a community speaks out against an outside incursion.

We also see that knowledge of the law is not a prerequisite for appealing to a legal official. There is little evidence from the villages of awareness of particular laws; in this regard it has been pointed out

---

1. On the meaning and importance of ὕβρις in Athenian law, see MacDowell 1976. Although this is a useful philological discussion, it does not address what I believe to be the central point of importance about ὕβρις, namely that it relates to concepts of shame and honour as these affect one's status in a community. ὕβρις is the Greek equivalent of Latin *iniuria*, which clearly involves intended insult to status by the perpetrator. For the supposed legal distinction between ὕβρις and βία, see Taubenschlag 1955: 435-52, although I did not find any clear distinction between these two terms in the papyri I looked at, where the two terms frequently occur in the same text.

that they seem distinctly different from the metropolites, whose petitions contain a number of indications that they were aware of the applicability of specific laws to their cases.[1]

The judicial system, such as it is, is heavily dependent on self-help, as I have shown. Since those who are strongest are best able to help themselves, the weak and defenseless are doubly disadvantaged. Thus the system inevitably must work to reinforce the rights of those who are most powerful. In this sense one might conclude that though the imperial legal system was omnipresent to the little villager, as a source of authority and obligation, it is unlikely to have functioned very effectively as a source of protection and a guarantee of his personal rights.

BIBLIOGRAPHY

Baldwin, B.
　　1963　　'Crime and Criminals in Graeco-Roman Egypt', *Aeg* 43: 256-63.
Bastianini, G.
　　1972　　*Gli strateghi dell'Arsinoites in epoca romana* (Papyrologica Bruxellensia, 11; Brussels: Fondation Egyptologique Reine Elisabeth).
　　1975　　'Lista dei prefetti d'Egitto dal 30a al 299 p', *ZPE* 17: 263-328.
　　1980　　'Lista dei prefetti d'Egitto dal 30a al 299 p, Aggiunte e Correzioni', *ZPE* 38: 75-89.
Bowman, A.K.
　　1976　　'Papyri and Roman Imperial History, 1960–75', *JRS* 86: 163.
　　1986　　*Egypt After the Pharaohs* (London: British Museum Publications).
Brunt, P.A.
　　1975　　'The Administration of Roman Egypt', *JRS* 65: 124-47.
Coles, R.
　　1966　　*Reports of Proceedings in Papyri* (Papyrologica Bruxellensia, 4; Brussels: Fondation Egyptologique Reine Elisabeth).
Crawford, D.
　　1974　　'*Skepe* in Socnopaiou Nesos', *JJP* 18: 169-75.
Davies, R.W.
　　1973　　'The Investigation of Some Crimes in Roman Egypt', *Ancient Society* 4: 199-212.
Davies, W.
　　1985　　'Disputes, their Conduct and their Settlement in the Village Communities of Eastern Brittany in the Ninth Century', *History and*

1.　On this point see also Katzoff 1972, *passim*. The documents cited in this study of legal precedents tend to emanate from a metropolis or from a privileged member of a rural society, rather than from a typical native without special status.

Anthropology 1: 285-312.

Foti Talamanca, G.
1974   Ricerche sul processo nell'Egitto Greco-Romano. I. L'organizzazione del 'conventus' del 'praefectus Aegypti' (Milan: A. Giuffrh).
1979   Ricerche sul processo nell'Egitto Greco-Romano. II. L'introduzione del giudizio 1 (Milan: A. Giuffrh).
1984   Ricerche sul processo nell'Egitto Greco-Romano. II. L'introduzione del giudizio 2 (Naples: A. Giuffrh).

Hobson (Samuel), D.W.
1981   'Greeks and Romans at Socnopaiou Nesos', in R.S. Bagnall (ed.), Proceedings of the XVI International Congress of Papyrology (Chico, CA: Scholars Press): 389-403.
1983   'Women as Property Owners in Roman Egypt', TAPA 113: 311-21.
1988   'Towards a Broader Context for the Study of Greco-Roman Egypt', Echos du Monde Classique/Classical Views 32 NS 7: 353-64.

Hohlwein, N.
1969   Le Stratège du Nome (Papyrologica Bruxellensia, 9; Brussels: Fondation Egyptologique Reine Elisabeth).

Humbert, M.
1984   'La juridiction du Préfet d'Egypte d'Auguste à Dioclétian', in F. Burdeau, N. Charbonnel and M. Humbert (eds.), Aspects de l'Empire Romain (Paris: Presses Universitaires de France): 95-138.

Katzoff, R.
1972   'Precedents in the Courts of Roman Egypt', ZSS 89: 256-92.
1978   'The Validity of Prefectural Edicts in Roman Egypt', in Bar Ilan Studies in History, I (2 vols.; Bar-Ilan: Bar-Ilan University Press): 45-56.
1980   'Sources of the Law in Roman Egypt: The Role of the Prefect', in Aufstieg und Niedergang der Römischen Welt II.13 (Berlin: de Gruyter): 807-44.
1981   'On the Intended Use of P. Col. 123', in R.S. Bagnall (ed.), Proceedings of the XVI International Congress of Papyrology (Chico, CA: Scholars Press): 559-73.
1982a   'Prefecturial Edicts and Letters', ZSS 48: 209-17
1982b   'Responsa Prudentium in Roman Egypt', in Studi in onore di Arnaldo Biscardi, II (Milan): 523-35.

Lesquier, J.
1918   L'armée romaine d'Egypte d'Auguste à Dioclétien (IFAO Mémoires, 41: Cairo: L'institut français d'archéologie orientale du Caire).

Lewis, N.
1981   'The Prefect's Conventus: Proceedings and Procedures', BASP 18.3: 119-30.
1983   Life in Egypt Under Roman Rule (Oxford: Oxford University Press).

Lukaszwicz, A.
1983   'Petition Concerning a Theft: P. Berol. 7306', JJP 19: 107-19.

MacDowell, D.M.
1976   'Hubris in Athens', Greece and Rome 23: 14-31.

Meyer, P.M.

1920   *Juristische Papyri* (Berlin: Weidmann).

Mitteis, L.

1912   *Grundzuge und Chrestomathie der Papyruskunde* (Leipzig: B.G. Teubner).

Modrzejewski, J.

1952   'Private Arbitration in the Law of Greco-Roman Egypt', *JJP* 6: 239-56.

1970   'La règle de droit dans l'Egypte romaine (état des questions et perspectives de recherches)', in D. Samuel (ed.), *Proceedings of the XIIth International Congress of Papyrology, Ann Arbor 1968* (Toronto: A.M. Hakkert): 317-77.

Montevecchi, O.

1973   *La Papirologia* (Turin: Societ' editrice internazionale).

Morris, R.B.

1981   'Reflections of Citizen Attitudes in Petitions from Roman Oxyrhynchus', in R.S. Bagnall (ed.), *Proceedings of the XVI International Congress of Papyrology* (Chico, CA: Scholars Press): 363-70.

Nader, L. and H.F. Todd, Jr (eds.)

1978   *The Disputing Process in Ten Societies* (New York: Columbia University Press).

Reinmuth, O.

1935   *The Prefect of Egypt from August to Diocletian* (Klio Beiheft, 34 NS 21; Leipzig: Dieterich).

1967   'A Working List of the Prefects of Egypt', *BASP* 4: 75-128.

Schiller, A.A.

1970   'The Fate of Imperial Legislation in Late Byzantine Egypt', in J.N. Hazard and W.A.J. Wagner (eds.), *Legal Thought in the United States of America* (Brussels: E. Biuylant): 41-60.

1971   'The Courts Are No More', in *Studi in Onore di Edouardo Volterra*, I (Milan: A. Giuffrh): 469-502.

Taubenschlag, R.

1955   *The Law of Greco-Roman Egypt in the Light of the Papyri, 332 BC to AD 640* (Warsaw: Panstwowe Wydawnictwo Naukowe).

1959   'Selfhelp in Greco-Roman Egypt', in *Opera Minora* (Warsaw: Panstwowe Wydawnictwo Naukowe): 135-42.

Thomas, J.D.

1982   *The Epistrategos in Ptolemaic and Roman Egypt: Part 2, The Roman Epistrategos* (Papyrologica Colonensia, 2; Cologne: Westdeutscher Verlag).

Toeppel, L.R.

1973   'Studies in the Administrative and Economic History of Tebtunis in the First Century AD' (unpublished PhD dissertation, Duke University).

White, J.

1972   *The Form and Structure of the Official Petition* (SBLDS, 5; Missoula, MT: Society of Biblical Literature).

Whitehorne, J.E.G.
    1978   'A Checklist of Oxyrhynchite Strategi', *ZPE* 29: 167-889.
    1981   'The Role of the Strategia in Administrative Continuity in Roman Egypt', in *Proceedings of the XVI International Congress of Papyrology* (Chico, CA: Scholars Press): 419-28.
Witt, P.D.M.
    1977   'The Judicial Function of the Strategos in the Roman Period' (unpublished PhD dissertation, Duke University, Durham, NC).

SLAVERY AND SOCIETY IN LATE ROMAN EGYPT

Roger S. Bagnall

1. *Introduction*

Slavery in Egypt may seem a singularly unpromising choice of subject if one hopes to find anything both new and true. Not only do we have a well-balanced synthesis by Iza Biezunska-Malowist (1974–77), but a host of specialized studies of the material have brought us to the point that Ramsay MacMullen can write, in an article on late Roman slavery, 'Egypt would be almost too richly documented to be treated in a summary paragraph or two, were it not that the numbers and employment of the servile element in the population have been so carefully evaluated already' (MacMullen 1987: 364). Biezunska-Malowist's select bibliography for the Roman period alone includes over 160 items, and Jean Straus, writing four years after the 1977 publication of Biezunska-Malowist's Roman volume, added another 40 or so (Straus 1981).

If one is to add to this pile yet another treatment of slavery, some excuse is needed. And one lies ready to hand. Biezunska-Malowist stopped with the late third century, though she used fourth-century documents occasionally in her treatment of individual questions. And there is no comprehensive treatment of slavery in the Byzantine period at all. On the other hand, MacMullen found no difficulty in discerning a scholarly consensus on the subject.[1] Two examples from the long-standing consensus will suffice. In Johnson and West's standard work on the Byzantine economy of Egypt (Johnson and West 1949: 132-35) we are told that most slaves were household slaves:

---

1.   Given the extensive bibliographic resources in the works of Biezunska-Malowist, Straus and MacMullen cited, I have kept my references to the secondary literature to a minimum.

> Egypt has never been a slave-owning country as that term is generally
> used or in the sense that Italy was in the first century. The dense population
> of Egypt has always provided an abundance of laborers for every need.
> Wages have been so low, owing to this superabundance of labor, that
> there has never been a need for slave labor or any additional profit to be
> obtained from its use.

E.R. Hardy, in his work on large estates, describes the situation in the
Apionic documents of the sixth century (Hardy 1931: 112):

> Slaves do not seem to have been very common, although there were still
> some in great households. Curiously enough several of our references to
> them show them carrying on businesses of their own—a slave of Flavius
> Apion renting a house at Oxyrhynchus [*PSI* 709], a slave of Cyril, tribune
> of Arsinoë, borrowing money from another member of the household
> [*BGU* 725], or a slave of the patrician Athanasius in the Thebaid holding
> a government position [*P. Cair. Masp.* 67166]. The Hermopolis estate
> owned slaves who received food and clothes, but the purposes for which
> they were used are not stated [*P. Bad.* 95].

In short, the main elements of MacMullen's summary of Egypt would
probably find few dissenters—'slaves are perceptibly fewer'. 'As in
earlier centuries, slaves are employed as domestic servants but are
little or never attested in manufacture and agriculture. When we find
large estates in the early or late fourth century with their own bakers
or potters, those resident workers are freeborn' (MacMullen 1987:
365). Apart from Egypt, however, MacMullen argues that late
antiquity saw less change in the numbers and employment of slaves
than has usually been thought, largely on the grounds that they had
never been so numerous or economically important in most areas as
some scholars have claimed.

Now there is a little inconsistency here. On the one hand, we find
that slavery supposedly declined in Egypt in the third century and
later. On the other, we find little change in the employment of slaves.
For the empire as a whole, however, slavery is supposed to have
remained fairly constant in both numbers and uses. Indeed,
MacMullen goes so far as to suppose that 'the number of slaves may
then have remained very nearly on a level, from Augustus to Alaric'
(MacMullen 1987: 376). Now it is not impossible that the Egyptian
trend was very different from that of the rest of the empire, of
course; but we may still be a little uneasy that this should occur precisely when Egypt in so many ways seems to be in a process of
becoming more like the rest of the empire, from the introduction of

councils into Alexandria and the metropoleis of the nomes by Septimius Severus, through Diocletian's unification of the currency and the administrative changes of the early Dominate which made the empire more uniform, to the increased imperial prominence of the Egyptian municipal aristocracy in the fourth and fifth centuries.

There is a still more compelling reason for uneasiness with this synthesis. Numbers and functions of slaves are not totally independent variables. It is difficult to imagine that a decline of, say, a half in the supply of slaves would not radically alter their availability to various classes of society and the uses to which they would put them. Moreover, no reason for the supposed decline in numbers has been offered. It seems to me worthwhile, therefore, to ask on how secure a basis rests the current synthesis. To that I will add an attempt to look again at the structural place of slaves in Egyptian society in late antiquity: not merely what jobs they held, but what role they played in the total fabric of society and economy. This, surely, is what we would really like to know about this institution which occupies such a prominent place in ancient and modern works on Roman law and society.

2. *The Numbers Game*

MacMullen's assertion that slaves were 'perceptibly fewer' from the third century on appears to be based on evidence, since he has just noted that the papyri sometimes preserve sufficient evidence for us to know just how many slaves there were in a particular time and place. What it is in fact based on[1] is an important article of 1973 (Fikhman 1973), in which the Soviet historian of late antiquity I.F. Fikhman drew attention to the radical decline in attestations of slaves in fourth-century and later documents from Oxyrhynchus. With characteristic carefulness, he showed that this drop in evidence is not the result of a smaller overall number of documents. For example, the Roman period up to AD 284 had yielded about 1700 total documents from Oxyrhynchus, of which 117, or about 6.9 per cent, mentioned slaves by name. For the period from the late third century through the seventh century, on the other hand, about 1130 documents name slaves only 60 times, about

---

1.   Apart from a reference to an assertion of Westermann and a brief remark of Marie Drew-Bear (1984: 326), based on one Hermopolite papyrus in which a well-off councillor of that city left 'only' six slaves in his will.

5.3 per cent. The decline is actually steeper than that, however, for most of the late texts seem to refer to a handful of slaves holding important positions in the Apionic estates. For the period from the late third century through the fifth century, the figure is only 2.2 per cent, less than a third of that for the Roman period. Fikhman shows clearly that this is not some Oxyrhynchite peculiarity, and he points out that the virtual disappearance of manumissions and freedmen from the documentation confirms the picture already drawn. He concludes that the diminution in the number of attestations of slaves is not simply a consequence of deficiencies in our documentation, but a reflection of the real situation.

A closer look at the instances of sales of slaves might seem to give strong confirmation to Fikhman's view. There are ten known from the first century, 16 from the second, 23 from the third and only five from the fourth.[1] And of the third-century sales, only three of 23 come from the last quarter. It would be easy to conclude that there were simply not very many slaves being sold and, with Fikhman, that there were simply fewer slaves around, and fewer still involved in production, than in earlier centuries. And yet we ought to be suspicious. One telling detail is that there are only three Ptolemaic slave sales in the Egyptian papyri, one of them from outside Egypt. Are we to suppose that the number of slaves in three centuries of Ptolemaic rule was only 6 per cent of that in three centuries of Roman rule? This can hardly be the case. Slavery was not uncommon in Ptolemaic Egypt, but it generated a documentation which rarely included contracts of sale. The coming of the Romans produces a dramatic rise in such contracts, a rise which peaks in the third century, then declines, so that there are no such contracts from the second half of the fourth century (apart from one concluded outside Egypt but preserved in it), and very few from later centuries.[2]

Here we have a *reductio ad absurdum*. This item of evidence supports Fikhman's conclusion so strongly as to throw it into doubt. We

---

1. See for references to published slave sales *P. Köln* IV 187, introd., supplemented most recently by the fourth-century sale *P. Köln* V 232 (the editor's proposed date of AD 314 is certainly wrong; good possibilities are AD 330, 332, and 337), with references to texts published more recently.

2. For the one contract from AD 350-400, see *BGU* I 316 (Askalon, AD 359). There is an extraordinarily verbose sixth-century example in *Archiv* 3 (AD 1906): 414-24; and for a late declaration of freedom, Wenger 1922.

cannot rationally maintain, faced with the Ptolemaic evidence, that preserved contracts of sale for slaves are a useful index of the presence of slaves in a society. Are we any better off with the other documentation? Our evidence, abundant though it is, has some insidious characteristics. Almost all of it, for one thing, comes from the viewpoint of the propertied classes of the metropoleis of the nomes, telling us little about village life. Most of the documents from the fourth century come from Oxyrhynchus or Hermopolis, fewer from Antinoopolis, Panopolis or Arsinoe, and very few indeed from other cities. These reflect the preoccupations of those who were literate in Greek or could pay scribes who were; transactions petty and large in money or commodities, leases, loans, deliveries, payments; legal complaints and records; the voluminous documentation of tax collection on behalf of the imperial authorities and the management of the finances and services of the towns; private letters.

A papyrological voice may be heard objecting that this description ignores the archives of Arsinoite villages, principally Karanis and Theadelphia. That is only partly true. These archives are rich in documents emanating from the same apparatus and processes at work in the cities, by which the villages sent their taxes in to the cities, by which urban residents lent money or grain to villagers at high interest, and by which villagers tried to move the machinery of the cities to do something on their behalf. In other words, village archives are largely the result of demands and relationships originating from the cities. How much would be left of the archive of Aurelius Isidoros if his liturgical work, tax payments, leases and loans were removed?

Where in this highly archival[1] body of documentation do we expect slaves to turn up? In point of fact, they appear mainly in documents concerned with inheritances, in petitions and court proceedings, and in letters, apart of course from slave sales and manumissions. Slaves did not generally borrow money, lease land, submit petitions, have responsibility for tax collection, pay taxes, buy and sell land, hold official positions, and so forth. It is, of course, possible that some—even many—of the people who appear in various occupations are

---

1. See Bagnall and Worp 1980, 1982 for the character of the documentation of this period. A very high percentage of our Arsinoite texts, for example, come from two large archives plus the Karanis ostraka. The Oxyrhynchite material is very heavily drawn from certain types of official documents. The Hermopolite sources are dominated by a handful of related family archives.

slaves without our being able to detect the fact. If a landowner writes to his phrontistes, his steward, ordering him to deliver ten jars of wine, we do not know the legal status of the steward. It is not irrelevant to the nature of the interchange, perhaps, but it need not be mentioned in an informal note from one to the other. Slaves, in general, tended not to produce documentation except when they were purchased, sold, manumitted, bequeathed, or reported in a census; when they paid taxes or performed compulsory duties, or when they got into some sort of trouble. In a time when census declarations did not include slaves, one born into a family who lived with it throughout life would not generate much paperwork.

To return to Fikhman's numbers, if we subtract slave sales (whose usefulness for this purpose I have challenged above) from the figures, 4.3 per cent of the pre-Diocletianic Oxyrhynchite papyri mention slaves while only 1.6 per cent of those from Diocletian through the fifth century do. The Roman papyri include seven nursing contracts and related texts (a type virtually extinct after Diocletian),[1] four census declarations (practically absent after the third century), ten manumissions and related texts (only three known after AD 284[2]), nine wills (very scarce after AD 300[3]), six epikrisis documents, three death notices (not found after AD 300 [see Brashear 1977: 3-5]), three marriage documents (a genre lacking between Roman times and the sixth century[4]). In all, about 62 per cent of the documents Fikhman lists for the Roman period represent genres which are scarce after Diocletian. Subtracting these and the sales, the remaining quarter amount to only 2.6 per cent of the Oxyrhynchite papyri; the comparable figure for the period after AD 284 is 1.9 per cent. When we remember that the latter figure covers a total of twelve documents, the difference may no longer impress us.

Another approach casts still more doubt on the enterprise. Sales of land from the Roman period totalled 115 when Montevecchi compiled her lists a half-century ago, those from after AD 284, only 35

---

1. One instance after AD 258, out of 40 known: M. Manca Masciadri and O. Montevecchi, *I contratti di baliatico* (*C.Pap.Gr.* 1) (Milan 1984).

2. For example, *P. Oxy.* IX 1205 (AD 291), *P. Mich.* VII 462 (fourth cent.), *P. Edmondstone* (see *BASP* 15 [1978]: 235-36; 355).

3. See Bagnall 1986: 1-2: only 16 of 131 known wills are after AD 300.

4. Except for *P. Ross. Georg.* III 28, a remarkable piece which I cannot discuss here.

(Montevecchi 1943: 12-19). Sales of building property were 105 for the Roman period, 34 later (Montevecchi 1941: 94-98). If these figures are computed as percentages of the total Oxyrhynchite documents as enumerated by Fikhman, sales of land are 6.8 per cent of the Roman total, those of buildings 6.2 per cent. For the Byzantine period, on the other hand, the comparable figures are 3.1 and 3.0 per cent. Now, more sales have been published since, and the figure is based on all provenances, not just Oxyrhynchus. But I do not think that matters for our purposes. What is clear is that documents recording sales of all sorts decline as a proportionate part of the documentation after AD 284.

This investigation is a bit crude and could certainly be refined. But I think it suffices to show that the numerous and profound changes in the nature of the surviving documentation for the second half of the third century are sufficient to account for the entirety of the decline of our documentation of slaves in the papyri. To what extent those changes in documentation reflect simply the archives we happen to have for the fourth century, or rather embody more profound alterations in the whole structure by which social relations and status were recorded, I cannot go into here. At all events, I believe the numbers game must be abandoned for this subject. There is no reliable basis for any claims about the relative abundance of slaves in Roman and Byzantine Egypt.

We have little information about how people became slaves in this period. A few were acquired abroad;[1] most were no doubt born slaves, and there are explicit attestations of such origin.[2] A slave of a military officer describes himself as *threptos*, exposed and rescued, brought up by the owner (*P. Abinn.* 36). It was also possible to fall into slavery through debt. For example, one letter complains that the addressee has taken the writer's money in order to get him released but has failed to do so. 'Now then [he says], do not neglect this, master, for God's sake; for you have already given my children as securities to the money-lender on account of the gold' (*P. Herm.* 7). In another

---

1. *BGU* I 316 (Askalon, AD 359) is the best known; but the power of attorney in *P. Oxy.* XXXVI 2771 (AD 323), whereby a husband in Cos is authorized to sell a slave on behalf of his wife, presumably travelled with the slave to Oxyrhynchos as part of the title papers.

2. For example *P. Lips.* 26 specifies that two of the four slaves are house-born; the origin of the other two is not specified.

letter, the writer recounts (to his wife) his seizure in Alexandria by a creditor; since he has nothing to pay him with, he asks her to put their little *paidion* Artemidoros in hypothec and send him the proceeds (*P. Amh.* II 144 [fifth century, no provenance]). One supposes that the luckless Artemidoros is already a slave and not their child, but the seizure of the writer himself suggests that the insolvent could wind up in indefinite bondage.[1]

Roman society, as we know, contained plenty of people whose exact status may have been unclear to those around them, as well as those who moved from free to slave and slave to free. We have two graphic illustrations of the difficulties which could ensue. A papyrus from Hermopolis reports proceedings about the status of one Patricius, evidently because his owner had sold him and the purchaser wanted to register the sale. The slave himself is asked if he is free or slave; he answers that he is a slave. He then answers questions about where he was bought, from whom, who his mother was, what her status was (slave), whether he has siblings (one, a slave); and on the basis of all this the registrars agree to register the sale, but at the purchaser's risk if the facts turn out to be wrong (*P. Herm.* 18 [323p?]).

The reverse case is found in a petition to the prefect, in which the complainant alleges that his wife and children were carried off by another couple (one member of which seems to be a prytanis), on the grounds that they were their slaves. The petitioner claims that his wife is of free descent and married to him, and that her brothers are free; he claims that her parents were also free. The case was probably not quite so clear, we may think, but it is striking just how much one might have to prove simply in order not to be enslaved.[2]

3. *Rural Slavery*

In saying that 'in the second and third centuries, the work of slaves did not play an important role in Egyptian agriculture', Biezunska-Malowist was not denying its existence, for she goes on to say that 'it is essential to point out its existence, even if only in a minimal amount, in the Roman period' (Biezunska-Malowist 1977: 83). She proceeded to enumerate a number of items of evidence, concluding

1. Another example of creditors seizing children occurs in *P. Lond.* VI 1915 (c. AD 330-340).
2. *P. Grenf.* II 78 (Great Oasis, 307, cf. Bagnall and Worp 1979: 31).

that it is impossible to evaluate their significance. This seems to me unnecessarily pessimistic, even if statistically true. Let us look at what there is. An Oxyrhynchus papyrus (*P. Oxy.* XIV 1638 [282]) preserves a division of the inheritance from one Psenamounis, who lived in a village in the western toparchy of the Oxyrhynchite nome, among the members of his two families by different wives. The estate was divided among seven people; the older family of two got a house, $3\frac{1}{2}$ arouras of grainland, and $\frac{2}{7}$ share of four slaves; the remaining five got the rest of the property and a $\frac{5}{7}$ share of the slaves. Of the slaves, one is apparently male, one undescribed, one an adult female aged 25 and one a child, her daughter aged ten. There is no sign of any actual assignment of slaves, merely division of ownership of the entire group. A family of moderate means thus owned four slaves. Unfortunately, the total amount of land owned by Psenamounis is not mentioned, but the older family's allotment of $3\frac{1}{2}$ arouras suggests a very modest total estate, perhaps no more than ten or fifteen arouras.

From the well-known archive of Aurelius Isidoros from Karanis, there is evidence that the wife of Aurelius Isidoros's brother Heras, one Taesis, owned slaves. Her paternal inheritance, shared with her sister Kyrillous, included 61 sheep, 40 goats, one grinding mill, six talents of silver, two artabas of wheat, and two slaves (*P. Cair. Isid.* 64 [c. AD 298]). It also included land. Each sister seems to have inherited about ten or eleven arouras of grainbearing land, for a paternal total of about 22 arouras; this is a very middle-range holding for a villager of moderate means.[1] About the slave holdings of the central figure of the archive, Aurelius Isidoros himself, we know nothing; since his and his siblings' landholdings far exceeded those of Taesis and Kyrillous, it seems hard to suppose that they did not include slaves. The one census declaration by Isidoros preserved (*P. Cair. Isid.* 8 [AD 309]), states that the household consists only of himself and his son. Similarly, in the census declaration of Sakaon, the central figure of the Theadelphian archives of this period, there are eight free persons and no slaves mentioned (*P. Sakaon* 1 [AD 310]). Sakaon was moderately prosperous by the standards of his village, but the village was in very rocky shape. Unfortunately, we do not know whether

---

1.   The evidence for landholdings is found in or deduced from *P. Cair. Isid.* 6 and 9, using the methods of analysis from Bagnall 1977: 330-31 n. 1. For the landholdings of village liturgists, who are the more prosperous part of village society, see Bagnall 1978: 16; 22 arouras is a very decent holding.

slaves were required to be listed. Sakaon's return contains eight men and no women. Was this really such a bachelor establishment, even though four of the eight men were over twenty? It seems very unlikely. It appears, in other words, as if these declarations of persons simply include only free males. It is hard to test this generalization; these are the only two declarations of persons known for the entire period from AD 275–450.

Yet another small household with a few slaves is attested in a Hermopolite document (*P. Lips.* 26) of the early fourth century, in which two brothers divide up four slaves in their inheritance. Two are farmers, one a weaver and one a donkey driver. It seems likely that these slaves were part of the rural estate of the two brothers. Another Isidoros papyrus (*P. Cair. Isid.* 141) mentions the role of the female slave of another villager in carrying out a criminal raid.

In sum, the character of the evidence for slaves belonging to village families of moderate means suggests that ownership of a small number of slaves—one to four—was not remarkable. The economic importance of slavery in such households was perhaps not so marginal as has been thought by almost everyone. On a small family farm, say 10 to 25 arouras, the presence of even one able-bodied adult agricultural worker alongside the family is not a trivial advantage. A farmer without a number of sons or other suitable male relatives would find it hard to work his farm himself without help. The effects of such rural slaves, therefore, though made up of very small units, may have been pervasive and decisive in the structure of the working of the land.

That is not to say it was universal. The poorer families, with barely enough land to support themselves, would not have been able to afford a slave. The average slave represented a capital of perhaps 20 to 30 artabas of wheat; to own two such might be likened to having a year's income in human capital. And those metropolitan, absentee landowners who had small amounts of land or had it widely scattered normally leased it out to villagers; slaves probably had no role in the working of this land, either.[1]

We are, then, far from any statistical appreciation of the phenomenon—we do not even know what portion of independent

---

1. See the distribution of ownership in the Hermopolite land registers, as analyzed by Bowman 1985, with table on 158-59. 62% of the landowners listed (in Hermopolis and Antinoopolis combined) held fewer than 20 arouras in the countryside.

landowners had more than ten arouras, after all—but in qualitative terms the importance to this class of increasing by perhaps 50 or 100 per cent the available labor force was significant. Since this is the class which provided the villages with their rotating public officials of all kinds, it needed some means of freeing up time for these uncompensated duties. That precisely these men owned slaves can hardly be surprising. In terms of the economy and structure of the villages, then, the role of even a small number of slaves may well have been critical.[1]

There is still the question of slavery on larger estates to be considered. Large estates in the fourth century are of all will-o'-the-wisps the most elusive. As Bowman's study of the Hermopolite land registers has shown, the larger the landholdings of an individual, the greater the likelihood that they are spread over the nome rather than consolidated (Bowman 1985: 154-55). Great landowners certainly had a substantial number of staff, with stewards in charge, and there is abundant evidence for a constant flow of orders, information and goods between estates and the master or mistress in the city. But we normally know only the function, not the legal status, of the employees involved in these interchanges.[2]

The one item of useful evidence for slavery in the management of large agglomerations is the long account of income and expenditures in wheat and various other commodities coming from an estate centered on Hermonthis and dated to the first four months of AD 338 (*P. Lips.* 97).[3] Payments of wheat for salary, or at least subsistence, are made on a monthly or bimonthly basis to various groups of workers, whose numbers vary from month to month. Prominent are *organitai*, opera-

1.   It is true that some tasks in the agricultural year fell at times when official duties were probably light; but at harvest time the pressure may have been considerable.

2.   There are occasional indications, apart from *P. Lips.* 97, to be discussed below, of rations paid to slaves; see *P. Haun.* III 68 (AD 402) and *BGU* I 34; cf. *P. Charite* 36 for a discussion of date and purpose, along with re-edition of a small part of it. *SPP* XX 106, an account of payments by or for *paidaria* for contributions to the *vestis militaris* for the 14th indiction, seems to agree with this view also; it lists *paidaria* who are butcher, brickmaker and pastry-cook. The date seems likely to be AD 355–56 or later.

3.   *P. Lond.* I 125 (p. 192), which is to be dated to July, AD 336, seems to pertain to the same places and probably the same entity. It is interesting that the Leipzig roll has an extensive text of Psalms 30–55 on the back, while the London one has a magical text.

tors of irrigation machinery, of whom 21 are paid in Pharmouthi; staff for animal care (cowherds, shepherds, donkey rearers), who number 18; transport workers (wagoneers, donkey drivers, camel drivers), totalling 11 at the peak; and gardeners, 14. But there are also some more undifferentiated groups: 20 *ergatai*, laborers; four *boethoi*, assistants; and 15 *paidaria*, slaves. Occasionally some specific information is given about one of these: one *ergates* is identified as a *hypoboukolos*, sub-cowherd, and one slave is a breadmaker, another a weaver (*tarsikarios*). Most have no particular occupational identity. The identification of the *paidaria* as slaves seems to me certain. Not only does the term always seem to mean this in the papyri of this period, but none of the people in question, with one exception, appears anywhere else in the long account in another capacity. Moreover, that one exception, with the nice slave name of Philokyrios, master-loving,[1] appears in another place with his name adjacent to that of a *doule*, a female slave.

It would be easier to interpret this information if we knew to whom belonged the substantial properties connected with this account. The amounts are not small: wheat expenditures total almost 2200 artabas in the four months; annually that would come to 6600 artabas, the income perhaps on 1500-2000 arouras, in line with the largest holdings found in the Hermopolite registers. The editor, Mitteis, argued that the estates could not belong to an individual; he preferred to think of them as held by a temple. For reasons I cannot go into in detail here, this view seems to me impossible, and Mitteis's arguments against individual ownership are devoid of substance.[2] If this is correct, what

1. Hardly found otherwise in the papyri, cf. *NB* and *Onomasticon*. Solin 1982: II, 752, lists a fair number at Rome, none of them demonstrably free-born.

2. Mitteis pointed out that the addressees of the account were *apo epitropon*, which he thought lent an official cast to things. But the term means that they are retired, and the Hermopolite registers are sprinkled with such terms, which simply identify the persons by their status. Nor does the appearance of a couple of priests, *hiereis*, among the people with whom business is transacted (one of them as agent for the owners, it seems) mean much. Priests owned or leased land and engaged in normal economic transactions like other people. The term *ousia* (v. 12) does not help much, either, as it may have a completely nontechnical meaning here. The term *phoros* can mean either rent or taxes and is thus unhelpful. An official government account would not be organized in this fashion, and there is no evidence for temples having large properties of this sort in the fourth century. In fact, it is well known that temple estates were confiscated by Augustus three and a half centuries earlier.

conclusions can be drawn about slavery in this context? The landholdings in question are distributed over several villages, and indeed in this pre-harvest season we have little evidence for the full extent of the property. Rather than think of an 'estate', we should perhaps think of the 'great house' which owned numerous properties and employed these people. But the conditions under which it employed them are obscure. The one obvious conclusion is that slaves coexisted with free labor in the pool of undifferentiated staff; those perhaps who filled multiple roles or who belonged to specialties whose members were not numerous enough to warrant their own heading in the account. The main groups of livestock and agricultural workers, however, were not slaves but free. Slaves make up about 15 per cent of the payroll in this particular establishment. I must emphasize that we cannot even be sure that these slaves were located in the countryside. The account could well have been drawn up at the urban headquarters of the great house, not at any of the rural locations mentioned, and the slaves could mainly have been located in the same place. The predominantly rural character of the free employees may speak against this possibility, but it does not quite exclude it.

In sum, rather than think about large estates and the role of slave labor on them, we will do better to think about great houses and their integrated operations, city and country. We are in no position to discern the pattern of these in general terms, but so far as slavery goes, we can see a significant slave component to the staff, but not any demonstrable role in agriculture or livestock raising themselves.

4. *Slaves in Urban Households*

Fikhman is undoubtedly right that little of the evidence for urban slaves shows any trace of their employment in craft production. The *tarsikarios* in the Hermonthis account, if he is in the city, is an exception. We do have one instance in which slaves—three Phoenician women—left behind for safekeeping by their owner with a brother were put out to work with an innkeeper until they could be taken upriver to Panopolis.[1] But they were doing it in Alexandria, after all,

---

Overall, the accounts impress one as highly similar to other accounts of wealthy landowners in Roman Egypt, not to official accounting.

1. *P. XV Congr.* 22 (Panopolis, earlier part of fourth century), a part of the archives of Ammon. Cf. also *SB* XIV 11929 for Harpocration's slaves.

not Panopolis. On the occupational front, it may also be worth mentioning that we have a bit of evidence for freedmen's work in a Karanis papyrus of the early fourth century, in which a freedman agrees to work in a workshop belonging to another person for a period of five months at a specified salary, part of which he receives in advance. We do not, unfortunately, know what kind of workshop.[1]

What we would call economic activities, however, play a small role in our documentation. Instead, the slaves we find are almost all household slaves or personal assistants for their master's business dealings. It is therefore hardly surprising that most of our evidence for urban slaves is connected with owners belonging to the upper stratum of society: members of the bouleutic class, the military, and the imperial civil service. The use of slaves in households for domestic purposes, with their number in proportion to the grandeur of the household, is so universal a fact of life in the Roman world as to need no comment.[2] The slave as confidential personal agent of the master in business dealings is also a common phenomenon;[3] it has been observed that the master's complete control over the slave and ability to torture him made slaves far more suitable than free persons for such positions. Even though production was hardly affected at all by slave labor, then, the importance of slave assistance for the ability of a small elite to manage business, civic, and military affairs should not be underrated.[4] The urban elite was as dependent as the village elite on the use of slaves as support for their own activities.

It is, however, at the social level that the effects of slavery are more determinative for the character of life. First, we do not get a very

1. *P. Mich.* IX 574. The salary is specified as 500 per day, with the unit being lost. But the advance payment total is given in myriads, which must be denarii. The editor has argued that they are drachmas, on the completely specious grounds that 'a daily wage of 500 drachmas is a reasonable figure'. Reasonable when? A monthly wage of 10 talents would be perfectly 'reasonable' around AD 325, when we find 8 talents per month paid to a *boethos* in *SB* XIV 11592.

2. Some examples from the papyri: *P. Ross. Georg.* III 9 = Naldini 77 (house servants in Memphis receiving goods); *P. Stras.* IV 296 (Hermopolis); *P. Oxy.* VI 903 (both members of a couple own slaves in the house).

3. Some examples from the papyri: *P. Oxy.* XLIII 3146 (AD 347); *pais* is surely 'slave' here; a business transaction; *P. Oxy.* XLIX 3480 (c. 360-390; the staff of a tax collector); *P. Abinn.* 36 (general agent of a *praepositus*).

4. Even so minor a testimony as the slave of a *praepositus* in *O. Bodl.* 2152 helps show such usage.

favorable impression of master–slave relations. Slaves ran away when they could,[1] even those working for important people in what were probably responsible posts, like Magnus, a slave of an *officialis* in the office of the prefect of Egypt, who fled to Hermopolis. His owner gave another *officialis* an authorization to arrest Magnus and bring him back.[2] An Oxyrhynchite, who had won many prizes and high rank as an athlete and had consequently been awarded Athenian citizenship, had a slave run away to Alexandria; he authorizes his representative to imprison the slave, accuse him, beat him, pursue those harboring him, and bring him back (*P. Oxy.* XIV 1643, 298). The correspondence of a nome strategos in the Panopolis rolls in the Chester Beatty collection includes an acknowledgment of instructions from the *magister rei privatae* to send up to him an absconding slave (*P. Panop. Beatty* 1.149 [Panopolis, 298]). A letter from a slave of Abinnaeus to his master remarks, 'I am again your slave and don't secede from you as I did before' (*P. Abinn.* 36).

If slaves did not run away, they tried to get their freedom. We have few manumissions and few freedmen attested, as I have noted already, but the nature of the human relationships involved is made clear by an Oxyrhynchus papyrus from the early fourth century. A female petitioner alleges that some slaves came to her and to her brother Eustochios by inheritance from their parents, and that they owned them jointly and equally. Without effecting any written division of ownership, they divided them in practice (evidently two for each).[3] The two slaves of her brother have persuaded him to manumit them, along with their child, but without the petitioner's consent. She objects and asks that the slaves be prevented from escaping the bonds of slavery.[4] Legally speaking she was probably correct, but it is obvious that her brother behaved as if there had been a division of the property, leaving him free to do as he pleased with his slaves. Another Oxyrhynchite petition concerns a jointly owned slave (the petitioner's sister is the other owner) who, since the death of their parents, has

---

1. See for the general problem Daube 1952.
2. *P. Oxy.* XII 1423 (mid to late fourth cent., according to the editor).
3. Where there was only one slave in an estate, presumably some sort of time-sharing arrangement was necessary; but our evidence mostly concerns families with multiple slaves, where a de facto division seems to have occurred.
4. *PSI* V 452. Biezunska-Malowist 1977: 125 n. 78, thinks that there were originally four slaves, two of whom had a child after the division.

paid them an *apophora*; but now he refuses to pay it. It appears, despite the petitioner's terminology, that the slave had been manumitted by the father in his will, and that *apophora* is his due to them as patrons of a freedman. The owner's attitude—and perhaps the reality of being a freedman—is made clear enough by her request that the former slave be compelled to pay the *apophora* and remain in their service (*P. Oxy. Hels.* 26 [AD 296]).

Those who remained in slavery and did not manage to run away or be manumitted seem often not to have behaved as their owners would like. The Roman law of slavery takes cognizance of theft by slaves, regarding the tendency as a vice which could be warranted against, and we find confirmation in a complaint by a member of the council of Hermopolis that his slave has been 'kidnapped'—corrupted, it sounds like—by another person. Last night, we are told, the slave opened the door of the house while he was asleep and stole some of his goods. He caught the slave with the goods in the house of the other man. He asks to recover his property; curiously enough, he does not ask specifically for any punishment for the corrupter (*P. Stras.* IV 296 [AD 326]). In an affidavit of a wife against her husband, the ultimate insult on his part in household matters is that he trusts his slaves with his keys but will not let his wife have them (*P. Oxy.* VI 903). This affidavit, moreover, gives a dismal picture of the state of the whole household. 'He shut up his own slaves and mine with my foster daughters and his superintendent and son for seven whole days in his cellars, having insulted his slaves and my slave Zoe and half killed them with blows, and he applied fire to my foster-daughters, having stripped them quite naked, which is contrary to the laws.' Later on, he ordered his wife to send her slave Anilla away. Slaves, in short, could not be trusted.

Moreover, slaves talked back to their owners, and to other free persons. The writer of a rather obscurely written Christian letter complains to the recipient that he has been unable to bear the constant *hybreis*, outrageous remarks, of the addressee's *oiketes* Agathos.[1] A petition preserves the complaint of one Sarapion about the female slave of Melas the silversmith; the slave had come to his house the day before and inflicted *hybreis* on his wife and virgin daughter in a way contrary to the laws and to their station in life. He requests that she be

---

1.   *P. Select.* 18 = Naldini 81 (provenance unknown; Bingen, *Cd'E* 41 [1966] 191 suggests the Hermopolite; IV century).

punished for what she shouted at them.[1] Ulpian tells us that the praetor's edict expressly provides the grounds for these complaints: 'One who is said to have loudly shouted at someone contrary to sound morals (*adversus bonos mores*) or one through whose efforts such shouting is effected contrary to sound morals, against him I will give an action'.[2] That particular remark has to do with the shouting of crowds, but individual acts are also punished if said for the sake of insulting someone. The jurists quoted in the Digest make it quite clear that the relative status of the parties involved was part of what defined how contumelious such remarks were, and the petitioners I have mentioned make it clear that their station in life makes such insults particularly reprehensible. That a slave's insults of a free person were punishable hardly needed to be said, indeed; the jurists were more concerned to deal with the less obvious cases, as where a slave insults another slave—and thus is taken to have insulted the other slave's master (*D.* 47.18.1).

With this matter we have passed from relations of slaves with their own masters to those of slaves with other free persons. It appears in general that though slaves provided much of life's comforts to the slave-owning class, they were also the cause of much of its trouble and even its danger.[3] Apart from insults and theft from their masters, slaves appear to have been sources of violence for others. This is true most obviously when they beat someone on their master's behalf, as someone complains happened to him at the hands of a tax collector and his slaves (*P. Oxy.* XLIX 3480). But we also find complaints such as that to the police magistrates at Oxyrhynchus by a man whose wife was attacked in their house during the evening hours by one Tapesis and the latter's slave Victoria; it seems (the text is fragmentary) that a theft of gold was also involved. He asks that a midwife be sent to check his wife, who was thus evidently pregnant, and that the culprits provide guarantees in the event anything happens to her (*P. Oxy.* LI 3620 [AD 326]).

The prize document of this sort, however, is *P. Lips.* 40, a

---

1. *P. Lond.* III 983 (p. 229; no provenance or date). The discussion makes it clear that *hybreis* here (and elsewhere) means verbal, rather than physical, attacks.

2. *D.* 47.15.2, from *ad edictum* 77. The entirety of Book 47 of the Digest is devoted to contumelious action.

3. Conversely, of course, one might use slaves to protect oneself from such dangers.

Hermopolite report of proceedings before the governor of the Thebaid from the late fourth century or early fifth century. The accuser, one Philammon, reports that his son had been attacked, beaten to within an inch of his life, and robbed of a substantial sum in public funds which he was carrying (10-12 gold solidi), by a party of four slaves. Philammon says that one of them held the victim's hands, one knocked him to the ground, and the other two beat and robbed him. Only two slaves are in court, Acholius and a young boy. Acholius claims that the supposed victim actually attacked them; that there were only two of them until a third joined them after the incident was over. Acholius is tortured but sticks to his story. His master, Sergius, was and is out of town. A neighbor who came out, with his own slaves, when he heard the noise of the scuffle, says that there were two or three of them, thus incidentally supporting the story of the defendants more than that of the plaintiff, though he seems to imply that the slaves were the aggressors. Since the neighbor happens to be the highest-ranking official in town, the *logistes*, his testimony carries some weight.

All of these accounts convey an impression of town life as involving for the upper class significant risks, not merely of verbal abuse but also of theft by their own slaves who were suborned by others, of assaults by free persons assisted by slaves, and of physical violence in the streets at the hands of unsupervised slaves. Like all crime reports, this one no doubt gives such incidents more prominence than they occupy in normal daily life, but their contribution to the tone of urban existence is nonetheless unmistakable.

The society of later Roman Egypt was hardly unique, in antiquity or otherwise, in having a high concentration of wealth and a large degree of dependency of part of the population upon a rich elite. It has often been claimed that this concentration was growing, but so far the evidence stubbornly resists all attempts to make it show that it was (cf. Bowman 1985: 155). It was not only the very top elite in society which relied on a social structure in which some were relatively free and others relatively not. Plenty of farmers of modest means had a few slaves, as we have seen. The wealthy of the towns had more slaves and perhaps depended on them less for their economic survival. In fact, they had dependent tenant farmers of ostensibly free status to work their lands and provide them with their income in rent. Slavery is only one aspect of this pervasive set of relationships of power. If it was declining in importance in the face of other such relationships in the fourth century—and I am not yet persuaded that this was the case—it had lost nothing of its character, either as a part of the rural and urban economy, or as a necessity for the public lives of the elites, or as a kind of human relationship.[1] MacMullen denies that the Roman world was a 'slave-owning society', on the grounds that slaves played a very small role in agricultural production. But that standard is excessively narrow in focus. Having slaves set the tone of existence; and the human face of slavery in the fourth-century papyri is on the whole an ugly one.[2]

1.   This paper has perforce looked at slavery from the point of view of the slave in society—an owner's point of view, for the most part. Bradley 1984 offers an attempt to look at the mechanisms of control from the slave's point of view.

2.   An earlier version of this paper was presented to the Israel Society for the Promotion of Classical Studies, meeting at Bar-Ilan University in May, 1986. I am grateful to Ranon Katzoff for the invitation to speak on that occasion.

BIBLIOGRAPHY

Bagnall, R. S.
1977   'Bullion Purchases and Landholding in the Fourth Century', *Cd'E* 52:
            322-36.
1978   'Property-holdings of Liturgists in Fourth-Century Karanis', *BASP*
            15: 9-16.
1986   'Two Byzantine Legal Papyri in a Private Collection', in *Studies in
            Roman Law in Memory of A. Arthur Schiller* (CSCT, 13; Leiden: Brill):
            1-9.
Bagnall, R.S., and K.A. Worp
1980   'Papyrus Documentation in Egypt from Constantine to Justinian', in
            R. Pintaudi (ed.), *Miscellanea Papyrologica* (Pap.Flor.,7; Florence:
            Gonnelli): 105–16.
1982   'Papyrus Documentation in the Period of Diocletian and Constantine',
            BES 4: 25-33.
Biezunska-Malowist, I.
1974-77   *L'esclavage dans l'Égypte gréco-romaine* (2 vols.; Wroclaw: Polska
            Akademia Nauk).
Bowman, A. K.
1985   'Landholding in the Hermopolite Nome in the Fourth Century AD',
            JRS 75: 137-63.
Bradley, K.R.
1984   *Slaves and Masters in the Roman Empire* (Collection Latomus, 185;
            Brussels: Latomus).
Brashear, W.
1977   '*P.Sorb.Inv.* 2358 and the New Statistics on Death Certificates', *BASP*
            14: 1-10.
Daube, D.
1952   'Slave-Catching', *Juridical Review* 64: 12-28.
Drew-Bear, M.
1984   'Les conseillers municipaux des métropoles au IIIe siècle après J.-C.',
            Cd'E 59: 315-32.
Fikhman, I.F.
1973   'Sklaven und Sklavenarbeit im Spätrömischen Oxyrhynchus',
            Jahrbuch für Wirtschaftsgeschichte II; 149-206.
Hardy, E.R.
1931   *The Large Estates of Byzantine Egypt* (New York: Columbia University
            Press).
Johnson, A.C., and L.C. West
1949   *Byzantine Egypt: Economic Studies* (Princeton University Studies in
            Papyrology, 6; Princeton: Princeton University Press).
MacMullen, R.
1987   'Late Roman Slavery', *Historia* 36: 359-82.
Montevecchi, O.
1941   'Ricerche di sociologia nei documenti dell'Egitto greco-romano III: I
            contratti di compravendita', *Aeg* 21: 93-151.

1943   'Ricerche di sociologia nei documenti dell'Egitto greco-romano III: I contratti di compravendita', *Aeg* 23: 11-89.

Solin, H.

1982   *Die Griechische Eigennamen in Rom: Ein Namenbuch* (3 vols.; Berlin: de Gruyter).

Straus, J.A.

1981   'Remarques sur l'esclavage dans l'Egypte romaine', *Anagennesis* 1: 125-28.

Wenger, L.

1922   'Ein christliches Freiheitszeugnis in den ägyptischen Papyri', in *Beiträge zur Geschichte des christlichen Altertums und der Byzantinischen Literatur: Festgabe Albert Ehrhard* (Bonn: Kurt Schroeder Verlag): 451-78.

PALESTINE AND JUSTINIAN'S LEGISLATION ON NON-CHRISTIAN RELIGIONS

Patrick T.R. Gray

How was legislation generated in the age of Justinian? The fact that, in Byzantium, all power to legislate was administratively invested in the emperor does not justify the conclusion that the emperor had therefore the de facto ability to impose legislation arbitrarily on the empire, or that he ever did so.[1] The following investigation of a specific province (Palestine) and of a specific class of legislation (legislation against non-Christian religions) will suggest a quite different set of conclusions. Justinian's legislation appears to have responded, not to the personal whim of an autocrat, but to pressures generated in the social and intellectual matrix of life in the provinces. Bishops, monks, landowners and military commanders formed a network which, by its ready means of access to the court, regularly and freely applied those pressures to the emperor. The generation of legislation was the achievement of this network, of which the emperor was the centre, but by no means the sole moving force. If these conclusions are at all correct, there is every reason to believe that simplistic notions about the generation of other classes of legislation, with reference to other parts of the empire, need to be similarly re-evaluated. The reality in practice of what is so often dismissed as Byzantine 'caesaropapism' may be quite different from what one imagines.

The choice of Palestine for this study is not entirely arbitrary. When it came to quarrels within Christianity—quarrels which absorbed

---

1. A parallel mistake is made when the eastern empire's expectation that the emperor would act as the legislator and police force for the Christian church is thought to imply that, on religious matters, the emperor could and did impose his will on the church. That conclusion, as I have attempted to argue elsewhere, is not borne out by the evidence. See P.T.R. Gray, *The Defense of Chalcedon in the East (451–553)* (Leiden: Brill, 1979), pp. 44-79.

a great deal more of the empire's energies than non-Christian religions ever did—Palestine was a particularly fertile matrix for the neo-Chalcedonian ideas which found their way into Justinian's ecclesiastical policy, into his legislation and eventually into the anathemas of the Fifth Council.[1] Palestine, in other words, had a direct connection with the court that tended to induce legislation in one area; there is at least reason to suspect that it played the same role when it came to legislation on the non-Christian religions.

The total population of Palestine in the sixth century has been estimated at 1,000,000 to 1,300,000.[2] In rural areas, the population was largely Jewish or Samaritan.[3] Of these, perhaps 150,000 to 200,000 were Jews. The majority of the population was concentrated in the Galilee, where 31 villages and 12 towns have been identified as Jewish.[4] Their leadership as a religion was a sanhedrin in Tiberias, presided over by an official designated the archipherecite.[5] Even in Jerusalem, from which Jews had of course been banned, there were apparently at least some Jewish inhabitants.[6]

The Samaritans, like the Jews, had doggedly retained their faith against a hostile world for centuries. They comprised a population of probably not more than 100,000 (we hear of 20,000 killed and 20,000 deported in the Samaritan Revolt of AD 529, but such figures are notoriously unreliable)[7], spread out among villages in the area of Neapolis, the nearest city to their ancient shrine on Mount Gerizim. There were dispersion Samaritans in many cities of the empire as well.

Christians were relative newcomers in Palestine,[8] most of them

1. See, for instance, L. Perrone, *La chiesa di Palestina e le controversie cristologiche* (Brescia: Paideia, 1980), pp. 175-222 as well as Gray, *Defense*, pp. 104-41.

2. M. Avi-Yonah, *The Jews of Palestine* (New York: Schocken Books, 1976), p. 240.

3. So W.H.C. Frend, *The Rise of the Monophysite Movement* (Cambridge: Cambridge University Press, 1972), p. 152.

4. Avi-Yonah, *Jews*, p. 240.

5. *Novella* 146 mentions the archipherecitae among those forbidden to impose the ban on users of Greek translations, but little is known of the office beyond the title.

6. Cyril of Scythopolis, *Vita Sabae* 57.

7. John Malalas, *Chronographia, PG* 97. 656B-657A.

8. Barsauma, a visitor to Palestine c. AD 400, found few Christians there, and experienced persecution from them as did his fellow-Christians. See J. Parkes, *The*

having arrived with the growing stream of rich pilgrims from all over the empire whom the holy places attracted. The permanent population seems to have depended to a considerable extent on these pilgrims, though there were many monks and some landowners. Through the pilgrims the Christians of Palestine were in direct contact with the affairs, religious and secular, of the wider empire.

Included in this 'international' character of Palestinian Christianity, and in constant touch with the life of the cities despite their geographical separation in the deserts, were the numerous monastic communities which sprang up in the fourth and fifth centuries. Typically, the influential Euthymius, founder of the strongest monastic settlements near Jerusalem, was from outside the province, as were most of his disciples.[1] The Christian monastic settlements, 'tended to remain somewhat isolated Greek-speaking enclaves, more tied to the international and pro-Chalcedonian world represented by the holy places than to any form of rural or provincial piety. Their security and even their existence depended on Constantinople.'[2] They were also unusual in that they did not follow Anthony's model of illiterate monasticism, and instead comprised 'a somewhat aristocratic monastic society' with pretensions to culture and learning.[3] It was no doubt for this reason that Palestine came to be the matrix for the neo-Chalcedonian ideas mentioned earlier, and perhaps for the analysis of how to undermine Judaism that will be discussed towards the end of this study. As will be seen, the monastic population and the urban church were in close contact, but their interests should not be seen as necessarily identical.

We can speak, then, of several religious groups, the rural representatives of which would often be separated by geography (monks in the desert, Jewish and Samaritan farmers in their own villages) with some intermingling of landowners and farmers in agricultural areas, and of

Conflict of the Church and the Synagogue (New York: Hermon, 1977), p. 233.

1. Frend, *Rise*, p. 152.

2. Frend, *Rise*, p. 153. It is misleading, however, to suggest (p. 153) that they were by the sixth century necessarily a minority in the midst of a hostile non-Christian population. Cyril of Scythopolis says they were 'few and preyed upon' in the area of Neapolis after the Samaritan Revolt, not before.

3. D.J. Chitty, *The Desert a City* (Oxford: Basil Blackwell, 1966), p. 88. As Chitty goes on to note (p. 105) the same qualities are to be found on the anti-Chalcedonian side. Zacharias the historian, for instance, was at one time a law student in Beirut, and later had close contact with Aeneas, a sophist in the prosperous school of Gaza.

others in the cities and their environs. Among the people there were to be found some pagans as well. The impact of Justinian's legislation was to be felt on every one of these populations in the course of his long reign.

Paganism

Pagan religion had, of course, been under attack by the Christian empire ever since Constantine. The early legislation of the Christian period, however, contented itself with forbidding *haruspicia*, magic and astrology; pagan emperors had already done as much.[1] It was Theodosius who, beginning in 379, prohibited the institutionalized pagan religion of the pre-Christian empire in a series of laws against public discussion of religion, sacrifice, libations, burning of incense to statues, and ordering the destruction of holy places, temples and shrines. His laws had judicial penalties attached to them, including severe fines and death.[2]

Pagan religion nonetheless survived in the Christian empire. We are used to the idea of the fifth-century pagan intellectuals of Athens and Alexandria carrying to new heights the interest in theurgy and mysticism, a new private version of what had in large part been public religion. Geffcken speaks of 'ascetics, half-formed hermits, mystics and learned scholastics, all devotedly seeking the knowledge of God'.[3] Our investigation, however, has to do, not with such as these, but with popular paganism. It has, moreover, more to do with Near Eastern cults than with the Hellenistic religion reinterpreted by the Athenian scholars.

At the popular level, it is clear, not all pagan holy places were ever destroyed, in Palestine or elsewhere. In nearby Arabia, at Zorawa, it was AD 515–516—the beginning, virtually, of the age of Justinian— before a triumphant Christian inscription could proclaim that the cult of Theandrites had been replaced by Christianity, and 'the hiding-place of demons' had become 'a house of God'.[4]

1. E.g. *Codex Theodasianus* 9.16.2, 1.
2. See translations of the main texts in J. Hillgarth, *Christianity and Paganism, AD 350–750* (Philadelphia: University of Pennsylvania Press, 1986), pp. 46-49.
3. J. Geffcken, *The Last Days of Greco-Roman Paganism* (trans. S. MacCormack; Amsterdam: Noord-hollandsche Uitgevers-Maatschappij, 1978), p. 262.
4. Geffcken, *The Last Days*, p. 237. The Arabian cult of Theandrites, though

Some interesting evidence of popular paganism in the Gaza area is provided by the correspondence of Barsanuphius and John with their pious interlocutors. Writing in the 520s, these hermits gave advice by correspondence on religious issues faced by quite ordinary people. One questioner asks 'if a Jew or a pagan invites me to dine on his festival, if he even sends me presents, should I accept or not?' On being told that to do so is contrary to canon law,[1] he presses the point: 'but if it is an important personage, who is my friend, and if he is sad at my refusal, what should I say to him?'[2] Another asks whether it is right to buy merchandise in the market during pagan festivals.[3] The reader has a clear impression that pagans and Christians, whatever the legal sanctions against the former, could be on a cordial footing, both in the day-to-day world of commerce, and in the world of private friendships, but that the Christian partners in such relationships were more than a little disturbed at the situation.

The most significant case in point is that of a certain military commander—a duke—in this area. The duke was a pagan. His soldiers had harrassed some Christian rustics. The 'town leaders' and the bishop decided to appeal to the emperor, but were afraid of reprisals from the duke. What, they ask Barsanuphius, ought they to do?[4] There is a small flurry of correspondence as the bishop and town leaders procrastinate, and Barsanuphius urges them to inform the emperor.[5]

This little scene brings together all of the people who normally played a part in generating legislation in the empire of Justinian. Dagron has pointed out how power over local affairs shifts under Justinian, the new authorities being the closely teamed pair of the *defensor civitatis* (ἔκδικος τῆς πόλεως) and the *defensor ecclesiae* (ἔκδικος τῆς ἐκκλησίας).[6] There is coming to be a 'homogeneity of

---

little is known of it, was apparently widespread and long-lasting. Proclus, among others, prayed to Theandrites.

1. *Codex Thedosianus* 8.8.8 = *Codex Iustinianus* 1.9.13.
2. L. Regnault, P. Lemaire and B. Outtier, *Barsanuphe et Jean de Gaza, Correspondence* (Sable-sur-Sarthe: Abbage Saint-Pierre de Solesmes, 1972), pp. 775-76.
3. Regnault *et al.*, *Barsanuphe*, p. 777.
4. Regnault *et al.*, *Barsanuphe*, p. 831.
5. Regnault *et al.*, *Barsanuphe*, pp. 832-33.
6. G. Dagron, 'Two Documents concerning Mopsuestia', in A.E. Laiou-Thomadakis (ed.), *Charanis Studies: Essays in Honor of Peter Charanis* (New Brunswick, NJ : Rutgers University Press, 1980), p. 21.

provincial society', as he puts it, in which,

> laymen are attentive to discussions concerning orthodoxy just as the
> bishop and his clergy care for the administration of the city and the
> appointment of its magistrates. Bishops, clergy, κτήτορες καὶ
> οἰκήτορες [owners and inhabitants]: here we see the coherent social
> group upon which all responsibility in the *polis* is conferred by law.[1]

At the same time, governors were losing power to military commanders. And, of course, there was great consolidation of functions in the
imperial office. The new power relations are graphically illustrated by
a plaque dated AD 559 or 560, from Mopsuestia (in Cilicia), on which
the memorials to Marthanius, the military commanders, and Antonius,
the bishop, flank the name of Justinian.[2] In Palestine, the existence of
large Jewish and Samaritan populations meant that the power-structure
could not function so smoothly as it did where the population was
more homogeneous; nonetheless, in Gaza the alliance of the bishop
and the local authorities even against another member of the power-
structure, the military commander, spelled trouble for the latter, as
will shortly be seen.

Another centre of power not mentioned, but one whose influence is
amply illustrated by the history of Palestine and indeed the whole of
the eastern empire during the preceding century, was the monastery.
The alliance of the monastery with the bishop and local authorities
was to be virtually all-powerful in effecting legislative changes.

Thus, in Palestine—to return to the correspondence of Basanuphius
and John—we see the combination of the local officials and the bishop,
urged on (typically) by a powerful and holy monk, at least contem-
plating an appeal directly to the emperor against a military commander
who happened to be pagan. If, as in this case, the emperor happened to
be fanatically Christian, the fact that the duke was in the—at least
technically—illegal position of possessing military rank while
remaining pagan was a telling point for the local authorities to make.
In this case we do not have any evidence that the appeal ever was
made. What is clear is that a combination of power centres was in
place that could, and in many cases did, operate to agitate for legislation aimed at religious uniformity, where there was a community of

---

1. Dagron, 'Two Documents', pp. 21-22. The laws were not yet in place in the
time of Barsanuphius, but no doubt the trend was under way. See *Novellae* 86, 128
and 134 (*Novellae = Corpus Civilis Iuris*, III).
2. Regnault *et al.*, *Barsanuphe*, p. 26.

interest among the power-holders in favour of such legislation.

The appeal was never made, it would seem, precisely because imperial action—I think no doubt in response to similar situations all over the empire—moved too swiftly in the direction this particular situation suggested. As the bishop and local authorities were dithering about whether to write to Justinian, the latter enacted with his uncle Justin his first piece of legislation on religion, *Codex Iustinianus*, dated to AD 527. It is a major attack on heretics, Jews, Samaritans, and pagans. Such people had been illegally accepting military appointments. They were therefore cut off from all such things—'participating in honours, being invested with the girdle, attaining any official rank, whether political or military' as also from positions in the legal system itself as advocates or judges or orators. There is the clear expectation that there will be difficulty with enforcement; not only are those who have gained illegal honours to be denied all profit from them and fined heavily, but 'we impose a fine of eight pounds of gold on the one whose job it is to inscribe people if, being aware that such a one enjoys an honour, they do not speak against and reject him...' Moreover, bishops are instructed to keep watch over the whole business and refer to the emperor 'about the way, and the extent of violence, that is to be used if necessary when we prosecute those who are remiss about the things defined concerning the orthodox faith'. There could be no clearer indication than this last sentence of the direct access bishops now had to imperial power and its expression in both legislation and enforcement.

Our monastic correspondence shows just how quickly this legislation worked. The duke immediately 'embraced Christianity, out of zeal for the Christian emperor' reports one correspondent to Barsanuphius.[1] The latter's advice to the bishop and others under these new circumstances is to send a letter of friendship to the duke, pointedly suggesting that their great joy at his entry into the faith will be even greater 'when we see spiritual fruit flourishing in you...' Barsanuphius adds a loaded postscript of his own: 'I want your excellency to know that, if the one taking power had been a pagan and opposed to the faith, whatever he did, we would have had no choice but to close the churches and wait to open them under Christian emperors'.[2] In other words, while Barsanuphius was glad that Justinian had shown himself a zealot

---

1. Regnault *et al.*, *Barsanuphe*, p. 834.
2. Regnault *et al.*, *Barsanuphe*.

in the correct orthodox cause, the emperor would have had a battle royal on his hands had he been a pagan. Paganism was no longer an option either for emperors or for those who wished to hold office in the Christian empire. The Christians would not allow it.

The effects of this imperial legislation raised issues for the simple souls of Gaza. 'An ordinance of the emperor has forbidden pagans to follow their customs any more, and the same for schismatics. Therefore certain have presented themselves after Easter, asking to be baptized; others ask to be received at communion. Should one then receive them? When should we admit them to baptism and to holy communion?'[1] 'Someone has seized a pagan in the ranks of the faithful, and many say we should kill him or burn him.'[2] These questions show that the legislation had the desired effect of converting pagans, though obviously some attempted to retain their paganism secretly. Feelings on the Christian side ran high, and even the eirenic Barsanuphius was willing to suggest that the offended Christians in the case of the pagan who went to church should beat him and 'impose a fine on him—that really touches people!—and then you are to commit him to someone who fears God to teach him the way of God, and in the end you are to baptize him'.[3] In short, the Christians had extra-juridical force to use effectively, and it, in combination with the juridical force they could appeal to, was expected to prove sufficient to produce submissive converts.

Further legislation was enacted in *Codex Iustinianus* 1.11.9-10 (unfortunately undated, but evidently before AD 534) to enforce earlier laws against pagan sacrifices and temples. The pagan population of Palestine was not large, it seems, and we have no evidence of this legislation's needing to be applied there. Neither do we see in Palestine anything to parallel John of Ephesus's great campaign of AD 542, commissioned by Justinian, to convert pagans in Asia Minor.[4] The fact that the novellae refer to pagans only in passing, never as a main topic, shows that the legislation before AD 534 was effective in bringing paganism as a real religious force in places like Palestine to

1. Regnault *et al.*, *Barsanuphe*, p. 496,
2. Regnault, *et al.*, *Barsanuphe*, p. 497.
3. Regnault, *et al.*, *Barsanuphe*, p. 822.
4. John of Ephesus, *Vitae sanctorum orientalium*. I. *Patrologia Orientalis* 18 (1924), p. 681. One does not know how to assess his claim that 80,000 were converted.

an end.[1] There is one small and rather pathetic seventh-century sign of continuing but secret paganism among the officially converted: a little pagan statuette was buried with the 'Christian' Mary in a Roman cemetery of Byzantine Beersheeba.[2] The statuette—a nude representation of a fertility goddess of the Astarte type so sensual that the reviewer found it 'trop inconvenante pour être présentée à nos lecteurs'[3]—shows the lingering attraction of Near Eastern religion even for Roman citizens.

The pagans were devotees of many cults, often entirely local, and paganism as a whole had never developed the kind of institutional structures that had been instrumental in Christianity's conversion of the empire.[4] The case was very different with the Samaritans.

Samaritanism

The Samaritans' relations with the empire were always stormy. Origen says they failed to share in the Jewish exemption from laws against circumcision.[5] They were frequently involved in revolts against an empire whose heavy sanctions must have seemed intolerable. Shortly after the Council of Chalcedon (AD 451) Samaritans were involved in a battle, either joining with troops in an attack on anti-Chalcedonian monks, as the Monophysite historians claim,[6] or they were themselves attacked by troops.[7] Later, in AD 484, in the wake of Illus's revolt and its violent suppression by the emperor Zeno, the Samaritans revolted in Neapolis. The revolt was quickly suppressed, and a church was built on Mount Gerizim, a stockade being erected around the Samaritan shrine there.[8]

---

1. *Novella* 131, for instance, includes pagans in the usual catalogue of the religiously suspect—Jews, Samaritans, Montanists, Arians, for example—to whom Christian institutions may not alienate property.

2. R. Savignac, 'Chronique', *RB* NS 1 (1904), pp. 88-89.

3. Savignac, 'Chronique', p. 88. It can hardly be the case, as he suggests (p. 89), that this is just an example of the persistence of pagan motifs in Christian art.

4. See R. MacMullen, *Christianizing the Roman Empire AD 100–400* (New Haven: Yale University Press, 1984) for a powerful exposition of this point.

5. Origen, *Contra Celsum* 2.13.

6. E.g. Zachariah of Mitylene, *Chronicon* 3, 5-6.

7. Evagrius, *Historia Ecclesiae* 2.5.

8. Procopius of Caesarea, *De aedificiis* 5.7.

Samaritan accounts, with a certain plausibility, ascribe their revolt to Christian attempts to move the bones of the patriarchs, to eliminate Samaritan worship, and to convert Samaritans to Christianity.[1] Certainly the building of a church on Mount Gerizim clearly reflected a Christian conviction—voiced explicitly in Justinian's time by Procopius in his account of the matter—that Jesus' prophecy in John 4 that the Samaritans would one day not worship there, but rather the true worshippers (τοὺς Χριστιανοὺς παραδηλώσας ['he was hinting at the Christians'] explains Procopius)[2], was long overdue for fulfilment. Procopius describes a later revolt, during Anastasius's reign, this time led by a woman.[3]

There is, then, clear evidence on both the Christian and the Samaritan side of a deep-seated popular Christian desire to see the end of Samaritanism. If, as has been argued by some, the Samaritans had since the return placed a special emphasis on gratitude to the Persians, there was an additional reason for Justinian, locked in a perennial struggle with Persia on his eastern borders, to respond to that popular animosity with further persecution of Samaritanism.[4] One of the instruments of persecution was legislation, and that legislation triggered a new revolt. Given the events of Justinian's reign, it is perhaps no wonder that Samaritan chronicles consider the Roman period to have ended with Zeno!

Our interest is the social context for the new legislation. We turn first to one of our most reliable and nearly contemporary accounts of the period, Cyril of Scythopolis's *Vita Sabae*. In AD 491 Sabas became the archimandrite of all of the monks in the lavras of the Judaean desert east of Jerusalem. The creation of this office gave him considerable power that was independent of the city and its secular

---

1. J.A. Montgomery, *The Samaritans* (Philadelphia: J.C. Winston, 1907), pp. 111-12.

2. Procopius, *De aed.* 5.7.

3. Procopius, *De aed.* 5.7.

4. E.g. S. Winkler, 'Die Samariter in den Jahren 529/30', *Klio* 43–45 (1965), pp. 447-48. The existence of a large Monophysite population in the province of Syria was, it is often thought, tolerated by a succession of emperors in this period at least partly because it guaranteed a population hostile to Persia (which was host to a Nestorian Christian population). A fifth column for Persia made up of Samaritans in Palestine was hardly likely to be welcomed by an empire which so clearly understood the logistical implications of local populations' religious positions.

clergy.[1] As happened so often in this period, the monks were able to influence the stance of the entire Christian community.[2] Sabas was a champion of Chalcedonian orthodoxy, and it was not long before he established Jerusalem as a bastion of that position.[3] The monastic captivity of the patriarch is graphically illustrated by the story of the patriarch John, personally wavering towards anti-Chalcedonianism, who was wheeled through his official functions by the pair of grim monastics, Sabas and Theodosius, one gripping him firmly on each side![4] Sabas's reputation as a holy man, and his influence over the patriarch, meant that he was often chosen—as he was, for instance, when the news reached Jerusalem of the accession of an orthodox emperor, Justin, in AD 518—to act as the patriarch's representative announcing the good news throughout the patriarchate.[5] Sabas expected to influence the church; as will be seen, he had no hesitation about extending that influence to the imperial court. When such influence was applied against Samaritanism, it would not be ineffective.

Consider the following account as circumstantial evidence. Sometime in the period immediately preceding the legislation of *Codex Iustinianus* 1.5.12 in AD 527 and the Samaritan Revolt of AD 529, Sabas was approached by a certain John, a lawyer from Scythopolis. John had a complaint against a Samaritan named Silvanus. The laxity of the pre-Justinianic period in enforcing earlier laws on religious conformity is evident, for Silvanus enjoyed imperial dignities and power, John reported that this Samaritan was 'laying snares' for Christians, an unfortunately imprecise expression.[6]

---

1. See Chitty, *Desert*, p. 110.

2. One thinks, for instance, of the immense influence of the Acoimetae in Constantinople.

3. Chitty, *Desert*, pp. 110-15. 'Especially we note how an international Orthodoxy centred on Jerusalem, and achieved not by force but by patience, is seen standing up against imperial monophysitism', p. 114.

4. Cyril of Scythopolis, *Vita Sabae* 56. I am indebted to Frend, *Rise*, pp. 230-31, for pointing out this illustrative passage.

5. Cyril of Scythopolis, *Vita Sabae* 61.

6. Cyril of Scythopolis, *Vita Sabae* 61. Cf. the account in Procopius, *Historia arcana* 27 (trans. R. Atwater; Ann Arbor: University of Michigan Press, 1963), p. 131: '[Arsenius's] father and brother, encouraged by his authority, continued in their ancestral faith in Scythopolis, where, with his consent, they persecuted the Christians intolerably'.

Whatever the nature of his harassment of Christians, it was evidently serious enough to rouse Sabas's ire. The holy man prophesied, 'he will be consumed by fire in the midst of the city',[1] a prophecy which, one suspects not entirely by divine agency, was fulfilled at the hands of a vengeful Christian mob after the revolt when Silvanus, adventuring unwisely into Scythopolis to see the damage for himself, and forgetting his imperial safe-conduct, was seized and burned to death.[2]

The story shows again, as did the story of the pagan duke who bothered Christians in Gaza, the power of an influential monk to mobilize public opinion against religious non-conformity wherever and whenever a real or suspected outrage against Christians occurred. Such a monk, using his ready access to the episcopacy, and, through it or along with it, to the emperor, could apply pressure for new action from the political centre. Action from the centre in the age of Justinian meant legislation and its enforcement. It cannot, unfortunately, be shown that *Codex Iustinianus* 1.5.12 was the direct result of initiatives from either Barsanuphius in Gaza or Sabas in Judaea. These stories illustrate the *kind* of social forces that were at work to elicit such legislation. Our two images of Justinian—'the sleepless emperor'—working late into the night, in one discussing theology on and on with ageing clerics,[3] in the other labouring over legislation, point the connection between the influence of the church on the emperor, and the legislation he enacted in Christianity's favour.

Another source reveals the level to which Christian–Samaritan tension had risen where both groups inhabited a single community:

> A custom prevailed in the Province of Palestine. [Unfortunately no city is specified.] On the Sabbath Day, the Christian young men would come out of church after the reading of the Gospel, and go into the Samaritans' synagogue to sing mocking songs and to throw stones at their houses.[4]

Clearly the Palestinian Christians of Justinian's time were encouraged to think, as they had not it seems thought previously, that the time had come when religious non-conformity would no longer be tolerated, but that their own vigilante action against them would. Something like Sabas's 'inflammatory' remark about Silvanus gave a clear indication　.

1. Cyril of Scythopolis, *Vita Sabae* 61.
2. Cyril of Scythopolis, *Vita Sabae* 70.
3. Procopius, *De bello gothico* 3.32.9.
4. John Malalas in T. Mommsen, 'Johannes von Antiochia und Malalas', *Hermes* 6 (1872), p. 376.

to ordinary Christians of where the most forceful church leaders stood on the matter. Not unnaturally, the Samaritans responded with hatred.[1]

The sanctions against heretics and pagans of *Codex Iustinianus* 1.5.12 were extended to include Jews and Samaritans. Section 13 made provision against the disinheriting of orthodox Christian children of heretics either by will or through the legal provisions applying to intestate estates, insisting that 'the same rules apply to Jews and Samaritans'. This law was of crucial importance to Samaritans. Largely self-sufficient agricultural communities, the Samaritan villages must have depended for their long-term survival on the passing of Samaritan land to Samaritan heirs. If sons who converted were entitled to inherit real property, the break-up of the Samaritan communities was possible. It is not surprising that Procopius reports that, 'those, indeed, who lived in my own Caesarea and in the other cities, deciding it silly to suffer harsh treatment over a ridiculous trifle of dogma, took the name of Christians... by which precaution they were able to avoid the perils of the new law'.[2] In the cities, conversion made life much easier; the pressures to convert to Christianity were, after all, enormous, especially if, as section 12 ruled, there could be no rising to preferment in the many ranks the empire had at its disposal if one were not Christian. No wonder, then, that urban Samaritans ('the most reputable and better class of these citizens', as Procopius puts it, with typical snobbery) responded as was hoped, remaining Christians ever after. It was 'the country people', he says, who took up arms.[3] Naturally—the country people were the most cohesive social group, and therefore the most tenacious of their religion. They were also the ones with the most to lose.

The details of the revolt itself do not really concern us. It occurred too soon after the legislation not to be at least in part caused by it, though clearly Arab incursions sponsored by Persia influenced the timing too.[4] The proximate cause was local rivalry. Malalas reports that, 'at that time' (that is, at the start of the revolt),

---

1. J. Parkes (*The Conflict of the Church and the Synagogue* [New York: Hermon], p. 259), points out some evidence in Antoninus Placentius of the degree of Samaritan loathing for Christians.

2. Procopius, *Hist. arc.* 11, p. 59.

3. Procopius, *Hist. arc.*, p. 59.

4. See Avi-Yonah, *Jews*, p. 242.

the Samaritans did not allow the Christians to leave the place. When... the Christian young men invaded the Samaritan synagogue and stoned it, the Samaritans rushed out, charged against the intruders, and killed many by the sword. Many youths fled to the altar of St. Basil's church, in the area where they were, and several of the Samaritans followed them and killed them in front of the holy altar.[1]

Surprisingly, the outcome of the revolt was not favourable to the Christians at first. Unfortunately for them, Silvanus's son Arsenius enjoyed considerable influence in Constantinople, having risen to senatorial rank. 'I do not know how', says Cyril of Scythopolis, 'but he had access to our emperor... and to the empress Theodora. He deceived their piety by means of false arguments, and excited their anger against the Christians of Palestine.'[2] Justinian had some reason to be angry at the Palestinian Christians if vigilante action against Samaritans had provoked a revolt that all too clearly coincided with Persian initiatives against the empire (and many Samaritans did flee to Persia when the revolt was crushed).[3] As happened so often with Justinian and his predecessors, however, the personal influence of powerful individuals like Arsenius simply could not override the dominant social pressures, which all ran in favour of the Christians.[4]

The story of the swift Christian response, and of Justinian's dramatic reversal, is quite astonishing. The ecclesiastical authorities in Palestine sent a letter to Justinian outlining their version of events, and chose Sabas—now 92 years of age—to deliver it. Winkler nicely summarizes the story of his journey:

1. John Malalas, in Mommsen, 'Johannes', p. 376.
2. Cyril of Scythopolis, *Vita Sabae* 70. This view is supported by Procopius in the *Hist. arc.* 27, though his ascription of special blame to Theodora has to be taken with a very large grain of salt. See A. Cameron, *Procopius and the Sixth Century* (London: Gerald Duckworth, 1985) for a thorough analysis of the worth of Procopius's testimony.
3. John Malalas, *Chronographia*, *PG* 77, 668A-C. Procopius says that many religious non-conformists left the empire in response to Justinian's legislation against them, quite apart from those Samaritans who left in the wake of the revolt (*Hist. arc.* 11, p. 59).
4. A particularly close parallel can be found in the case of Theodore Ascidas, the Origenist, whose influence was reportedly great with Justinian, yet who could not prevent the condemnation of Origenism.

> Informed by an advance notice from Peter [Patriarch of Jerusalem]
> Justinian sent imperial messengers to meet him, among those personally
> represented being Epiphanius [of Constantinople] and Eusebius, the
> Bishop of Ephesus. These noble attendants led the modest and humble
> envoys of Palestine before the Emperor. The latter set all etiquette aside,
> hastened to meet Sabas, kissed him on the head with tears of joy, sought
> his blessing, and received in his own hands the complaint and petitions
> prepared by the patriarch.[1]

In short, the aged holy man, representing as he did monastic sanctity,
Christian orthodoxy, and the power of popular Christian feeling,
could sweep aside the influence of any particular Samaritan in court or
any lingering sense that the Christians had behaved badly at the start of
the revolt or in burning Silvanus to death. An emperor who considered
himself the champion of Christian orthodoxy and the man destined to
realize the orthodox Christian empire was least of all equipped to
resist this kind of delegation. The icing on the cake was Arsenius's
dramatic capitulation—he and his family went to Sabas for baptism.[2]
Sabas's list of requests, which included remission of taxes for the years
AD 530–32 (with the money to be used for church repairs) and support
for other Christian enterprises in Palestine, was granted *in toto*.[3]

Further legislation against the Samaritans followed swiftly. *Codex
Iustinianus* 1.5.17 (undated, but evidently springing from this context)
ruled that,

> the synagogues of the Samaritans are to be destroyed and, if they
> undertake to make others, they are to be punished. They cannot have heirs
> apart from orthodox persons, whether by means of wills or by means of

---

1. Winkler, *Samariter*, p. 446.

2. Cyril of Scythopolis, *Vita Sabae* 71. There were many conversions, it seems,
but as with the pagans not all converts were to be counted on. The *Chronicon
Paschale* for the year AD 530 remarks that 'certain of them, being afraid, came into
Christianity by necessity and, being received, were baptized, but to this very day
they play both sides and, though by being deceptive in outward appearance... they
make themselves appear to be Christians, yet these Samaritans and haters of
Christianity and people who thus do not know Christianity, because of the folly of
money-loving officials, manage to win the officials over to Samaritan ways through
wealth', *PG* 92, 872. Procopius tells of a Samaritan named Faustinus who feigned
conversion, was denounced, then was reinstated when he paid off Justinian (*Hist.
arc.* 37, p. 133). The charge against Justinian can be discounted as just another
example of Procopius's diatribe, but it indicates all the same that Samaritans could
and did bribe officials to wink at their religion.

3. Cyril of Scythopolis, *Vita Sabae* 73.

provisions for intestate estates, nor are they to give or otherwise give out for adoption their children to those who are not orthodox.

The drastic implications of such legislation on the survival of the Samaritan villages was obvious; the provision about adoption was evidently an attempt to close off one obvious means of evading the law, that is by arranging for Samaritan children to be adopted by co-operative non-Samaritans, who could then be sold or 'given' land under the terms of the law, and could then legally will it back to the Samaritan children they had adopted. Given the extensive use of adoption as a means of retaining real property within a family in the ancient world, this last provision was quite necessary if the law was to achieve its goal.

Somewhat later—again, dating is a problem—another law sets aside the witness of various heretics and the Jews in cases against Christians, though their witness is permitted in litigation among themselves. This last exemption is specifically denied to Samaritans and certain others 'for whom every legitimate action is forbidden... We judge that for these... every witnessing, as equally any other legitimate transaction, is forbidden'.[1]

A glimpse of further social interraction behind legislation is provided by the procemium to *Novella* 45 of 537. 'Your eminence [the eparch John] has passed the information to us that certain men among the *curiales* are Jews, or Samaritans... and, since we hate heretics, they think to be free, by means of this pretext, of their conciliar duties'. The eparch has slipped the word to Justinian, but who slipped the word to him? One suspects the ever-vigilant monks of Palestine. The body of the legislation ruled that Jews and Samaritans were to lose their curial privileges—as earlier legislation had ordered—but that their curial obligations were to remain. Curial privileges included mostly empty honours,[2] but curial obligations involved taxes; members of the decurionate 'were responsible for the collection of taxation, and compelled to make good the deficit from their own fortunes'.[3] The earlier legislation against the validity of heretical testimony in court was reinforced.

Justinian's last legislation concerning the Samaritans, *Novella* 129,

---

1. *Codex Iustinianus* 1.5.21.
2. There were, however, valuable rights under penal law, such as rights against being beaten or imprisoned. See J. Juster, *Les juifs dans l'empire romain* (Paris: P. Geuthner, 1914), p. 181.
3. Parkes, *Conflict*, p. 178.

is dated to AD 551. 'There is no sin of any of our subjects so great that it does not warrant our clemency.' So Justinian begins the prooemium. And indeed, clemency is the watchword of the law. Admitting that the law about real property had been the principal punishment imposed on Samaritans 'who formerly rose up audaciously against Christians'—a recognition of the revolt as fundamentally an interreligious riot rather than a political rebellion in the first instance—Justinian suggests that, 'we did not observe the same strictness in practice as we did in the writing'. His new approach is to decree that 'there should be freedom for Samaritans to write wills and to dispose of property belonging to them... to write donations, both to give and to receive legacies, and to enter into legal arrangements of this kind...'[1] The only exception is the case of persons who die intestate, 'leaving children who differ on the things that concern God'. In that case only orthodox Christian children are entitled to inherit. The same is true for others who would be entitled to inherit under the rules concerning the line of inheritance, though even here a Christian who is more remotely related may not inherit over someone more closely related to the deceased, 'even if they are best in religious observance'.[2]

How does one explain this rather startling change in direction, even in an era of more eirenic and chastened approaches? The novella itself contains a clue:

> Now that we see them returning to moderation', says Justinian, 'and considering it unworthy of us or of them to remain in the same rage against those who do not suffer such things, *and above all giving in to the just request of Sergius, the most reverend Metropolitan Archbishop of Caesarea* made by him on their behalf—he who is a witness that they have improved, but who promises their quiet conduct for the future—we have arrived at our present divine law...[3]

A Christian archbishop appealing on behalf of Samaritans? Yes. Procopius, who was from Caesarea and can probably be relied upon here, tells us why:

> Ten myriads of men are said to have perished in this engagement, and the most fertile country on earth thus became destitute of farmers. To the Christian owners of these lands, the affair brought great hardship: for while their profits from these properties were annihilated, they had to pay

1. *Novella* 129, 1.
2. *Novella* 129, 2.
3. *Novella* 129, 1.

heavy annual taxes on them to the Emperor for the rest of their lives, and secured no remission of this burden.[1]

The reference must be not only to general taxes on land the Christians actually owned, but also to the ἐπιβολή, a tax introduced at the end of the fifth century under the terms of which farmers in a community were considered a fiscal unit responsible for a certain tax each year.[2]

The ἐπιβολή meant that, if Samaritans could not pass land to their Samaritan heirs, and Christians could not be found to take over the land, the remaining Christian landowners would bear the whole tax. There must have been a serious problem in Palestine finding Christians who could or would farm land in the Samaritan communities. The refusal of Samaritans even to accept Christian money or to associate with them in any way would make life virtually impossible for Christians in the village agricultural areas.[3] (One thinks of the black Muslims who in the 1960s purchased ranches in the American South, determined to practise farming in formerly all-white areas. They had to give up a few years later because of the monolithic resistance of the rural white population. Integration came more easily in the cities.) Agriculture is a difficult, even impossible, enterprise to pursue among hostile neighbours. In such a case, the practical concerns of Christian landowners evidently had more influence with the bishop than the ideological zeal of monks, and the combined appeal of landowners and bishop could change the approach even of a zealous emperor.

It is worth looking briefly at a further novella (*N.* 144) enacted, not by Justinian, but by his successor, Justin II, in AD 572. Observing that most of the Samaritans have not been brought to Christianity by the earlier leniency, and that, 'certain of them have given way to such great madness that, though they obtained saving baptism, they went back to the evil whence they had come', the novella reimposes sanctions against any inheritance or other transfer of property by Samaritans. Clearly, Samaritan intransigence remained a riddle to the Christian empire which it could find no way of addressing satisfactorily. When leniency did not work, it returned to stringent measures.

Such measures did not, however, go so far as to cause hardship again to the Christian landowners who were so influential two decades

1. Procopius, *Hist. arc.* 11, p. 60.
2. L. Bréhier, *Les institutions de l'empire byzantin* (Paris: P. Geuthner, 1949), pp. 250-51.
3. Parkes, *Conflict*, p. 259.

earlier with Archbishop Sergius. The one exception to the law
disinheriting Samaritans is the case of children of farmers. They may
inherit the land, but they may not abandon farming. The tax base
provided by Samaritan farmers was still felt to be necessary, and, if
agriculture was to be preserved in the Samaritan areas, it would
evidently have to be done largely by Samaritans.

Jews

Judaism enjoyed a special status in the Christian empire, recognized in
Roman law. According to Juster,

> Christianity become the religion of the state... did not generally impose
> on them penalties that deprived them of life or of liberty, but rather
> forfeitures; the right to existence therefore did not imply, for the Jews,
> immunity from these forfeitures.[1]

As he goes on to point out, 'theology desires the existence of the Jews
to serve its end, to demonstrate the truth of the Christian religion—
but also the truth of the gospel predictions, the realization of the
misery and penalty of the Jews'.[2] Only in North Africa at the
'liberation', and there only in Borion, were Jews forcibly converted.[3]

Anti-Jewish sentiment showed itself everywhere, of course, not least
in the contemptuous references of Christian theologians to 'the Jewish
doctrines' of someone like Nestorius—an identification used to
powerful effect, for example, by Cyril of Alexandria. So dependably
could the association of a Christian position with Judaism discredit it,
that some anti-Chalcedonians in Palestine, early in the sixth century,
created an effective weapon for their cause by forging a letter—
purported to have been sent by some Jews to Marcion after the
Council of Chalcedon—saying,

> For a long time we were regarded as descendants of those who crucified a
> God and not a man, but since the Synod of Chalcedon has met and
> demonstrated that they crucified a man and not a God, we ask by that that
> we be forgiven for this offence, and that our synagogues be restored to
> us![4]

---

1. Juster, *Juifs*, p. 167.
2. Juster, *Juifs*, p. 250.
3. *Novella* 37.5; cf. Procopius, *De aed.* 6.2.
4. Cited from several sources by S.W. Baron, *A Social and Religious History of
the Jews*, III (New York: Columbian University Press, 1957), p. 5.

The passage clearly illustrates the ever-present roots of Christian anti-Semitism.[1]

In the case of Jews, nonetheless, as in the case of pagans, there is some surprising evidence of communication and even friendship with Christians across the boundaries imposed by religion, though in most areas the de facto separation of the populations made this unlikely. We have already noticed that one of the Christians who corresponded with Barsanuphius and John in the region of Gaza was concerned about what to do if invited to dine with a pagan or Jewish friend during one of their festivals.[2] Another said, 'I intend to press the wine of a Jew in my wine-press', and asked, 'Is it a sin?'[3] The passage shows how the advantages of rural co-operation—evidently in one area in which the populations mixed fairly freely—could overcome religious differences, though not without troubling the conscience. (John's answer, by the way, is worth recording for its eirenic spirit: 'If, when it rains, God makes it rain on your field and passes by the Jew's field, then you should not press his wine. If, however, He is full of humanity for all and makes the rain fall on the just and on the unjust, why should you be inhumane, and not rather merciful?')[4]

That eirenic spirit is not so evident in the politically much more important centre of Jerusalem. Sabas's notice of Jews (and particularly of Jews in the sight of whom orthodox Christians were humiliated), in the forbidden Jerusalem was not a good sign.[5] Neither was the fact that at Hammath-Gader, one member of a prominent Jewish family there,

---

1. Severus could state quite baldly, 'No Punishment is severe enough for the arrogance of the Jews' (*The Sixth Book of the Select Letters of Severus*, II [trans. E.W. Brooks; London: Williams and Norgate, 1904], p. 60).

2. Regnault *et al.*, *Barsanuphe*, pp. 775-76.

3. Regnault *et al.*, *Barsanuphe*, p. 441.

4. Regnault *et al.*, *Barsanuphe*. Cf. Pseudo-Anastasius Sinaiticus's *Quaestiones et Responsiones*, several questions of which betray a humane concern for the spiritual status of Jews. For example, question 79 asks 'If anyone without faith—a Jew or a Samaritan—will do many good works, will he then enter into the kingdom of heaven?' *PG* 89, 708 BCE; and question 81 asks 'Where do we say the innocent children. . . of Jews and those not baptized go? To Judgment or to Paradise?' (709 BCE).

5. Cyril of Scythopolis, *Vita Sabae* 57. The presence of Jews in Jerusalem is noted in a libellus to the Emperor Anastasius submitted by Theodosius and Sabas, yet another example of the direct access monks like Sabas expected to have to the emperor through the device of direct appeals (a legal practice Justinian himself had made legitimate).

Pheroras, became a *comes*. He had not deserted his Judaism, for he is listed as a donor to the synagogue there.[1] Once again it is evident both that earlier laws disallowing the enjoyment of such honours were being ignored before Justinian's accession to power, and that that fact did not go unnoticed by the Christian leaders who could and did have access to the emperor.

The often-discussed legislation of *Codex Iustinianus* 1.5.12-21 applies as directly to Jews as to heretics, pagans and Samaritans. They are deprived of honours (12); their Christian children have rights of inheritance whatever they themselves attempt to determine by will (13); and their testimony against Christians in court is disallowed—though, unlike Samaritans, their testimony in cases amongst themselves is permitted (21). Likewise, *Novella* 45 of 537 denies to Jews, as to Samaritans and Montanists and other more extreme heretics, the privileges of being *curiales*, but insists that the duties connected with that status be performed. We have, unfortunately, no evidence to show how these laws affected the Jewish communities of Palestine.

More interesting is *Novella* 131 of 545. Here we have an example of legislation which frankly assumes the integration of the empire with the Christian church. 'We decree therefore', begins the law, 'that the holy ecclesiastical canons set forth or established by the four holy councils... have the status of laws'.[2] The main focus of this legislation is the church—it concerns itself only in passing with any other group—and its main effect was confirmation of the imperial duty to depose heretical clerics when they were condemned by what looked like the majority of the church. The novella's title is apt, therefore: 'Concerning Ecclesiastical Canons and Privileges'. The translation into concrete terms of the ideal of the orthodox empire means, that is, denying to heretics the right to function as clerics, for clerical functioning is one of the two concrete expressions of the reality of church. The other, of course, is possession of church property.

Section 2 of the novella addresses precisely this question of church property. Its main point is directly parallel to that of section 1—just as no heretic is to function as a cleric, so now no church property is to be possessed by heretics. The weapons used by Diocletian against Christianity at the beginning of the fourth century were thus turned against heretics by Justinian. Translated into the possibilities of legal

---

1. Avi-Yonah, *Jews*, p. 240.
2. *Novella* 131.1

proscription, this objective is to be achieved by forbidding the alienation or rental of church real property to heretics, by imposing penalties on administrators who knowingly engage in such arrangements, and by allowing for confiscation by the orthodox church of both the property and the revenues obtained in any such illicit real-estate transaction. Any new construction of buildings by heretics for religious use, or rental of existing buildings, is likewise forbidden, the same penalties of confiscation being imposed.

This last clause leads, really in passing, to sanctions against non-Christians who rent or construct buildings for religious purposes, and here something can be said about the social setting in Palestine. We have no accounts of rentals, but the matter of construction is relevant to our investigation. Here is the applicable sentence from the novella: 'If any of the heretics... should have the effrontery to build a cave of his unbelief, or Jews should construct a new synagogue, the holy church of those places is to appropriate the structures under its own absolute control'.

The attempt to create both an orthodox and an entirely Christian empire by manipulating rights of property was a not unintelligent approach, relying on attrition over an extended time to reduce the non-Christian population, rather than on unrealistically legislating conformity. In Palestine, however, and probably elsewhere too, it failed because of local realities. Excavations at en-Nabratein in the Galilee provide evidence of these local realities as they obtained in the period in question. The site of en-Nabratein was abandoned after the earthquake of AD 363, but re-occupied in AD 550, to enjoy continuous occupation through to sometime between AD 650 and 700. 'There is every indication', say the investigators, 'of a thriving Jewish village in the late Byzantine era, possibly absorbing villagers from nearby Gush Halav, whose village was destroyed c. AD 550 by earthquake...'[1] Inscriptions from such synagogues show that, while there continued to be support for the synagogue, the amount each donor gave tended to be reduced in this period over earlier periods. 'It seems', concludes Avi-Yonah, 'that the dominant class among the Palestinian Jews were small proprietors or merchants, who could afford to give, but not overmuch'.[2] Evidence of Palestine is also, apparently, to be found in

---

1. E.M. Meyers *et al.*, 'Preliminary Report on the 1980 Excavations at en-Nabratein, Israel', *BASOR* 244 (1981), pp. 6-7.

2. Avi-Yonah, *Jews*, p. 240.

the material of the Cairo Genizah. There are suggestions that it too points to a community carrying on in its ancestral ways, largely untouched by the concerns of the empire.[1] We get a picture of local Jewish life in the villages of the Galilee turning in on itself to some extent in an era of increased hostility from Christians and the empire, but still vital, still devoted to its religious identity. The point is not just that the Judaism of the villages was a durable phenomenon—like the Samaritanism of a nearby area—unlikely to be susceptible to the kind of change Justinian's legislation was aimed at producing. The point is also that such village-based Judaism could and did simply ignore the legislation.

One of the most interesting finds at en-Nabratein, in fact, was the lintel of a new synagogue built there—on the ruins of an earlier synagogue, but expanded by some 21 per cent—after the re-occupation of the village.[2] On it is found an inscription: '[According] to the number four hundred and ninety-four years after the destruction [of the Temple], the house was built during the office of Hanira son of Lezer and Luliana son of Yuder'.[3] The completion of the synagogue can thus be clearly dated to AD 564, a date supported further by the numismatic evidence.[4] Nineteen years had passed since the publication of *Novella* 131, so that there can be no question of the legislation's not having had a chance to be publicized, and yet the congregation of en-Nabratein went ahead with its construction programme in blithe disregard of the law. Furthermore, we are talking about a major construction project: 'The effort of reconstruction would surely have not gone unnoticed', say the archaeologists, 'especially given the highly attractive nature of the building'.[5] As-yet-unpublished reports of digs at other Galilean sites like Gush Halav show that there was other building going on in this period—for instance the building of new benches, and the re-arrangement of entrances in the synagogue at Gush Halav—though these are less startling than the clear evidence at en-Nabratein of the

1. See, for instance, M. Margulies, *Palestinian Halacha from the Genizah* (Jerusalem: Mosad ha-Rav Kuk, 1973 [Hebrew]).

2. E.M. Meyers *et al.*, 'Second Preliminary Report on the 1981 Excavations at en-Nabratein, Israel', *BASOR* 246, (1982), pp. 35-54.

3. Meyers *et al.*, 'Preliminary Report', p. 4.

4. Meyers *et al.*, 'Preliminary Report', p. 20.

5. Meyers *et al.*, 'Preliminary Report', p. 6.

ineffectuality of *Novella* 131.

Why was *Novella* 131 not effectual in these villages? Part of the answer may lie in the instruments specified by the law for its publication and enforcement. We have considerable evidence that local officials were supposed to post notices of new legislation.[1] On religious matters, however, the main instrument of disseminating legislation was the church. We have seen how Sabas was employed, for instance, to spread the news of Justin's accession. Moreover, *Codex Iustinianus* 1.3.54, forbidding Jews to own Christian slaves, provided—and it was the first legislation to do so—for enforcement by the clergy as well as by civil officials. We have seen how Justinian relied more and more on the alliance of local officials and bishops as the point of contact with local realities. *Novella* 131 instructs 'the holy church of those places', 'the church of the town where the property is located', to confiscate the property, buildings or rents involved. In Palestinian Jewish villages, where churches and bishops simply did not exist, the infrastructure for disseminating and enforcing laws did not exist, with the result that local life went on, to a very large extent, as if imperial legislation too did not exist. The absence of a system of genuinely public prosecution in Roman law meant that, where there was no party moved or entitled by law to lay charges, laws could be ignored with impunity. The alliance of bishops, monks and the emperor could see that laws were promulgated. Where Christians were not present *in situ*, however, laws might well prove ineffective.

We may now turn to Justinian's last legislation against Jews, *Novella* 146, of 553. This is a very long novella, which raises some intriguing issues. The novella is a response to internal dissension in Jewish communities over the issue of whether or not the Old Testament could be read in Greek and other translations at synagogue services. Certainly its main legislation is to provide that scriptures must be read in a language understood by the majority of a congregation, the LXX being used normally as the Greek translation, and others (such as the Latin translation) being used where appropriate. 'We have judged those to be better who wish to take up also the Greek language for the reading of the Holy Scriptures, and indeed any language that makes it more to

---

1. See the interesting discussion in R. Scott, 'Malalas and Justinian's Codification', in *Byzantine Papers* (Canberra: Humanities Research Centre, Australian National University, 1981), pp. 12-31 of the evidence from Malalas for the way in which laws were disseminated.

the purpose and better understood by the listeners', asserts the procemium. Synagogue leaders are expressly forbidden to use the most effective disciplinary measure at their disposal—anathema and the ban—against those who follow the law:

> The *archipherecitae*, or elders, or so-called teachers, are not to have freedom to prevent this by any ban or anathemas, unless they want because of these things to be punished with corporal punishment so that, being deprived of their possessions, they may concede better and more-beloved things to us who both wish and order it.[1]

The legislators expect opposition, for the epilogue goes on at some length to ensure compliance nonetheless:

> The things, therefore, which we have in hand and which are being made clear by this divine law, your excellency will protect and the office which is entrusted to you. He who in time will be appointed to the same authority will protect it, and will not entirely give in to the Jews to act contrary to these things, but submitting those who resist or even attempt to prevent [the law] altogether first to corporal punishments, he will force them to live in exile, despoiled of their possessions, lest they be emboldened against God and Empire by this same. Commands will be necessary also to those of the eparchs who are in charge, themselves posting our law, so that those who learn this set it up in each city, knowing that it is necessary to protect these things for fear of our anger.

Something is certainly at stake here, and it is not difficult to tell what. The point of enforcing the reading of scripture in popular languages is to prevent the Jewish teachers from maintaining their exclusive control over its interpretation. 'We decree that there is no license for those exegetes among them who accept only Hebrew, so as to falsify it as they will, concealing their own malignity by the ignorance of the many.'[2] The words of the opening of the procemium, at first dismissible as rhetoric, suddenly appear with their intended force:

> It was necessary for Jews who heard the Holy Scriptures not to cling to mere words, but to look to the prophecies stored up in them, through which they declare Jesus Christ, the great God and Saviour of the human race. Nonetheless, even though they wandered from the correct teaching up to this moment, giving themselves over to irrational interpretations (ἑρμηνείαι), the time has come to ensure that Jewish listeners can discern

---

1. *Novella* 146.1.2. Before this, the right to excommunicate had been treated as a purely internal concern of Jews. See Juster, *Juifs*, pp. 159-60.
2. *Novella* 146.1.

the Christian truth of the Old Testament, free from the perverted interpretation of the Jewish authorities, and so be converted.

This legislation is an outright attempt to make the conversion of Jews to Christianity more likely by, among other things, legislating something that can be enforced, namely, that the language used for reading of scriptures in synagogues be the common language of the hearers.

It is with exactly the same purpose that the legislation forbids the use of 'the second tradition' (δευτέρωσις), that is the Mishnah.

> We forbid entirely what is called on their part 'the second tradition' as not taken together with the Holy Scriptures nor handed down from on high from the prophets, but rather as being the invention of men who speak only from the earth and have nothing divine in them. And let them read the holy words themselves, opening the books themselves, but not concealing the things said themselves, receiving alien unwritten and vain talk that is invented by them for the destruction of the simple.[1]

It is not necessary to enter into the debate about whether Justinian's legislators thought the Mishnah was read in synagogue. As A. Baumgarten has convincingly argued,[2] the real point of *Novella* 146 is not what is or is not read in a synagogue service, but the belief of Justinian's advisers that access for Jews to the Old Testament without the filter of traditional Jewish interpretation of it will convince them that its whole point is to witness to Jesus Christ, thus enabling conversion without coercion. The issue of which language is used in the synagogue is thus superficial; reading in Hebrew is a problem only because it leaves the interpretation entirely in the hands of rabbis, who understand that language well, and for whom the Mishnah's intricate exploration of the Hebrew text provides the hermeneutic. 'To Justinian, a sixth-century Christian, the Christian interpretation of Scripture was so obviously the only possible and sensible one that if the Jews were only forced to read the Bible directly they couldn't help but see the truth of Christianity.'[3]

As Parkes says, 'it is surprising that in that age so serious an attempt at diagnosis should be made'.[4] Where did the diagnosis come from? Baumgarten has pointed out that Palestine was the locus of a relevant

---

1. *Novella* 146.2.
2. A. Baumgarten, 'Justinian and the Jews', in *Rabbi Joseph H. Lookstein Memorial Volume* (New York: Ktav, 1980), pp. 37-44.
3. Baumgarten, 'Justinian', p. 40.
4. Parkes, *Conflict*, p. 254.

Jewish–Christian quarrel in the fourth century.[1] The quarrel, dating back at least to Matthew's Gospel, was over which religion really possessed the Old Testament and could claim to be the true Israel. Jewish arguments had urged that Christian failure to keep the Old Testament commandments invalidated their claim, as Trypho had argued in his discussion with Justin in the second century.[2] In the fourth century, rabbis acting as apologists for Judaism argued further that it was δευτέρωσις which set Judaism apart as the true religion. Baumgarten cites the following revealing text:

> R. Judah. b. Shalom said: 'When the Holy One told Moses "write down [Exod. 34.27]",[3] the latter wanted the Mishnah also to be in writing. However, the Holy One blessed is He foresaw that a time would come when the nations of the world would translate the Torah and read it in Greek and then say: "We are Israel", and now the scales are balanced [that is their claim to be Israel is at least as good as the Jewish claim]. The Holy One blessed is He will then say to the nations: "you contend that you are my children. That may be, but only those who possess my mysteries are my children, that is [those who have] the Mishnah which is given orally".'[4]

The Christian response in the same period was best expressed by Jerome, who argued that the Jews, in turning to the Mishnah, were deserting the written word of God to follow 'the commandment of men [Isa. 29.13]'.[5]

It is evident that the sixth-century legislation's description of the Mishnah as 'alien unwritten and vain talk' clearly reflects the line taken by Jerome. However, the connection between this fourth-century Palestinian discussion and the sixth-century legislation is not clear. We have, in fact, very little material in the sixth century which involves Jewish–Christian debate, and what we do have is quite fictional (the Jewish advocate never refers to the Mishnah, and always ends up being converted).

Even if we leave Palestine aside, it may be worthwhile to look briefly at some of this literature. There is, for instance, a dialogue

---

1. Baumgarten, 'Justinian', pp. 40-43. I am relying on Baumgarten entirely in this section.

2. Justin Martyr, *Dialogus cum Tryphore Iudaeo* 8.

3. 'And the Lord said unto Moses, "Write thou these words; for after the tenor of these words I have made a covenant with thee and with Israel".'

4. Baumgarten, 'Justinian', p. 41.

5. Cited Baumgarten, 'Justinian', p. 42. See also p. 43.

purported to have been held between the Ethiopian Archbishop Gregentius and a Jew named Herbanus. Neither party mentions the Mishnah. The dialogue does, however, have Herbanus voice the following regret: 'It was an evil day when our fathers voluntarily translated the books of Israel into the Greek language, so that you, taking up residence in them, might put a bit in our mouths'.[1] In other words, it reflects the common Christian assumption shared by *Novella* 146 that Jews should feel threatened by the Christians' ability to demonstrate the truth of Christianity from the Old Testament, and so should regret having let it pass out of their private linguistic preserve.

More revealing is Anastasius Sinaiticus's *Viae Dux*, in which Anastasius attacks the Monophysite Severus for his work *Philalethes* on the grounds that its high-handed rejection and acceptance of texts from the fathers is just like 'what is called by the Jews δευτέρωσις, which encompasses the destruction of the correct [interpretation] of the Seventy Interpreters, and dissolution of the divine law...'[2] This passage shows that the Christian critique of the Mishnah first propounded in Palestine in the fourth century was still around, if not in Palestine itself, in a monastery which was in frequent contact with Christian Palestine and part of the same regimen of pilgrim sites as the holy places of Palestine itself.[3] This evidence thus makes it possible, though not by any means certain, that the diagnosis of *Novella* 146—so similar in spirit, in a way, to the neo-Chalcedonian diagnosis of the causes of the orthodox–Monophysite split, which certainly belonged primarily to Palestine—owed something to the Palestinian matrix.

Conclusion

Legislation in the age of Justinian, even—or perhaps especially—on religious matters, was not created in the vacuum of the court, but was generated and modified by the emperor in a complex dialogue with the social world of the empire, made possible by a network connecting the court with important persons in the provinces. The emperor enunciated legislation in response to social forces communicated through this network, and sometimes modified it subsequently when other forces emerged in response to its application.

1. Pseudo-Gregentius, *Disputatio cum Herbano Iudaeo, PG* 86. 624C-D.
2. Anastasius Sinaiticus, *Viae Dux, PG* 89.105.
3. The *Peregrinatio Egeriae* shows the connection clearly.

In the matter of legislation on the non-Christian religions, this study of the provinces of Palestine has shown that the persons at the local level most likely to be in the network were bishops and leading monastics. It is well known that Justinian consulted clerics—Procopius's image of their late-night conversations sticks in the mind. It is well known, too, that he and his predecessors made frequent use of the so-called home synod—an improvized council of any bishops who happened to be in Constantinople when an issue arose that required a semi-official decision from the church. What has not stood out with sufficient clarity is the direct influence local bishops and monks could have on the emperor. We have seen several cases in which the combined influence of bishops and monks could triumph even over that of military commanders and favoured courtiers.

That these people were not, for their part, individuals isolated from social realities is made quite clear by the case of Archbishop Sergius and his advocacy of the cause of the Samaritans. Bishops were caught between their 'idealistic' commitment to the notion of an orthodox empire and the more worldly concerns of their landowning parishioners caught by the burdens of taxation; in the end they supported the cause of those who paid the piper. The more independent monks could afford to be idealistic, but they could not carry the day against the combination of bishops and local authorities.

The fact that the emperor was both sole legislator and final court of appeal in the empire must have influenced profoundly the way in which legislation and social realities interacted. The usual kind of appeal that made its way to the emperor—an appeal for a ruling when lower courts had failed to satisfy one of the parties—meant that he was constantly made aware of the inadequacy of existing laws and the need for reformulating them. Justinian's laws frequently speak in the proœmia of previous laws as failed attempts to solve problems which the new law will attempt to solve in a new way.

There was also the possibility, however, of direct appeal to the · emperor without the requirement of previous submission to the courts. That possibility enabled local forces to have a direct effect apart from the inertia of the whole administrative structure of the empire, including local courts and authorities. These local forces came to form what we have called a network, all the more efficient because it was informal. We have seen the astonishing willingness of bishops and monks in Palestine to use this avenue. We have seen that their appeals, especially when delivered in person by a monk of great age and sanctity, could produce drastic changes in policy and legislation. The appeal procedure was, in fact, the main channel through which social forces in the provinces could bring their concerns to bear on the legislating power centralized in the emperor.

When we take account of the use of appeals, and consider the loss in Justinian's time of the authority of provincial governors which no proliferation of honorific titles could quite restore, we can see the emergence of a world—the world of later Byzantium—in which Dagron's picture of authority's concentration in the hands of bishops, civic authorities and military commanders (a list to which we should add monks) in partnership with the emperor was the dominant reality. That partnership was the matrix for the legislation on non-Christian religions we have examined.

The creation and modification of legislation did not always imply success in accomplishing the aims of that legislation. We have seen that the Christian social forces that were so successful in inducing the creation of legislation against the non-Christian religions were also often in publishing and enforcing it. Certain social realities—the coherent rural communities of Jews and Samaritans in Palestine, for instance—meant the failure of legislation, especially in areas where these instruments for publication and enforcement did not exist, or where the interests of some Christians were harmed by enforcement. These contrary social forces were particularly in evidence in Palestine, and there non-Christian religions more successfully resisted the Christian empire than elsewhere.

If the picture which has emerged here of a complex process leading to the generation of some specific legislation in the age of Justinian has any validity, then it is clear that the real exercise of the imperial office by Justinian cannot be understood in the simplistic way suggested by terms like 'caesaropapism'. That conclusion is not, of course, particularly surprising: it is difficult to imagine how any central legislating person or body could *not* be involved in some kind of dialectical relationship with the social forces affecting those for whom the legislation is destined. It is a healthy corrective to the theoretical rhetoric about the imperial office in Byzantium to realize how it really functioned in practice.

Truth or *pešāṭ* Issues in Law and Exegesis

Martin I. Lockshin

In the eleventh and twelfth centuries significant numbers of Jewish Bible scholars began to show an interest in the *pešāṭ*, the simple meaning of the biblical text. Until that point almost all Jewish Bible exegesis—with a few notable exceptions—could be characterized as midrash, interpretations that sometimes fly in the face of what the text, per se, is really saying. The question of why and how *pešāṭ* developed is difficult to solve and has not yet been sufficiently unravelled by scholarship (Lipshutz 1957: 266; Segal 1971: 62; Touitou 1982: 48-74). In any case, *pešāṭ* exegesis was a relatively short-lived phenomenon in Jewish circles. This paper will examine one of the major stumbling blocks that inhibited the growth of *pešāṭ* and perhaps dealt the death blow to the phenomenon of observant Jews taking an interest in the plain unadorned meaning of the biblical text. It is my contention that as soon as people realized what the religious problems would be when *pešāṭ* methodology was applied consistently to the biblical text—including and especially legal texts—the *pešāṭ* enterprise suffered a setback from which it has never really recovered. My proofs will be drawn from the works of one of the greatest medieval *paštānîm* (that is, *pešāṭ*-oriented exegetes), Rabbi Samuel ben Meir (c. 1080–1174;[1] henceforth Rashbam), from a consideration of both the innovative nature of his approach and the ultimate fate of his commentary.

First a few introductory words about the *pešāṭ*-midrash dichotomy in Jewish exegesis. Midrash, the traditional form of Jewish exegesis, is often not properly understood and overly maligned. The claim that midrash ignores grammar, context, syntax and the like is a gross exaggeration. In fact individual midrashic texts do reflect a concern

---

1. While no full biographical treatment of Rashbam has been written, see the discussion in Urbach 1968: 42-54.

for all such considerations. A midrash[1] that claims that Hagar and Keturah were actually the same person because of the defective orthography of the word *happîlagšîm*[2] (Gen. 25.6) is obviously not the simple sense of Scripture, but it has certainly noted and reacted to unusual orthography, as should any careful text reader. When the midrash (*b.B.Mes.* 86b; cited by Rashi, commentary to Gen. 18.1) claims that the phrase 'in the heat of the day' in Gen. 18.1 implies that God created some supernatural type of heat that kept passersby away from Abraham's house, it has obviously added a new unsupported element into the biblical text. And yet the midrash seems to show sensitivity to the reasonable literary question of why the text is providing such incidental information that, at first blush, seems to play no reasonable role in the story. Biblical authors do not usually tell you what the temperature was when a specific narrative took place. 'Why do it now?' asks the midrash.[3]

So midrash *is* sensitive to the various components of a good literary reading of a biblical text. Sarah Kamin (1986: 11-17) has explained well that what makes midrash midrash is its tendency when dealing with one specific text to highlight one aspect of the many factors that go into the reading of that text at the expense of all other equally relevant factors. The midrash will be willing to sacrifice pages of context because of a perceived orthographical difficulty or because of a phrase that appears to be unnecessary or redundant. Conversely midrash is sometimes willing for the sake of context to ride roughshod over the simple meaning of a word or phrase.[4]

---

1. The opinion of Rabbi Judah in *Gen. R.* 61.4, cited by Rashi (R. Solomon ben Isaac; the most famous Jewish exegete ever and Rashbam's grandfather) in his commentary to Gen. 25.6. Rashbam opposes that midrash in his own commentary to Gen. 25.6.

2. Curiously MT's spelling of *happîlagšîm* in all of our texts today is not defective, contrary to the claim of *Genesis Rabba* and Rashi.

3. Contrast Rashbam's attempt, in his commentary *ad loc.*, to explain why it is important for the reader to know that these guests arrived around mid-day.

4. See, for example, the claim of *b. Sôt* 35a that the word *mimmennû* in Num. 13.31 actually refers to God. The Talmud introduces that explanation with the formulaic words, *'al tiqrē'*, as it realizes full well that that is not the simple reading of the word. However the Talmud is actually providing a very reasonable interpretation of the larger context. It insists on seeing the complaints of the Israelites as ultimately directed against God, as is later done both by Moses (Num. 14.9) and by God (Num. 14.11).

Midrash then *does* read texts carefully. If many moderns find midrash off-putting it is because midrash fails to give reasonable weight to the full array of interlocking factors that ought to be considered when arriving at a text's interpretation. The *p^eŠāt* exegetes do just that. *p^eŠāt* exegetes consider all the same factors that midrashic exegetes consider but the *p^eŠāt* exegetes attempt to look at them all when analyzing each verse. At times, accordingly, the *p^eŠāt* exegetes are forced to conclude that a certain factor or 'difficulty' perceived by the midrash is simply without significance. An orthographical or grammatical or syntactical anomaly is most often seen by the *paŠtānîm* as simply an anomaly. 'Sometimes that's what happens', they say.[1] The midrash then in one sense is a closer reading, even a more literal meaning at times than the *p^eŠāt*.

Midrash really comes into its own when dealing with law and legal texts. The rabbis unashamedly admit that on numerous occasions entire blocks of Jewish law 'hang from a thread', that is, have little or no connection with the biblical text (*m.Hag.* 1.8). Five unlikely words about the boiling of baby goats (Exod. 23.19) are expanded by the process of midrash to become years later the basis for numerous pages of kashrut laws (*Šulḥān 'ārûk, Yôreh dē'â* 87-97). At other times midrash arrives at some very startling conclusions. Rabbinic literature correctly reacts to the cumbersome and repetitious syntax of Exod. 23.2. We witness, however, an amazing intellectual *tour de force* when it then reads the last three words of the verse as meaning, 'follow the majority' (*m.Sanh.* 1.6); virtually the precise opposite of what the verse is really saying.

In medieval times pious exegetes began looking for the *p^eŠāt* level of meaning of not only narrative but also legal passages of the Bible. Their biggest problem was to try to explain why it was permissible for them to look for the *p^eŠāt* if the ancients had not bothered. The medievals could only speculate about what the ancient rabbis thought about *p^eŠāt* since the ancient rabbis had never addressed the issue directly. Abraham ibn Ezra for one was certain that the earlier scholars must have known what the texts really meant (Lippmann 1839: 4b) while Rashbam argued that 'due to their piety' the ancient scholars had had nothing to do with the *p^eŠāt* (commentary to Gen. 37.2). Still, some way of justifying this newfangled *p^eŠāt* enterprise

---

1. See, e.g., ibn Ezra's commentary to Exod. 34.4 and Num. 24.8 or Rashbam's commentary to Gen. 29.30.

while still venerating traditional midrash had to be found. Obviously when dealing with a narrative, non-legal text, greater latitude for innovation would be allowed. But it is much more difficult to claim that a legal text has more than one level of meaning.

One should mention the two extreme options for solving the medieval *pᵉšāt*–midrash dialectic although these solutions obviously did not please the *paštānîm* of the Middle Ages. One can reject midrash as a worthless type of fanciful exegesis or one can reject *pᵉšāt* as a godless type of heretical intellectual pursuit that disregards hundreds of years of venerated tradition. The first model was in fact adopted by the Karaites and the second presumably appealed to some non-*pᵉšāt*-oriented exegetes. But how would rabbanite *paštānîm* deal with the problem?

The best thought-out position seems to be that of Abraham ibn Ezra who argues that midrash is authoritative but it is not exegesis. If the midrash reads a biblical verse in a particular way, the legal result of that midrash must be considered true and binding, but the midrash need not—and probably should not—be considered exegesis. If the rabbis derive from Num. 27.11 through some casuistic exegesis that a widower inherits his dead wife's estate, the legal conclusion is true but no rational person ought to consider the rabbis' reading of the verse to be the 'true' interpretation. The rabbis, argued ibn Ezra, never meant to claim that that is what the verse meant. They simply artificially attached a legal conclusion to an essentially irrelevant biblical verse, presumably for mnemonic reasons. Ibn Ezra called this type of exegesis *'asmaktā'*.[1]

Still ibn Ezra knew that there were limits to what could be accomplished through the *'asmaktā'* answer. Maybe one can argue that the text does not really say what the rabbis' *'asmaktā'* says that it says. But ibn Ezra realized that he could not solve all his problems through the *'asmaktā'* method and was willing to abandon the quest for *pᵉšāt* on a number of occasions for the sake of religious orthodoxy.[2]

A more radical approach was adopted by Rashbam, ibn Ezra's older contemporary. Rashbam claimed to see midrash as not only

---

1. See ibn Ezra's lengthy excursus on this verse in Numbers in his shorter commentary to Exod. 21.8 (Fleischer 1926: 162-63).

2. See for example ibn Ezra's conservative explanation of the word *lᵉ'ôlām* in Exod. 21.6 (both in his shorter and longer commentaries *ad loc.*) and his pious retreat from a *pᵉ'sāt*-like interpretation in his commentary to Lev. 21.2.

authoritative but also as a method of exegesis and the most important method of exegesis.[1] This never stopped him, however, from offering his own audacious and innovative interpretations that flew in the face of traditional exegesis.

Rashbam, a great Talmud scholar, knew full well that the rabbis derived from the verse, 'And there was evening and there was morning', that a Jewish day begins at sunset (*m.Hul.* 5.5). Rashbam argued cogently that that is not what the verse means. He argued (commentary to Gen. 1.5) that a creation day, one of the six days described in Genesis 1, began at sunrise.

> The text does not write, 'There was *night* and there was *day*'. Rather it writes, 'There was evening'—i.e. the light of the first day subsided and the darkness fell—'and there was morning'—that morning [that came at the end] of the night when dawn broke. At that point, 'one day' of those six described in the Decalogue (Exod. 20.11) was completed. Then the second day began when (v. 6) 'God said, "Let there be an expanse"'. The text has no interest in stating that an evening and a morning regularly constitute one day. The text is interested only in describing how those six days were constituted—that when the night finished and the dawn broke one day was completed and the second day began.

While many traditional Jews found such exegesis troubling,[2] one can argue, theoretically at least, that there is nothing inherently heterodox or antinomian about such a reading. If a non-legal, narrative biblical text describes a day as beginning at dawn it does not necessarily mean that from a legal perspective that is when all days begin.[3]

Still Rashbam was willing to offer some explanations of biblical legal texts that directly contradict the conclusions of traditional exegesis. Consider the question of the legal responsibility of a bailee when the object that he is guarding is stolen. The implication of Exod. 22.7-8 is that the bailee is not responsible but v. 11 of that same chapter implies that the bailee is responsible. The common Jewish answer is that some but not all bailees are responsible in the case of

---

1. See, for example, his programmatic statements in his commentary to Gen. 1.1 and to Gen. 37.2 and in his introductory words to Exod. 21.

2. See ibn Ezra's longer commentary to Exod. 16.25 and his *'Iggeret haššabbāt*. Still it is unlikely that the major thrust of ibn Ezra's comments is to be seen as directed against Rashbam, but rather as directed against the Karaites (Margaliot 1953, 357-69).

3. Furthermore, in Rashbam's own commentary a few verses later to Gen. 1.14 he clearly accepts the idea that a Jewish day begins when the stars first appear.

theft. What then distinguishes between those bailees who are and those bailees who are not responsible? Rashbam (commentary to Exod. 22.6) presented two possible explanations, that of the rabbis and his own:

> The rabbis explained (*b.B.Mes.* 94b) that the first bailee described is one who is not remunerated while the second bailee described is one who is remunerated. However, following the plain meaning of scripture the first section, 'When a man gives money or goods to another for safekeeping', refers to the guarding of removables that are commonly kept inside one's house and that are to be guarded in the same way that one guards one's own property. That is why if they were stolen from his house he is not responsible, for he guarded them in the expected manner, as one guards one's own possessions. But in the second section when 'a man gives to his neighbor an ass an ox a sheep or any other animal to guard', since animals commonly graze outdoors it is to be assumed that when he entrusted them to the bailee he expected that the bailee would protect them from theft. Accordingly if they were stolen the bailee is responsible.

So Rashbam offered two possible ways of understanding when it is that a bailee is responsible in the case of theft—either when he is remunerated or when he is guarding animals. But then what does the Bible have to say about a bailee who is being paid but is guarding chattels, not animals? Is he responsible in the case of theft? Rashbam said that according to the $p^e\check{s}\bar{a}t$ he is not responsible but according to the law he is. What could a distinction like that mean? What is the significance and relevance of $p^e\check{s}\bar{a}t$ if it directly contradicts the desired legal conclusion of the text?

Rashbam never really answered those questions directly. In fact what is sorely missing from Rashbam's trailblazing commentary is any explanation of why a traditional Jew ought to be interested in reading that commentary. Given Rashbam's repeated insistence on the primacy of midrash for halakhic Jews, and given the fact that $p^e\check{s}\bar{a}t$ often contradicts the result of such midrash, why should a traditional Jew read his commentary?

This same question can be rephrased in a theologically more troubling manner. How did Rashbam himself, as a pious medieval Jew (Urbach 1968: 42), understand the intentions of the divine law-giver? Why would God, whose primary purpose in writing Exod. 21.6 was to teach that a slave with a pierced ear is freed at the jubilee year, have purposely written that text with a plain meaning that, according to Rashbam, dooms that same slave to perpetual servitude? Why would God, whose primary purpose in writing Lev. 21.1-4 was to teach us that a priest may (in fact, must!) defile himself through contact with the dead when his wife dies, have written those verses in such a way that their plain meaning, according to Rashbam, forbids a priest to do so?

In theory, there are a number of possible solutions to this problem. One might claim that the *pešāt* level of understanding is relevant to some non-practical level of the traditional Jew's edification, his moral enlightenment, for example. Rashbam, however, nowhere made this claim nor, to my mind, could he have explained systematically all his non-halakhic interpretations in this manner.

Alternatively, one might attempt to solve this problem by adopting some version of ibn Ezra's *'asmaktā'* approach. The authority of laws, according to this approach, comes from tradition and from their status as oral law, and has nothing to do with the meaning of biblical texts. *pešāt* and Jewish law are then compatible because midrash has nothing to do with exegesis.

Again such an understanding cannot be imputed to Rashbam. He clearly understood halakhic midrash as a form of exegesis, based on textual superfluities, redundancies, etc., not as an artificial wedding of tradition to text (e.g. commentary to Gen. 1.1 and 37.2). Yet Rashbam does not hesitate to offer *pešāt* interpretations that directly contradict the traditional understanding. Why then did the divine author, to Rashbam's mind, write a text whose plain meaning contradicts its intended primary meaning?

David Weiss Halivni recently discussed these problems (1986: 105-107). He concluded that, for Rashbam, the *pešāt* level of the text must have been seen as having value only inasmuch as studying it fulfils a *miṣwâ*, a religious duty. The Torah then has only one way of being properly understood and that is through halakhic midrash. When one reads the text without the tools of halakhic midrash and one finds the *pešāt*, one is fulfilling a divine commandment but one is not finding out anything about what the text means.

Halivni's theory is attractive but, as he notes, Rashbam never explicitly made such a claim. Furthermore, one must recall that Rashbam often became quite strident and vituperative (e.g. his commentary to Gen. 37.2, Gen. 48.28, Exod. 3.11 and Deut. 15.18) when defending the superiority of his interpretations over previous midrashic ones. If he really thought that *pešāt* had nothing to do with the true meaning of the text would he react in that way?

My speculation is that Rashbam had not thought through the issue in all of its ramifications. He was clearly a committed halakhic Jew who subscribed to accepted theories about the authorship of the Torah and the derivation of Jewish laws from the Torah text. On the other hand he was an accomplished exegete, who was attracted by his grandfather's pioneering attempts to determine the $p^e\check{s}\bar{a}t$ of biblical texts. He was disappointed with his grandfather's hesitant blend of $p^e\check{s}\bar{a}t$ and midrash and decided to carry his grandfather's work to what Rashbam considered its consistent and logical conclusion (Lockshin 1989a: 391-99).

In his own commentary, he produced a work almost devoid of midrash. This commentary often arrives at interpretations that were later to be accepted by non-traditional modern critical scholars. It did not succeed, however, in capturing the attention of later generations of traditional Jews, perhaps as a direct result of Rashbam's disregard of the inevitable tensions between $p^e\check{s}\bar{a}t$ and $h^al\bar{a}k\hat{a}$.

In the words of the author of the one super-commentary (Ashkenazi 1727: introduction) written on Rashbam's commentary:

> I have heard many people asking themselves, amazed about his [Rashbam's] stature... 'What good has he done, what has he accomplished, what did he improve for us with this commentary of his on the Torah? Why should we indulge in such matters, wasting our days and years?' They take only quick glances at his words and do not delve into them. In passages wherein it is difficult to understand the meaning of his words they retort that there is no duty incumbent upon us to devote our energies to understanding his interpretations...

Rashbam did not manage to convince later generations of traditional Jews that the study of $p^e\check{s}\bar{a}t$, in and of itself, is a worthwhile pursuit.

Moses Mendelssohn, the founder of the modern Jewish Enlightenment, once wrote (1801: introduction) that Rashbam, 'due to his exceeding love of $p^e\check{s}\bar{a}t$ sometimes missed the truth'. The contention that $p^e\check{s}\bar{a}t$ and truth are not coterminous seems strange, especially from this supposed champion of intellectualism, but it is understandable within a religious framework where truth is often not the result of human intellectual effort.

Rashbam's commentary, a great Bible commentary, has been treated with benign neglect by eight centuries of traditional Jews. The conclusion could be that if $p^e\check{s}\bar{a}t$ exegesis is applied consistently not only to narrative but also to legal passages then it cannot yet claim a place within the confines of traditional Judaism.

BIBLIOGRAPHY

Ashkenazi, S.Z.
    1727   *Qeren š^e mû'ēl* (Frankfurt).
Fleischer, E. (ed.)
    1926   A. Ibn Ezra *Shorter Commentary to Exodus* (Vienna).
Halivni, D.W.
    1986   *Midrash Mishnah and Gemara* (Cambridge, MA: Harvard University Press).
Kamin, S.
    1986   *Rāši: p^e šûtô šel miqrā' ûmidrāšô šel miqrā'* (Jerusalem: Magnes).
Lippmann, G. (ed.)
    1839   A. Ibn Ezra *Sāpâ b^e rûrâ* (Fürth).
Lipshutz, E.
    1957   Rashi [Heb.] in Y. Maimon (ed.), *Sēper rāši*, (Jerusalem: Mosad Harav Kook): 165-285.
Lockshin, M.I.
    1989a   *Rabbi Samuel ben Meir's Commentary on Genesis:* An Annotated Translation (Queenston: Edwin Mellen Press).
    1989b   'Tradition or Context: Two Exegetes Struggle with Peshat', in J. Neusner, E.S. Frerichs and N.M. Sarna (eds.), *From Ancient Israel to Modern Judaism: Essays in Honor of Marvin Fox* (Atlanta: Scholars Press).
Margaliot, A.
    1953   'The Relationship Between Rashbam's Commentary and ibn Ezra's Commentary to the Torah' [Heb.], in U. Cassuto (ed.), *Sèper 'āsāp* (Jerusalem: Mosad Harav Kook): 357-369.
Mendelssohn, M.
    1801   *Bē'ûr* (Fürth).
Samuel ben Meir
    1882   *Torah Commentary* (ed. D. Rosin; Breslau).
Segal, M.Z.
    1971   *Paršānût hammiqrā*, (Jerusalem: Kiryat Sefer).
Touitou, E.
    1982   *Šitātô happaršānît šel hārašbam* in Y. Gilat *et al.* (eds.), *Studies in Rabbinic Literature Bible and Jewish History* (Ramat-Gan: Bar-Ilan University): 48-74.
Urbach, E.
    1968   *Ba^'a lê hattôsāpôt* (Jerusalem: Mosad Bialik).

INDEXES

INDEX OF REFERENCES

OLD TESTAMENT

JEWISH SOURCES

OTHER SOURCES

INSCRIPTIONS AND TABLETS

PAPYRI

INDEX OF AUTHORS

JOURNAL FOR THE STUDY OF THE OLD TESTAMENT

Supplement Series